The Beyoncé Effect

The Beyoncé Effect

*Essays on Sexuality,
Race and Feminism*

Edited by ADRIENNE TRIER-BIENIEK

McFarland & Company, Inc., Publishers
Jefferson, North Carolina

LIBRARY OF CONGRESS CATALOGUING-IN-PUBLICATION DATA

Names: Trier-Bieniek, Adrienne M.
Title: The Beyoncé effect : essays on sexuality, race and feminism /
   edited by Adrienne Trier-Bieniek.
Description: Jefferson, North Carolina : McFarland & Company, 2016 |
   Includes bibliographical references and index.
Identifiers: LCCN 2016022666 | ISBN 9780786499748 (softcover :
   acid free paper) ∞
Subjects: LCSH: Beyoncé, 1981—Criticism and interpretation. |
   Sex in music. | Feminism and music. | Music and race.
Classification: LCC ML420.K675 B39 2016 | DDC 782.42164092—dc23
LC record available at https://lccn.loc.gov/2016022666

ISBN (print) 978-0-7864-9974-8
ISBN (ebook) 978-1-4766-2558-4

BRITISH LIBRARY CATALOGUING DATA ARE AVAILABLE

Front cover: Beyoncé Knowles, 2011 (Photograph by Tony Duran, Parkwood
Pictures Entertainment LLC)

Printed in the United States of America

*McFarland & Company, Inc., Publishers
   Box 611, Jefferson, North Carolina 28640
   www.mcfarlandpub.com*

For my friend Jennifer Wiles,
Official Defender of Human Rights.

Acknowledgments

Thanks go to all the contributors to this text for sharing their expertise and talent. Each essay is a reflection of outstanding scholarship and I have learned so much from all of you. It has been a privilege to work with you. An extra special thank you to Tia Tyree and Rachel Griffin for their help in recruitment.

Many thanks to my personal book-editing mentor, unofficial book-editing champion and feminist partner-in-crime Patricia Leavy. I also thank Angie Moe, the greatest dissertation chair in the universe. Thanks to the usual suspects in my life for their support: my soul-sisters Efua Akoma and Beatrice Yarbrough and their families, Lee Paulsen and family, the Clapper twins, Andy and Dan, and their families, the Spertis, the Triers, the Bienieks, Chastity Orrship, Melissa Sierra and Bethany Kelly. And thanks to my four-legged pals Mara and Charlie for the constant company, and to my two-legged husband Tim Bieniek, who is just as handsome as he was in 1997. You make my heart happy. Thanks to Rick and Deanne Trier—you raised me right.

Vadzim Sheika, your girl is Flawless. Go get that ring.

Catherine Kelly, hopefully this book helps in making your own band. Thanks for being my Galentine.

Finally, the idea for this work was born not just from Beyoncé but from watching the women in my life who are embodying the spirit of "killing it." Collectively they are academics, nurses, health care providers, costume designers, mothers, attorneys, writers, dancers, police officers, teachers, public servants, business owners, counselors, survivors and community leaders. Thank you all for the inspiration and the continued motivation to be better than I was yesterday.

Table of Contents

Introduction

Few contemporary entertainers in the pop music world have had an impact equal to Beyoncé's. Her talents as a songwriter and entertainer, coupled with her powerhouse vocals and a desire to challenge gendered norms, has catapulted Beyoncé to a level of stardom and influence few performers will ever see. Yet what is perhaps most interesting about her cultural impact is the ways she has embraced feminism. Her songs can be read as mini-lectures in feminist theory and methodology—she has introduced feminism to new generations of young women and given feminists the world over an opportunity to rally behind a woman who is perhaps the world's biggest pop star.

Much is connected to the title that comes with "Queen Bey." Her lyrics eschew the typical pop music fare and cover topics like women's independence from men, healthy sexuality, post-partum depression, feminism and identity, to name a few. Yet, as diverse as her songs are, the images and statements she makes through her performances and media are perhaps more impactful. Beyoncé often tours with an all-female band, something unheard of for a pop star of her caliber. She has mixed her music with speeches from author Chimamanda Ngozi Adichie, a writer whose stance on feminism was highlighted in Beyoncé's song "Flawless." One December night in 2013, she released her album *Beyoncé* via iTunes without fanfare and without the industry standard press junket that accompanies the release of new albums.

Since her introduction as a member of Destiny's Child during the pop music scene of the late 1990s, Beyoncé has been a lightning rod for both praise and criticism from scholars, feminists and critics alike. While some see Beyoncé as an empowering presence and in every way celebrating the "independent women" she praises in her music, others view her as detrimental to women's rights, feminism and as a negative portrayal of a woman of color. Recently, feminist theorist and writer bell hooks, during a talk at the New School in New York City, referred to Beyoncé as a terrorist and an "anti-feminist," and described her image as her "collusion in the construction of herself as a slave."

1

The response to hooks' words from the feminist and music community was overwhelmingly critical. Many feel that Beyoncé represents a new face of feminism: the woman who forms her own opinions and actions regarding gender equality. As evidence of the relevance of these discussions, academic courses have popped up across the nation focusing on Beyoncé's effect on the dialog about race and gender, the female body, sexuality and the politics of media representations. Additionally, much focus has been on Beyoncé's philanthropy to help women and girls worldwide via the non-profit project "Chime for Change."

These discussions also lend themselves to analysis of Beyoncé's presentation of self. They raise debate about the place of a Black woman in the music industry, as well as of the wealth and privilege she has gained via her marriage to Jay-Z. Arguments about her ability to represent "Blackness" have abounded almost as frequently as deliberations about her use of sex and sexuality in her songs. Some scholars posit that Beyoncé is owning her sexuality while others argue that her status as a married woman allows her the privilege to talk about her sex life, or that she is a product of the male gaze, requiring submission to hegemonic media culture. Much focus has also rested on her body, everything from politicizing nudity in her videos to sensual performances on stage. Beyoncé-inspired body politics challenges notions of race and gender, questioning whether her body (naked or clothed) is oppressive or empowering.

Additionally, Beyoncé has become the focus of debate surrounding theories of intersectionality and privilege, raising the question "Does fame cancel out inequality based on race, class or gender?" This collection of essays focuses on these concepts, offering an analysis of Beyoncé the person, the entertainer and the brand, and examining the music industry's representation of gender and Beyoncé's connection with her fans.

A Brief Biography of Beyoncé Knowles

Beyoncé Giselle Knowles-Carter was born on September 4, 1981, in Houston, Texas. She began her musical career at the age of eight, as part of an all-girl group that would eventually become known as Destiny's Child. Their massive success throughout the 1990s and early 2000s led to Destiny's Child being named by *Billboard* magazine one of the most popular female groups of all time. The group became famous for songs like "Independent Women," which praised women's financial independence and urged female listeners to depend only on themselves. Their song "Survivor" was released after the members had a falling out and media reports about "cat fighting" among the group led Beyoncé to write the song, declaring that the group had chosen to focus on the positive and "survive." Eschewing support from others became a theme of the trio's music.

After Destiny's Child broke up in 2006, Beyoncé began to focus on a solo musical career. She quickly became known for lyrics promoting women's empowerment in their personal lives and romantic relationships. In a pair of songs released in 2008, "Single Ladies (Put a Ring on It)" and "If I Were a Boy," Beyoncé encouraged men to commit to marrying their long-term girlfriends, and criticized the double standard that allows men to care little about their appearance, "hook up" with little fear of repercussion, and take their female partners for granted. "Run the World (Girls)" was released in April 2011 from Beyoncé's album *4*. Continuing in the vein of earlier songs like "Independent Women," "Run the World" celebrates women, including female college graduates, who are taking over the world, and mothers, who she depicts as strong women who can give birth and also be successful in the business world. She praises men who love and support educated, independent women (Trier-Bieniek and Pullum 2014).

These earlier records seemed to be leading up to the release of *Beyoncé*, her self-titled fifth album. It presented a side of the artist not previously seen, particularly songs dealing with sex, feminism, monogamy, post-partum depression, politics, and miscarriage. *Beyoncé* was released without publicity at midnight on December 13, 2013. Regardless of the lack of promotion, the album shot to the top of the Billboard charts and was praised as one of the best of 2013.

With the album's release, Beyoncé began what could be considered a feminist campaign to raise awareness about gender inequality. The track "Flawless," which is discussed in depth in this collection, featured a voice-over from a speech by Nigerian author Chimamanda Ngozi Adichie, amid heavy beats and lyrics about being more than just a wife and mother. In "We Should All Be Feminists," Adichie says, "We say to girls, 'You can have ambition, but not too much. Otherwise you will threaten the man'" (2013). She also offers this definition: "Feminist: A person who believes in the social, political and economic equality of the sexes" (2013). This sample, in the middle of a song about declaring personal independence from patriarchy, was Beyoncé's feminist statement. In addition to "Flawless," Beyoncé wrote a piece for *The Shriver Report* on women's pay equality. The piece, titled "Gender Equality Is a Myth!," read,

> Men have to demand that their wives, daughters, mothers, and sisters earn more—commensurate with their qualifications and not their gender. Equality will be achieved when men and women are granted equal pay and equal respect [Knowles-Carter 2014].

Beyoncé went on to write, "Humanity requires both men and women, and we are equally important and need one another. So why are we viewed as less than equal?"

In addition to bringing discussions of gender equality into her music and public service, Beyoncé also presented her feminism to young people via major media appearances. At the 2014 MTV Video Music Awards (VMAs) Beyoncé did a medley of almost all the songs from *Beyoncé*. In the middle of the performance, after a series of explicitly sexual moments, another quote of Adichie's appeared on a huge screen: "We teach girls that they cannot be sexual beings in the same way that boys are" (2013). As words from the quote flashed, the women who had been dancing on stripper poles along with Beyoncé were moved across the stage. Presumably this was a pre-emptive moment, staged to head off the coming critique that Beyoncé's performance was too sexual. The moment ended with Beyoncé standing in front of a lit up sign that simply read "Feminist." For many feminist pop culture scholars this moment was an achievement. As *Slate* writer Amanda Marcotte said, "The VMAs statement was next level—an unusually mainstream flaunting of feminist pride in our image-driven culture. And man did it feel good" (Marcotte 2014). This text is an examination of many of the themes and reactions to Beyoncé's brand of feminism and her pursuit of women's rights via her music. Along with being a benchmark for her stunning career, the VMA performance also served as a reminder of how women are claiming their own roles in pop music.

Gender and Pop Music

Gender presentation has a long and varied history in pop music, from the risqué "Empress of the Blues" Bessie Smith in the 1930s and 1940s declaring that she will not marry or settle down, to the ladylike do-wop girls of the 1950s and 1960s. Female fans are usually given the role of "watcher" as it is assumed they are present to see the boys in the band. This relationship was first addressed in Frith and McRobbie's 1979 study of what they called "cock rock" and "teeny bop," in which male musicians perform masculinity for female fans.

> The male musician is typically portrayed as aggressive, dominating, boastful, and constantly seek[ing] to remind the audience of their prowess, their control. Their stance is obvious in live shows; male bodies on display, plunging shirts and tight trousers, a visual emphasis on chest hair and genitals [65].

Further, as noted in my first book *Sing Us a Song, Piano Woman: Female Fans and the Music of Tori Amos*, Frith and McRobbie's observations can be applied in the 21st century:

> An important concept in Cock Rock, especially when applying it to contemporary music, is that it is defined by hyper-masculine behavior in music. I would argue that contemporary pop acts such as Justin Bieber, Usher and Chris Brown

certainly fit this definition. In another vein, "Teeny Bop" revolves around the female fan who is always the consumer of music, rarely the performer or producer of music [Trier-Bieniek 2013, 19].

Performance and gender display is also grounded in gendered theory, such as West and Zimmerman's concept of "doing gender." They contend that gender is not just taught—it is performed in everyday life. This was expanded in Judith Butler's famous 1999 book *Gender Trouble*; she explained that gender is an identity created by dress, physical appearance, etc. Gender in pop music is illustrative of society's expectations of men and women.

In her 2009 book *Gender in the Music Industry*, Marion Leonard surveys the music industry (and its journalists) to demonstrate how gender stereotypes get reproduced in music. Because the music industry is constructed by men who dominate the positions of record executive, music journalist, fan and academic listener, its product is distinctly gendered. "The concern is to uncover how this gendering of rock is articulated, with particular attention to how a masculinist tradition is established, reproduced and maintained" (2009, 23). Presenting phrases like "women in rock" or "the year of the woman in music" as problematic, she says, "Rather than simply pointing to the activity of female musicians within a particular music genre, the phrase usually works to peculiarise the presence of women rock performers" (2009, 32). Indeed, the presence of women in music as anything other than pretty performers is laudable. When performers like Beyoncé (one could add Taylor Swift and Miranda Lambert) take control by writing, producing and distributing their music, it is seen as an anomaly, but also a bit of a breakthrough.

Another component to the image of men and women in music is the press coverage. As Feigenbaum (2005) notes, many rock journalists have made attempts to examine the place of women in music. Lucy O'Brien's books *She Bop* and *She Bop 2* chronicle the history and trends of female musicians, including Memphis Minnie, Sister Rosetta Tharpe, Wanda Jackson, Aretha Franklin, Dolly Parton, Carly Simon, the Riot Grrrls, Alanis Morissette, Tori Amos and Ani DiFranco to name a few. Yet, as Feigenbaum notes, anthologies written about women in music are often used to combat the sexism published by news media, particularly the ways female musicians are addressed.

> Adjectival gender markers and gender binaries also work to support an authentic/inauthentic dichotomy that devalues women. This type of distinction often precedes a non-gender specific noun such as, "the girl rocker" or "the chick singer." These markings are usually employed only when women are being referred to. One does not often come across "the male rocker," just "the rocker" [2005, 40].

Essentially, when female performers are discussed, they are held up as notable for existing in a man's world. Yet, what makes Beyoncé stand out is her ability to not only exist in a male-dominated culture but to also continue to set a bar for what female performers should expect from the music industry.

When discussing the impact Beyoncé had on music in 2014, rock critic Ann Powers explained the connection between Beyoncé the performer and Beyoncé the game-changer.

> By the time she took the stage at the Forum, near the end of the summer *On the Run Tour*, Beyoncé had deflated assertions that her stand for equality was compromised by prurient onstage behavior in myriad displays of her integrated multiple identities: mother, mogul, activist, ass-shaker. In this way, Beyoncé set the bar for the several other women who scaled pop commerce's heights with her in 2014, to present selves and songs defined by a feminist concept of abundance [Powers 2014].

What has made Beyoncé stand out, and what makes her interesting to gender studies scholars, is her ability to traverse boundaries previously thought to be cemented in pop music standards. The contributors to this text address many of these factors including race, motherhood, social class, intersectionality, sex, marketing, feminism, gender, age and technology. Not many artists transcend all of these categories and few do it at the same time. It would also be over-simplifying to say that these are the products of an artist who continues to reinvent herself (something that is often attributed mainly to female performers.) Rather, Beyoncé has followed the lead of many definitive female singer-songwriters and presented various portraits of moments in time, sonic pictures which rest in both personal and political history. This text is, hopefully, the beginning of great scholarship focused on Beyoncé's impact as a musician.

About This Book

The text begins with Janell Hobson's essay "Feminists Debate Beyoncé." Hobson, who wrote the 2013 *Ms.* magazine cover story on Beyoncé, addresses the myriad reactions to her essay, couching them in the debate about feminism in general and Beyoncé in particular. Hobson applies an intersectional lens to the debate surrounding Beyoncé the feminist, and engages a dialog regarding who/what is a feminist.

In "Beyoncé as Intersectional Icon? Interrogating the Politics of Respectability," Marla H. Kohlman examines the persona of Beyoncé as an example of intersectionality. Using the "politics of respectability"—often held up as an ethical standard within the black community—Kohlman argues that Beyoncé both uses and ignores this standard depending on her needs.

In "Beyoncé as Aggressive Black Femme and Informed Black Female Subject," Anne M. Mitchell applies queer identity theory to discuss Beyoncé's public persona as a femme who simultaneously situates and eschews aggressive and submissive femininity. Mitchell argues that Beyoncé even can engage both of these personas while also being able to subtly critique submissive femininity. She argues that the "queer identities of femininity" are connected to the image of Black female bodies in popular culture.

Examining the performance of black women's bodies in popular culture is the focus of "Policing Beyoncé's Body: 'Whose Body Is This Anyway?'" Noel Siqi Duan uses both contemporary and historical references of the use of Black women's bodies as public areas for consumption. Discussing topics like fashion, dance, music and photography as potential sites for debate, Duan paints a complicated picture of the ways media have exerted control over Beyoncé's body.

Changing gears from identity to marketing, "I'm Not Myself Lately: The Erosion of the Beyoncé Brand," critiques Beyoncé as a brand. Kristin Lieb identifies three life events that changed Beyoncé's identity—marrying Jay-Z, firing her father as manager and giving birth to her first child—and argues that these upset Beyoncé's carefully cultivated commercial brand. Lieb asserts that Beyoncé is a complicated and groundbreaking musician, but notes that she relies on safe, conservative, and normative forms of pleasing men to walk the "impossible tightrope" of being a female popular music star.

Continuing discussion of marketing and branding, "*The Visual Album*: Beyoncé, Feminism and Digital Spaces" by Jamila A. Cupid and Nicole Files-Thompson addresses the connection between Beyoncé's identification as a feminist to the extension of her brand. Looking at the role of new media and the release of *Beyoncé* the album, the author's consider Beyoncé's engagement in a "feminist strategic communication." They address the ways new media permitted Beyoncé to have a certain amount of control over her cultural production, particularly with her fans, and the opportunities to expand and commoditize the Beyoncé brand.

This theme is rounded out with "Beyoncé and Social Media: Authenticity and the Presentation of Self" in which Melissa Avdeeff focuses on Beyoncé's use of Instagram as a means of celebrity-branding. Avdeeff considers the use of social media as an artist platform in light of Erving Goffman's theory of the presentation of self, arguing that while some may see the use of Instagram as shameless self-promotion, Beyoncé embraces it as a means to relay information to fans.

Addressing the communication style of Beyoncé is one component of "Flawless Feminist or Fallible Freak? An Analysis of Feminism, Empowerment and Gender in Beyoncé's Lyrics." Here Tia C.M. Tyree and Melvin L. Williams provide a textual analysis of Beyoncé's five albums for themes connected to black and Hip-Hop feminist theory. In addition they examine how her songs align with historic Black female stereotypes, sexual scripts and sexual roles.

With "Birthing Baby Blue: Beyoncé and the Changing Face of Celebrity Birth Culture," Natalie Jolly discusses the connections between the culture of childbirth and the impact of celebrity birth narratives. Looking at three aspects of "birth discourse" from Beyoncé's experience giving birth to her daughter, Blue Ivy, Jolly addresses how Beyoncé's experience challenged contemporary ideas about birth, particularly pain avoidance as standard labor protocol, women's general lack of body confidence and body shame connected with birth. Jolly contends that Beyoncé's birth experience relates to body politics focused on birth/body competency rather than body distrust/disgust.

Next Sonita R. Moss offers "Beyoncé and Blue: Black Motherhood and the Binds of Racialized Sexism." Inspired by a 2014 online petition demanding that Beyoncé take better care of her daughter's hair, Moss paints a portrait of the complex opinions contemporary society forces on Black women. These types of racialized sexisms particularly are aimed at Black woman and girls, whether it be through a take-down of how young Black women do their hair or the ways Black mothers are raising their children. Borrowing from Crenshaw's theory of intersectionality, Moss portrays Black womanhood as a dynamic as much linked to racism as it is sexism, interconnected with body politics and unique experiences with oppression.

Addressing Beyoncé's place within hip-hop feminism is the focus of "BDSM, Gazes and Wedding Rings: The Centering of Black Female Pleasure and Agency in Beyoncé." Evette Dionne Brown examines the album *Beyoncé* as a text for Black feminist identity. By placing Beyoncé in the company of other hip-hop Black feminist pop stars such as Janet Jackson, Nicki Minaj, and Rihanna, Brown asserts that Beyoncé also presents issues of intersections of race and gender via the use of pleasure. By illustrating five videos from *Beyoncé* Brown contends that, overall, Beyoncé is a hip-hop black feminist text focused on exploring women's pleasure.

Looking at Beyoncé's use of sexuality through her cultural roots is the centerpiece of "Creole Queen: Beyoncé and Performing Plaçage in the New Millennium." Kimberly J. Chandler draws from Beyoncé's Creole heritage to discuss how Black women can embody their sexuality, perform it, and be viewed as more than a spectacle. Through a discussion of the contradictions present when looking at Black women's bodies and addressing them as sexual objects, Chandler suggests that intersectionality is not at the root of this exploration. Rather it is a culturally informed performance of gender functioning as "new millennium placèe."

"Sex(uality), Marriage, Motherhood and 'Bey Feminism'" by Elizabeth Whittington Cooper brings together the major themes addressed in the book. Whittington Cooper uses online websites and blogs discussing Beyoncé's feminism as examples of the ways Beyoncé has translated across multiple social factors. Here Whittington Cooper illustrates the feminism found in

Beyoncé's identity and music while also addressing the ways the media have self-selected her persona.

This book demonstrates that there is something about Beyoncé that is striking a chord with people of varied backgrounds. Her brand of feminism, the way she markets herself, her use of sexuality and the connection between race, class and gender found in both her person and her persona is ripe for analysis. Further, while certainly not exhaustive, these essays do serve to fill a gap in studies of pop music. Presenting a pop star through the lens of feminist thought and intersectional social analysis demonstrates that more research is needed in order to fully understand the roles of women in music.

REFERENCES

Adichie, Chimamanda Ngozi. 2013. "We Should All Be Feminists." Speech.

Feigenbaum, Anna. 2005. "Some Guy Designed This Room I Am Standing In." *Popular Music*, 24:37–56.

Frith, Simon, and Angela McRobbie. 1979. "Rock and Sexuality." *Screen Edition*, 4:65–75.

Marcotte, Amanda. 2014. "Why It Felt So Amazing When Beyonce Stood in Front of That Glowing Feminist Sign." Accessed June 21, 2015. http://www.slate.com/blogs/xx_factor/2014/08/25/beyonc_goes_full_feminist_at_the_vmas.html.

Knowles-Carter, Beyoncé. 2014. "Gender Equality Is a Myth!" *The Shriver Report*, January 12. http://shriverreport.com/gender-equality-is-a-myth-beyonce/.

Leonard, Marion. 2009. *Gender in the Music Industry*. London: Ashgate.

Powers, Ann. 2014. "In 2014, Pop Followed Beyoncé's Lead." Accessed January 6, 2015. http://www.npr.org/sections/therecord/2014/12/12/370230607/in-2014-pop-followed-beyonces-lead.

Trier-Bieniek, Adrienne. 2013. *Sing Us a Song, Piano Woman: Female Fans and the Music of Tori Amos*. Lanham, MD: Scarecrow Press.

Trier-Bieniek, Adrienne, and Amanda Pullum. 2014. "From Lady Gaga to Consciousness Rap: The Impact of Music on Gender and Social Activism." In *Gender and Pop Culture: A Text-Reader*, edited by Adrienne Trier-Bieniek and Patricia Leavy, 81–102. Rotterdam: Sense.

West, Candace, and Don H. Zimmerman. 1987. "Doing Gender." *Gender and Society*, 1:125–151.

Feminists Debate Beyoncé

Janell Hobson

> I think I am a feminist in a way.... It's not something I con-
> sciously decided I was going to be.—Beyoncé (cited in Gor-
> don 2010)

Even before pop star Beyoncé took a stand (quite literally) in front of
the neon-lit "FEMINIST" sign at MTV's Video Music Awards (VMA) show
in 2014, her previous articulations of a feminist consciousness had already
garnered attention. Whether we point to her early years in the girl group
Destiny's Child—singing alongside Kelly Rowland and Michelle Williams
with such empowering hit songs as "Survivor" and "Independent Women"—
or to her more forthright "Run the World (Girls)," which was mobilized for
a graduation-type send-off and tribute to the final Oprah Winfrey Show in
2011, Beyoncé Knowles-Carter has generated popular narratives of feminism
writ large. These narratives, however, have not always been embraced by fellow feminists.

Some consider her too aligned with accepted patriarchal and white
supremacist standards of beauty and femininity. Some see her as too commercial and part of a neoliberal corporate structure that undermines feminist
agendas. Still others view her women's empowerment memes as too simplistic
to advance political perspectives that can meaningfully impact the lives of
women disadvantaged by the same economic, racial, and sexual systems that
have rewarded the pop star with class-based, color, and able-bodied heterosexual privileges.

On this last point, Beyoncé's perceived lack of sophistication is less about
her pop-stardom status. After all, feminists have often looked to pop stars to
represent the public face of feminism: from Camille Paglia's embrace of
Madonna (1990) to the "hip-hop feminism" of nineties-era women rappers
Queen Latifah and Lauryn Hill, as championed by such black feminist writers

as Tricia Rose (1994), Joan Morgan (1999), and Gwendolyn Pough (2004), to J. Jack Halberstam's celebration of "Gaga Feminism" (2012) in reference to Lady Gaga. Taylor Swift, who initially disclaimed the feminist identity, has also been eagerly claimed, even before she finally embraced the F-word (Little 2015). This begs the question: If other pop stars are more acceptable as "feminist" icons, then what makes Beyoncé unacceptable by comparison?

This was the question I sought to explore in my cover story, "Beyoncé's Fierce Feminism," which appeared in the Spring 2013 issue of *Ms.* magazine. However, the *Ms.* cover that featured the pop star drew the most attention, as the magazine's editors received a barrage of criticism and hate mail, while others praised their choice. Embedded within these responses to the cover is the recognition that Beyoncé's feminist credentials had been "officially" endorsed with her appearance on the longest running feminist publication co-founded by *the* feminist icon Gloria Steinem. In other words, no matter how hesitant Beyoncé may have previously responded to feminism no matter how negative other feminists have responded to her images and narratives, the *Ms.* proclamation settled the question. Or did it?

In her article, "The Beyoncé Wars," featured on Salon.com black feminist writer Brittney Cooper notes how feminists tend to respond to the pop star from a visceral level. As she argues:

> Beyoncé … triggers a lot for us: about desire and beauty and skin color politics and access and being chosen and being the cool kid…. Nerdy girls resent the popular pretty girls. We grow up to become the feminists who are beautiful in our own right, to critique patriarchy and challenge desire. And we have a sort of smugness that says, the pretty girl who gets the guy can have all that, but she can't be radical. That Beyoncé would even want to means she has stepped out of her lane, and lanes matter greatly [Cooper 2013].

These tensions certainly echoed in the various complaints by *Ms.* readers who responded to the Beyoncé cover. Indeed, one reader confessed: "Beyoncé makes me feel bad about myself." What does such a statement reveal about these representational politics of feminism? Moreover, without knowing the racial identity of such a reader, what do such personal sensibilities suggest about a black female pop star's ability to engender such "insecurities," as opposed to feelings of solidarity and shared politics and identities?

If the reader is white, we might recognize the need to reject Beyoncé's conventional depictions of beauty and femininity that have often been viewed as "oppressive" to a white womanhood, or—when these images are embodied by a woman of color—fueling feelings of "sexual inadequacy" within the white woman, when compared to the "hypersexual" black woman. If the reader is a woman of color, we might recognize someone who resents Beyoncé's abilities to fit closer to a white ideal of beauty and femininity due to her fairer skin. How do these sentiments then shape our views of Beyoncé the feminist?

In what follows, I will utilize an intersectional analysis to assess the complexities of Beyoncé through the prism of race and gender, which necessarily informs her representation as "feminist." I also explore how the feminist conversations about her reflect certain raced and gendered tropes that have marked a globally celebrated black female pop artist in particular ways. Nonetheless, the pushback created by these feminist debates also prompted Beyoncé to aggressively reclaim and redefine the feminist label, and to do so through bold contradictions, which lend themselves to subversive readings and critique.

The Popular Face of Feminism

In an interview for the online site *Makers*, featuring prominent feminist women, renowned black feminist Beverly Guy-Sheftall made an astute observation: "When popular media talk about feminism, you rarely ever see a black face" (Guy-Sheftall 2013). Her remark is salient in the way that it highlights a particular image that has been constructed around "what a feminist looks like." In the popular imaginary, the feminist is primarily configured as angry, humorless, in opposition to all signs of femininity, troublemaking, rebellious, and above all else, *white*. On the last point, it may seem strange to racialize the image of the feminist when we have numerous black feminists as examples—from Guy-Sheftall herself to Angela Davis to bell hooks to Audre Lorde to public intellectual Melissa Harris-Perry to Twitter activist Feminista Jones. However, now that we can add pop star Beyoncé Knowles-Carter to this list, the debate continues about just who counts as a feminist and who does not.

Women of color in particular have had a long contentious history with being excluded from feminist movements. Apart from those who may view feminism as a "white woman thing," others fought to be included, to reposition themselves "from margin to center," to quote bell hooks. We can point to the examples of Audre Lorde warning radical feminists that, when they dismissed women of color, they "encourage [their] own demise" (Lorde 1984, 69), or Barbara Smith working with the Combahee River Collective to boldly state, "If Black women were free, then everyone else would have to be free since our freedom would necessitate the destruction of all the systems of oppression" (Combahee River Collective 1982, 18). Feminists of color reasserted their presence in a movement that had become increasingly identified as white. Their insistence on creating the analysis of intersectionality, which would better reflect the experiences of women of color, queer women, and other marginalized groups who face multiple oppressions, led to the creation of alternative presses like the Kitchen Table Women of Color Press, which gave us important publications like *This Bridge Called My Back* and

Home Girls, and set off an avalanche of criticisms and scholarship by feminists of color.

These criticisms from the 1980s, which challenged the racism of white feminists, have overshadowed the earlier work of interracial coalition-building among feminists from the 1960s and 1970s, including black feminists Flo Kennedy and Shirley Chisholm. These black women helped to launch the modern women's movement as co-founders with Betty Friedan and Pauli Murray of the National Organization for Women (NOW). Kennedy's Feminist Party also launched Shirley Chisholm as a presidential candidate who became the first woman to run for the 1972 Democratic presidential nomination and the first major-party black candidate for president. The year before, in 1971, another black woman, Dorothy Pitman Hughes, posed with Gloria Steinem for *Esquire* magazine as she and Steinem kicked off a media campaign on feminism while also co-founding *Ms.* magazine. Hughes was also a child welfare advocate and is responsible for founding the first day care center in this country. She has recently been recognized as the aunt of Oscar-nominated actress Gabourey Sidibe of *Precious* and *American Horror Story* fame.

Because popular media rarely show a black face of feminism, it is easy to forget feminists like Dorothy Pitman Hughes, even though we all know Gloria Steinem. Indeed, the PBS documentary *Makers: Women Who Make America* examines how Steinem's introduction to the public sphere came at a time when mainstream media sought a more palatable, "prettier" face of feminism to calm their own fears of a radical feminism that championed lesbianism and the dismantling of patriarchy. As a conventionally attractive white woman and journalist, Steinem became the popular face of feminism, even given credit for such radical statements as, "A woman without a man is like a fish without a bicycle," a quote that was actually made famous by Flo Kennedy. More recently, Steinem has acknowledged that black women "invented the feminist movement," since she "learned feminism disproportionately from black women," even though "the white middle-class part of the movement got reported more" (cited in Tisdale 2015).

Given these representational politics, we often overlook the historical fact that black women were foundational to—not marginal within—the modern women's movement (if we consider the examples of Kennedy, Chisholm, Murray, and Hughes). These historical erasures and the privileging of whiteness have led to a "whitewashing" of the feminist brand. As such, the black feminist is rarely acknowledged. Hence, black feminists—especially in the academy—asserted their presence and theorized their existence from an oppositional framework, whether we look to publications like *All the Women Are White, All the Blacks Are Men, but Some of Us Are Brave*, Audre Lorde's *Sister Outsider*, bell hooks' *Feminist Theory: From Margin to Center*, or Patricia Hill Collins' *Black Feminist Thought*, this last work articulating intersectionality from a sociological perspective, also adapted for critical race feminist theory by legal scholar Kimberlé Crenshaw (1991). Even such celebrated black feminists as Alice Walker, who served as an editor for *Ms.* magazine and established friendships and alliances with Steinem, would enter into these oppositional discourses when she coined the term "womanist" to define a "black feminist"—a definition other black women would embrace to distinguish themselves from white feminists (Walker 1983).

During this post–Civil Rights era of the late twentieth century, black women entertainers in popular culture contributed their own narratives to feminism as they amplified their voices on issues of women's empowerment, independence, and resistance to male domination and racism. It is worth noting that when such black feminist scholars as Collins and Crenshaw were publishing their seminal works in the early nineties, popular black feminism hit the airwaves, as expressed in rapper Queen Latifah's "Ladies First"—featuring London-based emcee Monie Love. The rap song champions black women's political and musical leadership roles in the black community and within hip-hop culture. The video also highlights black women's transnational struggles in the contemporary scene, not just in the shared lyricism of African American and Afro-British subjects but also in the anti-apartheid resistance struggle in South Africa. Queen Latifah creatively demands space for black feminist voices in the public sphere, or as Gwendolyn Pough notes: "bringing wreck… [which has] meant reshaping the public gaze" (Pough 2004, 17). This vernacular term is taken from another Queen Latifah rap single, "U.N.I.T.Y.," which addresses sexual violence, including street harassment women of color face in urban communities.

This musical moment is part of a longer trajectory of black women's musicality and political consciousness, whether we look to blues singers Bessie Smith and Billie Holiday, jazz musician Nina Simone, or soul singer Aretha Franklin. Lesser explored is the pop-culture and "crossover" entertainment of 1980s singers like Janet Jackson, declaring "I'm in control," or internationally celebrated pop vocalists like Whitney Houston, who updated R&B singer Chaka Khan's "I'm Every Woman" anthem for the 1990s moment that saw the flowering of a hip-hop feminism. Joining Queen Latifah in her women's empowerment themes were fellow rappers Salt-N-Pepa and the R&B girl group TLC (including rapper Lisa "Left Eye" Lopes boldly sporting a condom over her left eye) who pushed for sex-positive sensibilities and HIV-awareness with their respective songs "Let's Talk about Sex" and "Ain't 2 Proud 2 Beg." Other examples abound, including rappers Yo-Yo, Da Brat, Missy Elliott, and Eve, as well as the raunchier acts Lil' Kim and Foxy Brown. Such articulations of sexually assertive and/or politically conscious black womanhood climaxed with rapper and singer Lauryn Hill, who integrated hip-hop and R&B with her much lauded and critically acclaimed 1998 solo album *The Miseducation of Lauryn Hill.*

After rising to popularity as part of the hip-hop trio The Fugees, with fellow members Wyclef Jean and Pras, Hill became the first female artist to be nominated for and to win the most Grammys in a single night and her album the first hip-hop-themed work to win the Grammy's top prize of Album of the Year. Her album, alluding to Carter G. Woodson's *The Miseducation of the Negro*, situates her concerns over love and heartache ("Ex-Factor"), pro-choice decisions toward motherhood ("Zion"), gender relations ("Doo Wop [That Thing]"), and nostalgia ("Every Ghetto, Every City") through the lens of radical racial politics. Interestingly, the same year of Lauryn Hill's solo album debut, a sixteen-year-old would later be known only by her first name—Beyoncé—also emerged on the pop scene when Destiny's Child released their self-titled debut album. And despite the many differences between the two icons—Hill cast as a natural-haired, dark-skinned beauty with black nationalist views in contrast to Beyoncé's lighter-skinned, blonde-haired presentation and more "universal" approach to women's empowerment—Hill is a definite influence on the pop star, as was illustrated at her 2014 *On the Run* world tour with her partner Jay-Z when she offered her own rendition of "Ex-Factor."

I mention this as a reminder that the black feminist groundwork had already been laid for Beyoncé, on which to build her musical brand. Not only that, but despite the obviously feminist work in black popular culture, few of these artists embraced the feminist label. As Whitney Peoples notes, "the ambivalence to the label 'feminism' expressed by many female rappers whose lyrics have been read by some as expressing feminist sentiment … speaks to the contested nature of the term 'hip-hop feminism'" (Peoples 2008, 27). This has not stopped certain writers like Tricia Rose from assisting such rappers as MC Lyte in understanding feminism as "a mode of analysis rather than a label for a group of women associated with a particular social movement" (Rose 1994, 176). Nonetheless, more often than not women like Queen Latifah and Lauryn Hill resist identifying as feminists.

Such rejection, I would argue, stems from the historical exclusion of women of color from dominant images of feminism, which give the impression that the movement does not speak to the specific struggles impacting black women. Beyoncé herself was initially hesitant before she more confidently claimed the word for her own identity, a development that I would argue only became possible with a millennial generation of black feminists who came of age during this 1990s era of women's empowerment as "daughters of feminist privilege" (Morgan 1999, 59), which allowed them to combine the popular rhetoric with the academic rhetoric of black feminism to which they had been exposed through their college education and which they can now expound upon through social media. Indeed, that Beyoncé could find on YouTube a fellow black woman, such as celebrated Nigerian author Chimamanda Ngozi Adichie, delivering a Tedx speech, "We Should All Be Feminists" (Adichie 2013), propelled her toward a more self-assured engagement with feminism, which she could later sample in her musical creations.

Beyoncé Talks Back to Feminists

Although my article, "Beyoncé's Fierce Feminism," explored the contradictions of the pop star's public delivery of feminism, I wish I had delved further into our queasiness over her sexiness and her embrace of wealth and capitalism, main points of contention in feminist debates in the wake of her *Ms.* cover. On *Ms.*'s Facebook wall, numerous comments flooded the page in response to this cover, in which several *Ms.* readers left harsh, derogatory comments: from calling the pop star "a fur-wearing stripper" and a "whore" to discrediting her feminism for "calling women bitches," in reference to her released track "Bow Down, Bitches/I Been On." The nature of these criticisms also seemed racially tinged in that black women's bodies are often aggressively policed and condemned for what is perceived as embodying a morally suspect sexuality. I therefore sought to address these racial politics in a post for *Ms.*'s blog, "Policing Feminism: Regulating the Bodies of Women of Color." However, one commenter seemed to critique Beyoncé from the perspective of a woman of color and responded to this blog post with the following derisive rant:

> Out of all the "fierce feminists" in the world, why are Black women and girls stuck with Beyoncé? That's all we get is Beyoncé? Is she worth the cover of a non-entertainment focused magazine? Is she more important than fracking? Is this journalism? Seriously? If you're listening Mrs. Knowles-Carter, which I know you're not, this isn't personal. Do your thang, gurl. Just don't call it feminism… [cited in Hobson 2013b].

Although this individual dismisses the pop star's relevance to a "serious" feminist magazine or to black feminism, instructive here is the assumption that Beyoncé would not be listening to these responses. However, Beyoncé showcased in many ways that she was not only listening to these dismissive criticisms against her but offered a complex rebuttal through her self-titled fifth solo album *Beyoncé*, which debuted seven months after her appearance on *Ms.* with its surprise release on December 13, 2013. Her strongest statements are often embodied through performance, even though she has sought more credentialed ways of expressing her feminism—from contributing the essay "Gender Equality Is a Myth!" to *The Shriver Report* to joining Facebook COO and *Lean In* author Sheryl Sandberg for the "Ban Bossy" campaign in 2014.

Interestingly, one could argue that, once *Ms.*, the premiere feminist magazine, featured and boldly claimed Beyoncé for its cover, the gauntlet had been dropped, with different feminists squaring off in a battle between "radical" feminists—wanting to focus their struggles against systemic oppressions—and "liberal" feminists, who continue to focus women's struggles on individual choice and social reform. The harsh comments on the publication's Facebook and Blog—roundly criticizing Beyoncé's upholding of standard portrayals of female beauty and sexuality—also jarred against those who defended the pop star for representing "sex-positive" feminism. Whether she intended to or not, Beyoncé ignited such debates, which then elicited her response that came in the form of an album.

The unconventional release of Beyoncé's album via iTunes, with a brief announcement on her Instagram as her only promotion, captivated audiences who eagerly greeted the news. Indeed, the album was rapturously described on MSNBC's *Melissa Harris-Perry* show as a "feminist manifesto" (Harris-Perry 2013). In particular, Harris-Perry's labeling of the *BEYONCÉ* album as "feminist" was in response to Beyoncé's sampling of Adichie's "We Should All Be Feminists" speech in her song "Flawless."

What is particularly striking, when reviewing Beyoncé's visual album of 14 songs and 17 music videos, is the multifaceted and contradictory ways she engages representational politics of beauty and sexuality. Opening with her song and video, "Pretty Hurts," which is a critique of the rigid beauty standards impacting women and girls, she wryly closes the album with the bonus video "Grown Woman," which willfully disrupts the visual aesthetics of video production—from grainy footage and "home videos" of herself as a young girl, to psychedelic animation sequences and pastiche images of the pop star dancing raunchily in the company of African women, thereby suggesting her black diasporic connection of sensual dancing (represented by booty-enhancing dances like twerking) to traditional African dance expressions, as well as the African-based rhythms of the song. She reinserts the "fertility" aspect of dance, best represented by her sensual evolution into motherhood (a role she also celebrates in the song and video "Blue," dedicated to her daughter Blue Ivy). "Grown Woman" is an irreverent video that colors outside the lines of the rigidity expressed in "Pretty Hurts."

And yet, other music videos and songs on the album reassert conventional images of sexuality, which are often positioned as "hypersexual" when represented through the black body. Given that so many "feminist" critics on *Ms.*'s Facebook and Blog coded Beyoncé as a "fur-wearing stripper"—a critique of her perceived lack of environmental consciousness combined with her hyper-feminine and hypersexual presentation—one cannot help but notice how the pop star aggressively mobilized this image for her videos "No Angel," "Yoncé," and "Partition." Indeed, these videos, taken together, position

Beyoncé within racialized and class-based contexts, as the first video situates her "fur-wearing" lingerie-clad body within the "Third Ward" of Houston's low-income black community, while "Yoncé" signifies on the "streets" display through black supermodels "posing" alongside her as "hood" girls. However, "Partition" opens on a scene of opulent wealth before we are transported to a Parisian strip club where Beyoncé embodies the "stripper" that so many feminists seemed to condemn. When the pop star aligns with the streets and then takes that same sentiment onto the world stage and to her million-dollar mansion, Beyoncé reconfigures the raced and classed meanings of her own black female body in her eroticized self-image. Nonetheless, her inquiry, "Don't feminists like sex?"—a loose translation from the French language heard in her song "Partition"—suggests that she is indeed responding to criticism that she is "too sexy" and questions how a "feminist" sexuality could be realized if we do not start with the existing images of sexiness, which she engages but also tries to subvert.

Tellingly, Beyoncé's sampling of Adichie is placed in dialog with the earlier released track "Bow Down, Bitches," as if Beyoncé invites us to listen to the "Flawless" single as both a definitive and satirical response to her critics who dismiss her feminist claims. The online-released track, "Bow Down, Bitches/I Been On," responded to the numerous criticisms she faced after a number of political "missteps": from "lip-synching" the National Anthem at President Barack Obama's second inauguration on January 21, 2013; to spending her wedding anniversary on the island of Cuba a few months later; to naming her world tour that year *Mrs. Carter.* Set against these politically charged attacks, Beyoncé's "Bow Down, Bitches" represents a sonic moment of articulating rage and self-defense.

Despite the feminist criticisms against this track for espousing chauvinistic language that subjugates women, Beyoncé invites us to recognize her own gender performance in the way she appropriates masculinity, or as Regina Bradley argues about the sonic deepening of Beyoncé's vocals: "Rather than remaining attached to the definition of bitch as directed at women, Beyoncé uses the sonic tropes at play to decentralize gender norms" (Bradley 2014). Such gender-bending sonic experimentation is also performed in the vein of hip-hop rhetorical bravado and "dirty dozen" trading in insults. Moreover, Beyoncé addresses those who have criticized her for naming her world tour *Mrs. Carter* by challenging her critics to not misread or misinterpret her gendered choices, to not dismiss her as a mere wife, since she embodies several identities simultaneously. Considering that Beyoncé legally hyphenated her surname to Knowles-Carter—and rumors suggest that her husband also goes by this surname in a gesture of gender equality and marital partnership—we are reminded of the separation between public persona and private identity, as well as the spectacle of performativity both in her case and the case of her partner. We are invited to contend with a much more complex rhetorical response when she remixes this track with her sampling of Adichie's "We Should All Be Feminists."

As Beyoncé described of her "Flawless" feminist anthem single, it "will make you feel real gangsta" in this exercise in verbal battling (Knowles-Carter 2014b). She especially invites a complication of the term "flawless" by placing asterisks next to the word and opening the video with earlier footage of her childhood days when she and her girl group Girls Time tried to break into show business, only to lose a competition on the show *Star Search*. She proclaims "flawlessness" by inserting a reminder that she didn't always "win," or what can be called a "humble brag" moment.

These issues are then given more gravitas with Adichie's words. Given the complex engagements with feminism in both the songs and videos "Partition" and "Flawless," it is telling that Beyoncé staged "Partition" at the 2014 VMAs, featuring her "stripper"-like pole-dancing performance, just before sampling in particular this segment from Adichie's speech: "We teach girls that they cannot be sexual beings in the way that boys are.... Feminist: a person who believes in the equality of the sexes" (Adichie 2013). Beyoncé may be flawed in her feminist expressions, but she sincerely challenges feminists to reconsider their relationship to sex and sexuality.

Selling Black Feminism

The feminist debates that proliferated over Beyoncé's *Ms.* cover intensified in the wake of her fifth solo album release. However, some of the more heated conversations occurred among black feminists, most notably when bell hooks labeled the pop star a "terrorist" and a "slave." These comments were made at the public forum, "Are you still a slave?" on May 6, 2014, at the New School, which featured hooks, as well as writers Janet Mock and Marci Blackman, and filmmaker Shola Lynch ("Are You Still a Slave?" 2014).

While hooks can admit to enjoying Beyoncé the entertainer—as illustrated in a video of the scholar dancing to "Drunk in Love," uploaded onto Janet Mock's Twitter account—she roundly rejected Beyoncé the feminist, whom she recast as doing active harm to other women and girls (a "terrorist") while simultaneously rendering her as an abject victim (a "slave") with no agency over her image and performative choices. However, Angela Davis found this construction problematic. Davis, who responded favorably to Beyoncé's sampling of Adichie, argues, "Whatever problems I have with Beyoncé, I think it is so misleading and irresponsible to use [the word "terrorist"] in connection with her. It has been used to [criminalize] struggles for liberation. But we don't use the word terror and terrorism to describe U.S. history and the racism of the pre-civil rights era.... So, to call Beyoncé a terrorist just does not work" (cited in Jeffries 2014). This critique has not stopped hooks from railing against what she characterizes as a neoliberal corporate take-over of feminism by Beyoncé, whom hooks views as "colonized" by white supremacist capitalist patriarchy (hooks 2014).

Such criticisms lead me to wonder: Is there a space for a commercially mass-marketed feminism that could co-exist alongside radical feminism? Is Beyoncé really the problem here, or is it the confining space of commercial media that silences more radical feminist discourses? And, with regards to what Carole Boyce Davies sees as the "blonding" of our black pop stars (Davies 2013, 200)—from Beyoncé to Nicki Minaj—do these appropriations of whiteness signal "colonization"? Conversely, Yaba Blay notes how this critique is often mobilized when black women attempt to fit white beauty standards—from hair straightening to skin bleaching—even though such critiques are not leveled against black men who desire such women or who perpetuate colonial definitions of power and masculinity (Blay 2013).

Curiously, in her analysis, Blay offers as an example of African men's own "colonial mentality" the Nollywood movie, *Beyoncé: The President's Daughter*, which conflates "successful" and desirable Nigerian womanhood with American-style class and color, signified through the naming of the pop star that is then consumed in the transnational cultural spheres of the African Diaspora. Of course, these power differentials exist beyond black cultural expressions, as the H&M clothing line, which globally marketed ads featuring Beyoncé, quickly learned that the wider public responded less favorably to her darker-haired ads in comparison to her blonder images (Grey 2013). Given the normalcies of whiteness across the globe, as well as the male-dominated music industry in which she operates, Beyoncé found ways to survive and thrive to a point where she could champion the feminist cause, which should not be summarily dismissed by other feminists.

Moreover, in conforming to white beauty standards that allow her more visibility on the world stage, Beyoncé complicates representations of black womanhood and resists racially essentialist meanings ascribed to the black female body. While she perpetuates images reifying whiteness through her appropriation of long blond hair and lightened complexion, she nonetheless utilizes this visibility to incorporate black women's vernacular dance and musical expressions, as well as to include a multiracial cast of supporting women routinely populating her concerts and music videos. Achieving "blonde ambitions," Beyoncé simultaneously undermines those same white beauty "model-thin size-zero" standards by embracing a "bootylicious" aesthetic of her (and by extension other black women's) natural curves. In these ways, she projects a black femininity that subverts the meanings of "racially pure" blondeness and white womanhood.

In addition, Beyoncé champions femininity, the expected gendered presentation for women that is often derided in feminist discourse while more masculine-presenting or androgynous-appearing women are lauded as symbols of resistance. However, femininity can take on subversive meanings when represented via the black female body. Within contemporary representations of black womanhood, the black female body is often portrayed, even scorned for being "too masculine"—from the powerful athletic bodies of Venus and Serena Williams in tennis to the lighter-skinned ballerina Misty Copeland, who is often depicted in advertisements and commercials that emphasize her muscular build, which engenders an "athletic" discourse in ballet that is never used to construct the more feminine and ethereal aesthetic of white ballerinas. While these women have transformed their respective arenas, they are nonetheless entrenched in what transgender blogger Shaaadi Devereaux calls a transphobic dismissal of black women as "real women" (Devereaux 2014). Such attitudes pertaining to black women's perceived lack of feminine embodiment prompted blogger Hannah Giorgis to celebrate Oscar-winning actress and fashionista Lupita Nyong'o for redefining beauty through her dark-skinned and short-haired appearance. As she posits, "Lupita is a beacon of hope for every dark-skinned, natural-haired girl who grows up being told she looks like a boy, a challenge to the racist, cissexist claims that Black women's short hair or musculature are inherently masculine" (Giorgis 2014).

Lupita Nyong'o, in many ways, is celebrated as a counterpoint to the representations of lighter-skinned black pop stars, including Beyoncé, Rihanna, and Nicki Minaj. However, rather than reduce these public figures through the colorist lens of "light skin" versus "dark skin," we can instead revel in a wider black sisterhood in which all these women offer diverse representations of black womanhood. Indeed, Beyoncé's discourse on femininity, sexuality, sex and sexiness has liberatory potential for black women. Certainly, as hooks contends, her engagement with a white supremacist capitalist patriarchal construction of beauty and sexiness does not advance new narratives of sexual liberation. Yet, I want to push back a bit on this because it is precisely her appropriation *and subversion* of white supremacist capitalist values that enabled her to build her enterprise and access economic and cultural power. As a black woman existing in a music industry infamous for exploiting and marginalizing black women's musical talents (whether they be light-skinned or dark-skinned, conventionally attractive or not), this is already an extraordinary feat for someone like Beyoncé, who now has the ability to *own* a feminist identity on a world stage—something that relatively few pop artists do.

Beyoncé's more recent performances are on par with her earlier tributes to feminism, as was envisioned in the futuristic takeover of women "running the world" in her 2011 song and video "Run the World (Girls)," which was actively dismissed by some feminists as juvenile and not particularly sophisticated in understanding the geopolitical scene of women's realities (Nine-teenPercent 2011). However, a vision for the future is still a vision worth considering, and Beyoncé does emulate this vision in practice, such as forming her all-female band, the "Sugar Mamas," and championing women's collective power on a worldwide, mass platform when given the chance, as had occurred with her Super Bowl halftime show on February 3, 2013. In this grand performance, Beyoncé interjected into the hyper-masculine arena of the football game a hyper-feminine display of female energy. She also disrupts the U.S. nationalist spectacle by infusing a transnational and black diasporic aesthetic, as evidenced by her performance of "Baby Boy" and its choreographic and linguistic invocation of Jamaican dancehall "dutty wine" and Indian music samplings, including Hindu allusions to the warrior goddess Durga.

Such a performance makes it possible to disrupt white supremacist and patriarchal visions of female beauty, sexuality, and feminist politics. There is a reason why mainstream American audiences decried her Super Bowl show as "too sexy," due to the booty-enhancing dances on display. The (white) body politic is being challenged, and such spectacles—coupled with feminist rhetorics *not* emerging from the institutional sphere of academic feminism—pushes the boundaries around which bodies, which aesthetics, and which politics are valid.

This spectacle was so powerful and so subversive that men (and women) found ways to undermine it through memes on social media that appeared after her show, which recast Beyoncé's dance moves through masculinized caricatures, or which criticized her "too sexy" display. Such defeminizing mockery of black women's bodies are a not-so-subtle reminder that, no matter how much Beyoncé tries to control her image, other "controlling images," as Collins once argued, will attempt to contain her through recognizable stereotypes of black womanhood. That Beyoncé consistently receives such criticisms from the dominant culture—including from right-wing conservatives ranting against "Beyoncé voters" (Basu 2014) and blaming her for black teenage pregnancies, despite her mature age when she married and gave birth to a daughter within the marriage—suggests that she is not nearly as "safe" as some feminists accuse her of being. Her very existence as a black woman codes her as disreputable, thus making her engagements with conventionality rather subversive in its repositioning for feminism.

Black Feminist or Just Plain Feminist?

To conclude, I would like to reiterate Guy-Sheftall's concern that black women are often not chosen to represent the popular face of feminism. Despite the many debates over Beyoncé's claim to feminism, there is no denying the massive influence that comes with the pop star boldly standing before a brightly lit "FEMINIST" sign during her fifteen-minute performance at the VMAs and doing so before millions of viewers. Not only was this moment remarkable for the popular rebranding of feminism, but it also signals something else: a black woman's reclaiming of the word without adjective— "BLACK FEMINIST"—or renaming—"WOMANIST."

What, specifically, does this moment in popular culture mean for a younger generation of women who have been raised to be suspicious of feminism? Granted, this suspicion is widespread. Countless women and men, across races, ethnicities, genders, and sexual orientations, are hard-pressed to define what a feminist actually is because they have already heard the stereotypes: "manhater," "domineering," "unattractive," "killjoy," and the list goes on. Then here comes today's most prominent sex symbol claiming feminism, exulting in her sexiness while her husband—renowned for his machismo—takes care of child duties (as was demonstrated during the VMA show). That Beyoncé is a black woman at the top of her musical enterprise propels this rebranding to another level. As Adichie noted in an interview with *Vogue* magazine: "My thirteen-year-old niece calls herself a feminist—not because I made a speech but because of Beyoncé" (cited in Frank 2014).

Although popular media rarely show a black face when talking about feminism, Beyoncé has most definitely changed the game in which black women can unhesitatingly embrace the "feminist" label and bring to the table all of their sexiness and contradictory selves. We have come a long way from the seventies era, when mainstream media sought Gloria Steinem as a "pretty face" of feminism. However, Beyoncé's *Ms.* cover provides the necessary "face-lift" for a multiracial feminism—where she appropriates a Steinem-like visibility while bringing to the forefront the political work of Dorothy Pittman Hughes and other black feminists. In her articulation of "Flawless" feminism, Beyoncé has shifted the terrain of gender, race, and sexual politics.

REFERENCES

Adichie, Chimamanda Ngozi. 2013. "We Should All Be Feminists." TEDx Talks YouTube Video (April 12). https://www.youtube.com/watch?v=hg3umXU_qWc (accessed October 25, 2014).

Anzaldúa, Gloria, and Cherríe Moraga, eds. 1982. *This Bridge Called My Back: Writings by Radical Women of Color.* New York: Kitchen Table Women of Color Press.

"Are You Still a Slave?" 2014. Live Stream Video from *The New School*, featuring bell hooks, Janet Mock, Marci Blackman, and Shola Lynch (May 6). http://new.livestream.com/thenewschool/slave (accessed October 25, 2014).

Basu, Tanya. 2014. "The Myth of the Beyonce Voters." *The Atlantic* (July 18). http://www.theatlantic.com/politics/archive/2014/07/the-myth-of-the-beyonce-voter/374297/ (accessed June 1, 2015).

Blay, Yaba. 2013. "Skin Bleaching, Self-Hatred, and 'Colonial Mentality.'" Yaba Blay

Pages. http://yabablay.com/skin-bleaching-self-hatred-and-colonial-mentality/ (accessed May 29, 2015).

Bradley, Regina. 2014. "I Been On: BaddieBey and Beyoncé's Sonic Masculinity." *Sounding Out!* (September 22). http://soundstudiesblog.com/2014/09/22/i-been-on-baddiebey-and-beyonces-sonic-masculinity/ (accessed October 25, 2014).

Collins, Patricia Hill. 1990. Black *Feminist Thought.* New York: Routledge.

Combahee River Collective. 1982. "A Black Feminist Statement." In *All the Women Are White, All the Blacks Are Men, but Some of Us Are Brave: Black Women's Studies*, eds. Gloria Hull, Patricia Bell Scott, and Barbara Smith, 13–22. New York: Feminist Press, 1982.

Cooper, Brittney. 2013. "The Beyoncé Wars: Should She Get to be a Feminist?" *Salon* (December 17). http://www.salon.com/2013/12/17/a_deeply_personal_beyonce_debate_should_she_get_to_be_a_feminist/ (accessed October 25, 2014).

Crenshaw, Kimberlé. 1991. "Mapping the Margins: Intersectionality, Identity Politics, and Violence against Women of Color." *Stanford Law Review* 43(6):1241–1299.

Davies, Carole Boyce. 2013. *Caribbean Spaces: Escapes from Twilight Zones.* Urbana: University of Illinois Press.

Devereaux, Shaadi. 2014. "Rollersets & Realness: Black Womanhood Defined as Drag Performance." *Black Girl Dangerous* (July 24). http://www.blackgirldangerous.org/2014/07/rollersets-realness-black-womanhood-defined-drag-performance/ (accessed May 29, 2015).

Frank, Alex. 2014. "Chimamanda Ngozi Adichie on Her 'Flawless' Speech, Out Today as an eBook." *Vogue* (July 29). http://www.vogue.com/946843/chimamanda-ngozi-adicihie-feminism-beyonce-book/ (accessed October 25, 2014).

Giorgis, Hannah. 2014. "Lupita Nyong'o and the Evolving Paradox of Black Femininity." *Youngist* (February 28). http://youngist.tumblr.com/post/78098418728/lupita-nyongo-and-the-evolving-paradox-of-black (accessed May 29, 2015).

Gordon, Jane. 2010. "Beyoncé: The Multi-Talented Star Reveals What She Is Planning Next." *Daily Mail* (August 15). http://www.dailymail.co.uk/home/you/article-1301838/Beyonc--The-multi-talented-star-reveals-planning-next.html (accessed October 25, 2014).

Grey, Judith. 2013. "People Don't Recognize Beyoncé in Ads Unless She's Blonde." *Business Insider* (May 9). http://www.businessinsider.com/blonde-beyonce-scores-better-with-consumers-2013–5 (accessed May 29, 2015).

Guy-Sheftall, Beverly. 2013. Online Interview. *Makers: The Largest Video Collection of Women's Stories.* http://www.makers.com/beverly-guy-sheftall. (accessed October 25, 2014).

Halberstam, J. Jack. 2012. *Gaga Feminism: Sex, Gender, and the New Normal.* Boston: Beacon Press.

Harris-Perry, Melissa. 2013. "Beyoncé Drops Her 'Feminist Manifesto.'" MSNBC *Melissa Harris-Perry Show* (December 14). http://www.msnbc.com/melissa-harris-perry/watch/beyonce-drops-her-feminist-manifesto-90969155971 (accessed October 25, 2014).

Hobson, Janell. 2013a. "Beyoncé's Fierce Feminism." *Ms.* (Spring): 42–45.

_____. 2013b. "Policing Feminism: Regulating the Bodies of Women of Color." *Ms.* Magazine Blog (June 10). http://msmagazine.com/blog/2013/06/10/policing-feminism-regulating-the-bodies-of-women-of-color/.

hooks, bell. 1984. *Feminist Theory: From Margin to Center.* Boston: South End Press.

_____. 2014. Keynote Address Delivered at the National Women's Studies Association Annual Meeting. San Jan, Puerto Rico. November 14.

Hull, Gloria, Patricia Bell Scott, and Barbara Smith, eds. 1982. *All the Women Are White, All the Blacks Are Men, but Some of Us Are Brave: Black Women's Studies.* New York: The Feminist Press.

Jeffries, Stuart. 2014. "Angela Davis: 'There is an unbroken line of police violence in the U.S. that takes us all the way back to slavery.'" *The Guardian* (December 14). http://www.theguardian.com/global/2014/dec/14/angela-davis-there-is-an-unbroken-line-of-police-violence-in-the-us-that-takes-us-all-the-way-back-to-the-days-of-slavery (accessed May 29, 2015).

Knowles-Carter, Beyoncé. 2013. *Beyoncé: The Visual Album.* Distributed by Columbia Records.

_____. 2014a. "Gender Equality Is a Myth!" *The Shriver Report* (January 12). http://shriverreport.org/gender-equality-is-a-myth-beyonce/ (accessed October 25, 2014).

_____. 2014b. "Self-Titled, Part 2: Imperfection." YouTube Video (January 13). https://www.youtube.com/watch?v=41WgKIeCRqs (accessed October 25, 2014).

_____. 2014c. "Self-Titled, Part 4: Liberation." YouTube Video (January 13). https://www.youtube.com/watch?v=0eZ0mzI37-A (accessed October 25, 2014).

Little, Anita. 2015. "We Heart: Taylor Swift's Feminist Evolution." *Ms.* Magazine Blog (May 21, 2015). http://msmagazine.com/blog/2015/05/21/we-heart-taylor-swifts-feminist-evolution/ (May 30, 2015).

Lorde, Audre. 1984. *Sister Outsider: Essays and Speeches.* Trumansburg, NY: Crossing Press.

Makers: Women Who Make America. 2013. PBS Documentary.

Morgan, Joan. 1999. *When Chickenheads Come Home to Roost: A Hip-Hop Feminist Breaks It Down.* New York: Simon & Schuster.

Ms. Magazine Blog. 2013. http://msmagazine.com/blog/ (accessed May 31, 2015).

Ms. Magazine Facebook. 2013. https://www.facebook.com/msmagazine (accessed May 31, 2015).

NineteenPercent. 2011. "Beyoncé—Run the World (Lies)." YouTube Video (May 20). http://www.youtube.com/watch?v=p72UqyVPj54 (accessed October 25, 2014).

On the Run: Beyonce and Jay Z. 2014. HBO (September 20).

Paglia, Camille. 1990. "Madonna—Finally, a Real Feminist." *New York Times* (December 14). http://www.nytimes.com/1990/12/14/opinion/madonna-finally-a-real-feminist.html (accessed June 1, 2015).

Peoples, Whitney A. 2008. "'Under Construction': Identifying Foundations of Hip-Hop Feminism and Exploring Bridges between Black Second-Wave and Hip-Hop Feminism." *Meridians: Feminism, Race, Transnationalism* 8 (1): 19–52

Pough, Gwendolyn. 2004. *Check It While I Wreck It: Black Womanhood, Hip-Hop Culture, and the Public Sphere.* Boston: Northeastern University Press.

Rose, Tricia. 1994. *Black Noise: Rap Music and Black Culture in Contemporary America.* Middletown, CT: Wesleyan University Press.

Smith, Barbara, ed. 1983. *Home Girls: A Black Feminist Anthology.* New York: Kitchen Table Women of Color Press.

Tisdale, Stacey. 2015. "Gloria Steinem on Black Women: 'They Invented the Feminist Movement.'" *Black Enterprise.* http://www.blackenterprise.com/lifestyle/arts-culture/be-womens-history-month-feminist-icon-gloria-steinem-talks-black-women-feminism/ (accessed May 29, 2015).

Walker, Alice. 1983. *In Search of Our Mothers' Gardens: Womanist Prose.* New York: Harcourt Inc.

What's Love Got to Do with It? 1993. Dir. Brian Gibson. Perf. Angela Bassett, Laurence Fishburne. Distributed by Touchstone Pictures.

Beyoncé as Intersectional Icon?
Interrogating the Politics of Respectability

Marla H. Kohlman

There are myriad ways in which contemporary female performers offer a positive message of sexual confidence and self-empowerment for all women and Beyoncé Knowles-Carter is no exception. In fact, Beyoncé is not the first to present this type of image to young women. But there are significant differences between the images projected by Dorothy Dandridge, Tina Turner, and Whitney Houston. In this essay, I reference the pervasive influence of a "politics of respectability" that remains an ethical high ground within the black community, and argue that Beyoncé has managed to alternatively invoke and eschew this doctrine as her whim dictates.

The persona of Beyoncé presents, for many, an example of intersectional agency. She is simultaneously a commoditized item to be consumed by the public gaze, an independent woman, a wife, a devoted daughter, and a mother. She has used her lyrics and her persona to become a powerful icon of black female sexuality because of the many ways in which she chooses to present herself to the world, but also because she interrogates many of the tropes of womanhood that are problematic for all women.

Establishing the Point of Reference

Fannie Lou Hamer once said "A black woman's body is never hers alone," and I am reminded of this quite often when I see videos featuring young, shapely, black women aggressively displayed for the male gaze of rap artists around whom they undulate, as well as for the audience consuming these video representations. Hamer's prophetic statement reminds us still that the commodification of the black female body remains a powerful force in the American imagination and in all forms of popular culture. In the pages that follow, I call for us to reflect upon the commodification of black woman in popular culture and film from the turn of the 20th century to the present.

The principal defining feature for us to consider, then, is the passage of time and the increasing influence and pervasiveness of popular media in all of its myriad forms of the 21st century. With that in mind, we must remember that the ubiquity of Beyoncé's influence is much greater in comparison to those who have preceded her by several decades in the popular imagination and cultural art forms. Think, for example, of the influence of Dorothy Dandridge, Lena Horne, and Josephine Baker. Now move forward in time to the examples of Aretha Franklin, Patti Labelle, and Tina Turner. Come closer in time to Beyoncé and think about the way in which Whitney Houston and Janet Jackson were what we may refer to as "packaged for popular consumption." What all of the aforementioned actresses and performers share is, indeed, the fact that they were specifically "packaged" for popular consumption to appeal to what was considered to be the mainstream audience of their time. What differs for each of these women, and the audience for which they were commodified, is the moment in time governing popular depictions and the media available for them share in formulating the architecture of their popular consumption. Notwithstanding these facts, all of the women named above were forced to contend with the politics of respectability in shaping their image for popular consumption and Beyoncé is no exception to this standard.

Understanding the Politics of Respectability

As Evelyn Higginbotham powerfully presents the concept of "the politics of respectability" in her text, *Righteous Discontent*, it is derived from the influential teachings of the black Baptist church at the turn of the 20th century in a deliberate attempt to circumnavigate racist depictions and stereotypical representations of black women in the United States. Black women were perceived during slavery, at the height of Jim Crow, and beyond as promiscuous, lazy, and lacking in self-respect on the one hand and as subservient and menial on the other. This may be seen especially well in the stereotypical images of black women as jezebel or mammy in popular culture then and now. You will recognize the Mammy stereotype from the character of the same name in the film adaptation of Margaret Mitchell's *Gone with the Wind*. Mammy is portrayed as a dark-skinned, overweight female servant who is fiercely loyal to the white family she is content to care for from birth to death. Jezebel is the flip side of mammy. Mammy does not start out as an older heavy woman, as we are reminded of in the character of Aunt Sarah, in Octavia Butler's fictional text, *Kindred*. Rather, mammy may have once been a shapely young black servant who was sexually exploited by her white male master. Thus, the black woman as jezebel is portrayed as lascivious and amoral, desiring of the male gaze and more. Both stereotypes, the mammy and the jezebel, have been used to justify the exploitation and oppression of black women during slavery and the sharecropping period that led us into the Reconstruction and Jim Crow Era. The continued prevalence of these stereotypes, however, presents a different issue for our consideration.

The politics of respectability, according to Higginbotham, was purposefully constructed by black women to serve two complementary functions: to encourage assimilation of black women into the hegemonic discourse of femininity ascribed to white women while also discounting class-based notions of poor black women as being innately inferior (Higginbotham 1993).

> Respectability demanded that every individual in the black community assume responsibility for behavioral self-regulation and self-improvement along moral, educational and economic lines. The goal was to distance oneself as far as possible from images perpetuated by racist stereotypes…. There could be no laxity as far as sexual conduct, cleanliness, temperance, hard work, and politeness were concerned [Higginbotham 1993, 196].

With this in mind, it is easier to understand why many black female performers were forced to walk a fine line in self-presentation and to maintain the audience they needed to ensure continued vitality as performers. It is also easier to understand why Josephine Baker chose not to perform for much of her adult life in the United States, abjuring the segregationist politics of her time for the greater freedom and creativity permitted her as a performer in France. It is important to note, however, that many black people in the U.S. shunned Baker at that time because it appeared that she disdained the dictates of the politics of respectability. Even so, it is also important to note that while Baker seems to have created the stage persona she presented, she was forced to rely upon the French patronage endemic to popular approval to maintain her career. In this way, it may be argued that she was no different than Lena Horne or Dorothy Dandridge who were forced to contend with the politics of respectability in a different way in the United States.

Lena Horne, for example, suffered the indignity of being packaged so that her race was almost undetectable for much of her career. In fact, she was prevented from playing a role as an octoroon in the MGM production *Showboat* in deference to Ava Gardner who had to be "blackened up" for the part. Moreover, Lena Horne was the voice of the character to which Ava Gardner had to lip sync. At that point in history, the white audience for whom the theater was "packaged" would not have tolerated Horne as a romantic lead to a white man, despite the racialized overtone of the character at issue (Lawrence). In anticipation of this societal double standard, and far before her career as a performer began, Horne's grandmother "drilled into her respectability at all costs. She was to use proper diction, no [black] dialect allowed, and always present herself as a lady" (Lawrence). It is instructive; nonetheless, that Lena Horne was the first black woman to obtain a recording contract with a major Hollywood production studio.

Dorothy Dandridge was the first black woman to be nominated for an Academy award, for her portrayal of Carmen Jones in the movie of the same name directed by Otto Preminger. Despite the fact that this popular movie featured an all-black cast (also starring Harry Belafonte and Pearl Bailey), Dandridge despaired of being offered too many roles that seemed to be reserved specifically for black actresses as "servants, slaves, or 'loose' women," some of which she was forced to take in order to make ends meet during her all too short career span (Gates and Wolfe).

Even as we move forward in history, we find examples of women performers who are limited by the vision of those who would mold them into a particular image for popular consumption and who, thankfully in some cases, had the ability to chart their own course. Think here of Tina Turner, Diana Ross, Patti Labelle, Aretha Franklin, and Janet Jackson. Whitney Houston presents a different discussion than these women because of the way in which her career was cut short, similar to that of Dorothy Dandridge. All of that being said, the ostensible freedom to present one's own talents to do the work does not mean that the dictates of popular opinion and expectation are any less important for more recent female performers. It does, however, provide an opportunity to explore the reasons why the politics of respectability does not have the currency and influence it once exerted on the choices made by black female actresses and performers.

And lest we think that the politics of respectability was only about black women, remember Higginbotham's warning that the point of this ideology was to dictate the tenets of black self representation, for black men and women alike. Langston Hughes calls our attention to this in his essay "The Negro Artist and the Racial Mountain," as he contends that blacks must move beyond the politics of respectability to embrace a self-defined set of identity politics:

> We younger Negro artists who create now intend to express our individual dark-skinned selves without fear or shame. If white people are pleased we are glad. If they are not, it doesn't matter. We know we are beautiful. And ugly too…. If colored people are pleased we are glad. If they are not, their displeasure doesn't matter either. We build our temples for tomorrow, strong as we know how, and we stand on top of the mountain, free within ourselves [Hughes 1926, 4].

Beyond Respectability Politics

In *Exotic Revolutionaries*, Shayne Lee presents an insightful analysis of current pop culture and media representations of black female sexuality. In so doing, Lee discusses black female celebrities across the entire spectrum of popular media coverage—recording and video artists, athletes, comediennes, talk show hosts, models, and the list goes on, as he argues that contemporary black female performers offer a positive message of sexual confidence and self-empowerment for all women, significantly exhibited by black women.

Citing the pervasive influence of a "politics of respectability" that remains an ethical high ground within the black community, Lee argues that black women's comfort level with sexuality, in both private and public forums, has been hampered by historical archetypes of promiscuity and exploitation that should no longer be regarded as prevalent in the 21st century of pervasive media images. He also cites the influences of black churches and idealized family configurations for continuing to enforce a prudish, unenlightened sense of morality that is sorely out of touch with much of the reality we find ourselves faced with in the popular media.

What does it mean to teach young black women that it is best to avoid the topic of sexual pleasure in an age when they find bold sexual imagery thrown at them in every form of media they consume, whether or not they explicitly understand the messages being conveyed? Lee presents a compelling argument that continuing to embrace obsolete notions of respectability is the same as actively teaching young black women not to be proactive agents in the process of developing individual sexual identities, and relegating them to have sex, and sexuality, defined for them. In short, I read Lee's argument as one that purposefully eschews preoccupation with the "politics of respectability" in the way that we regard black women as sexual objects in today's world because this causes black women to actively ignore their own sexual health and vitality.

Many will argue, I am sure, that Lee is ignoring the fact that we can still see examples of black women portrayed as the Jezebel and Mammy in popular media. In this vein, some might argue that Lee's analysis does not pay tribute to black women like Hamer, Rosa Parks, Ella Baker, and Anna Julia Cooper; all of whom helped to construct a "politics of respectability" for black women at a time when black women's bodies were still boldly regarded as commodities against their will. These women, through courageous activism and patient work, were quite deliberate in laying the foundation for black women to exercise sexual autonomy that was free of sexual coercion, sexual harassment, and instances of rape. The model of black female empowerment that Lee advances in his text may diminish, however inadvertently, the gains made by female activists of the civil rights movement who demanded that black women be regarded without reference to sexual objects subject to the power and control of others. In fact, the ways in which the self-declared "Video Vixen," Foxy Brown, or Lil Kim have chosen to commodify their sexual experience and sexual prowess could serve to underscore the need for a politics of respectability at this present moment in history. (See for example, the argument of Carolyn West 2008.) It could be argued that these women, all of whom Lee addresses in his text, have chosen to overlook much of the work accomplished by those I reference above who sought to provide a way for black women to earn self-respect and a living wage without having to rely upon the commodification of sexual desire (read jezebel). Parks, Cooper, Hamer, and many others beside them, were theorizing within, and perhaps also beyond, the politics of respectability in which political activism, racial uplift, and black female integrity were intricately intertwined and strictly separate from public expressions of sexuality that could be cause them to be commodified against their will.

Danielle McGuire provides fertile found to explore the beginning of the black feminist recognition that the politics of respectability does not adequately address the subjugation of black women as sexual victims in United States history. In her pioneering text, *At the Dark End of the Street*, McGuire presents the sexual subjugation of black women during the civil rights era as a continuation of the sexual violence visited upon slave women. Importantly, Danielle McGuire explains how the civil rights movement was a distinct battle for black women, separate from the imperative for racial uplift emphasized by the politics of respectability. *At the Dark End of the Street*, McGuire successfully illustrates how interracial rape was "used to uphold white patriarchal power," and "as a justification for lynching black men who challenge the Southern status quo" (McGuire 2010, xviii).

McGuire provides many accounts of sexual injustice against black women in order to demonstrate the ways in which sexual violence was used as a means to publicly and privately degrade black women and men with the goal of ensuring collective and individual complience. Importantly, her analysis guides the reader through the process of identifying the ways in which legal institutions were also complicit in undergirding both racial and gender hierarchies during the civil rights movement. The historical accounts presented in McGuire's text demonstrate the importance of recognizing the ascriptive power of institutional frameworks, while simultaneously illuminating the relative lack of agency available to individuals who are marginalized within society, focusing most especially upon the lack of agency black women had in demanding recognition of their bodily integrity. It can be argued, then, that McGuire's text provides the opportunity to acknowledge the significance of intersectionality as we attempt to understand gender stratification and how it manifests itself *within* other systems of stratification such as race, age, education, and class.

Thus it is at this point in history, as E. Frances White has noted, that with the influence of the Black Power movement alongside the civil rights movement,

> many became particularly concerned with questions of representation, broadly defined—for example, how blacks were represented in history and who represented them.... We, as blacks, began to realize the extent to which we needed to represent ourselves and to address issues beyond our own lives [White 2001, 45].

White then moves into a discussion of the Combahee River Collective, founded in Boston in 1974, which explicitly framed black women's oppression as an intersectional phenomena in "A Black Feminist Statement" published in 1981. As stated in that document:

> This focusing upon our own oppression is embodied in the concept of identity politics. We believe that the most profound and potentially most radical politics come directly out of our own identity, as opposed to working to end somebody else's oppression. In the case of Black women this is a particularly repugnant, dangerous, threatening, and therefore revolutionary concept because it is obvious from looking at all the political movements that have preceded us that anyone is more worthy of liberation than ourselves. We reject pedestals, queenhood, and walking ten paces behind. To be recognized as human, levelly human, is enough....We also often find it difficult to separate race from class from sex oppression because in our lives they are most often experienced simultaneously. We know that there is such a thing as racial-sexual oppression which is neither solely racial nor solely sexual, e.g., the history of rape of Black women by white men as a weapon of political repression [Combahee 1974, 264].

Consequently, we see that it is in this statement where the term "identity politics" is first specifically invoked to give voice to the conscious need of the black feminists at that time to define their own stake in self-representation. This was specifically to be separate from the strictures of a politics of respectability that required assimilation with white mainstream society and white feminist concerns that did not include their unique concerns as black feminists, the liberation politics of the civil rights movement and the Black Power movement that marginalized black women in the name of collective racial uplift, and the refusal to recognize the concerns of black lesbian women alongside those of all other black women. In short, this document crafted by the Combahee River Collective was a clear statement of intent to recognize and frame an oppositional consciousness to combat the collective oppressions suffered by black women due to historical forces that rendered them vulnerable to attack on several fronts, both within the black community and the larger "mainstream" society of the United States.

So we have to ask: where does the example of Beyoncé fall within the limits of the politics of respectability? I tend to agree with Lee's analysis of

Beyoncé to the extent that he reminds us that it is imperative for black women to purposefully develop a positive sense of sexual empowerment, even as we engage in difficult dialogue about black female sexual politics that span several generations of popular media.

The video and stage persona presented by Beyoncé, along with the messages in her music, interviews, and choice of filmic roles are designed to make us consider popular depictions of black women's body and call them into question. Beyoncé's use of sexuality plays at the margins of the "politics of respectability," highlighting the ways in which historical archetypes of promiscuity and exploitation are still prevalent and should be actively challenged. Furthermore, whoever may be helping Beyoncé to package the image she presents to her audience seems to be very well aware of this.

Beyoncé as Intersectional Icon

Beginning with the feminist statement of the Combahee River Collective and continuing to the current day, the concept of *intersectionality* has become integral to both theory and research endeavors as it emphasizes the interlocking effects of race, class, gender, and sexuality. Intersectionality highlights the ways in which categories of identity and structures of inequality are mutually constituted and defy separation into discrete categories of analysis. Intersectionality provides a unique lens of study that does not question difference; rather, it assumes that differential experiences of common events are to be expected. By noting the ways in which men and women occupy variant positions of power and privilege across race, space, and time, intersectionality has refashioned several of the basic premises that have guided feminist theory as it evolved following the 1950s. The intellectual vibrancy within and around intersectional theory is yielding new frontiers of knowledge production that include a purposeful interrogation with popular of images of the black body and sexuality that moves beyond the politics of respectability.

Perhaps as an echoed response to the words of Langston Hughes almost a century ago, Roderick Ferguson, in his book *Aberrations in Black: Toward a Queer of Color Critique* (2003), develops what he calls "queer of color analysis" that reveals the interconnections among sexuality, economic inequality, and race not only in the history of U.S. labor, but within various forms of knowledge production. His book lays out the historical role of labeling African American culture as deviant and, by carefully highlighting this process; Ferguson reveals how identity is inextricably linked to power, political representation, and the ever-shifting power dynamics of identity politics. Central to this discussion we must position the use of popular culture to appeal to what we are currently calling a mainstream audience. In so doing, we must continue to seek ways to overcome an image that suggests that these dimensions of inequality such as race, class, gender, etc. are separable and distinct and that it is only at certain points that they overlap or intersect with one another. This concern was specifically articulated by Deborah King in 1988 when she called for a model of analysis permitting recognition of the "multiple jeopardy" constituted by the interactive oppressions that circumscribe the lives of black women and defy separation into discrete categories of analysis. The modifier "multiple" refers not only to several, simultaneous oppressions but to the multiplicative relationships among them as well (King 1988, 47).

Beyoncé purposefully presents herself to us as a performer, a lover, a mother, a daughter, a wife, a scribe, and an actress. We saw this most explicitly and deliberately in her choice to release a new and original self-titled collection for sale on iTunes without prior notice in December of 2013. This collection included video clips as part of the purchase, which we by now recognize as a method for artists to guide our consumption of their music as they initially wish for us to experience it. But this also illustrates quite powerfully that even now, as Beyoncé has access to a larger media presence than the other female actresses and performers I have referenced above in this discussion, she remains subject to popular demand. Should we be concerned, then, with her provocative lyrics, dance moves, and scantily clad performances? We must acknowledge that this does not distinguish her from other mainstream female performers at this point in history. And how are we to view the images next to the thought-provoking lyrics she provides us for consideration? Take for example, the lyrics of "If I Were a Boy" or "Irreplaceable," from prior collections. In both of these songs, and the accompanying videos, Beyoncé provides her audience with the opportunity to examine how it is that we continue to sanction the agency of men differently than that of women in maintaining the continuity of positive intimate relationships. It would seem, in songs like these she has scripted, that she is invoking the politics of respectability as a point of demarcation for men and women alike, but especially for men. In the lyrics to each song, she is specifically addressing a putative lover, husband, or boyfriend. And she pulls us in, quite deliberately, to that intimate discussion.

Contrast this message with that presented by songs like "Crazy in Love," "Drunk in Love," and "Dangerously in Love" in comparison to songs like "Diva," "Grown Woman," and "Flawless." There is a very clear "I am talking to you, now hear me" message in each of these songs, even as she is directing her audience to engage with very different aspects of her experience. And she is clearly, very deliberately, eschewing any preoccupation with the politics of respectability as she performs each single. But she is sending the same message to a vast audience across the spectrum of race, age, gender, sexuality, class, etc.: "I've made it to where I want to be and you wish that you could, too." This message seems very simple on it's face, but I cannot help but to experience all that is Beyoncé—and, yes, I am aware that she is continuing to evolve—in relation to those who have come before her. Quite frankly, we have watched her move from her teenage years with Destiny's Child to the "Grown Woman" that she is now. This has to shape our understanding of her message and her ability to exercise intersectional identity politics that was not available to those who preceded her simply because they did not have the social media tools at Beyoncé's disposal nor the relatively unfettered ability to appeal to such a wide, cross-over audience.

On the other hand, we have to remember that Destiny's Child was packaged by Beyoncé's parents for public consumption. And now she regularly invokes the image, presence, and voice of her husband, Jay-Z, and her child, Blue Ivy, in her lyrics, performances, and television interviews. We are the audience, however, and we cannot always be sure of who is definitively guiding, directing, and ultimately determining the path of Beyoncé's career. Moreover, as the audience for whom Beyoncé is being packaged for popular consumption, we are always being guided to engage those entities of her life in a predetermined fashion. In that way Beyoncé is no different from every other performer of her time and those who have preceded her. Others guided her career, in its infancy, and we are now to believe that she speaks in her own voice and she is directing her own path.

It is in this way that I contend Beyoncé is an intersectional icon. She has not transcended race, gender, or sexuality; she has purposefully made them an intrinsic element of her audience's engagement with her. Think back to the sentiments expressed by Langston Hughes, as cited above in this discussion. Beyoncé is presenting an image of a black female artist who is "free within herself." She is answering the call of the Combahee River Collective to move toward her own sense of self, even as she is conscious of how her various modes of self-representation are consumed by a popular audience. Beyoncé has, in the end, a different kind of artistic agency than the female artists who came before her because she can make the choice to bring aspects of herself into her art that were not available to the black female performers who came before her.

This is not to say, however, that Beyoncé is never subject to the tenets of the politics of respectability. Rather, she has the agency to engage with it head-on in a manner unavailable to her forbearers. This is because the politics of respectability for black Americans operates differently in the current sociopolitical climate than it did during the 20th century. Rather than serving as an assimilationist imperative for all black Americans, only mentioned within the private confines of the black community and ever conscious of the regard of white mainstream America, the current iteration of the politics of respectability, commands blacks left behind in post–civil rights America to "lift up thyself." ... But now that black elites are part of the mainstream elite in media, entertainment, politics, and the academy, respectability talk operates within the official sphere, shaping the opinions, debates, and policy perspectives on what should—and should not—be done on the behalf of the black poor.

In fact, the current iteration of the politics of respectability is now meant to invoke an ostensible "common sense" notion of "unacceptable" behavior for black people from any walk of life (Harris).

It is for this reason that the politics of respectability has lost much of its potency in warning against "inappropriate presentations of self" in popular media. In short, the ideology has gone mainstream and become, predictably, increasingly irrelevant. This focus on policing the behavior of the black poor serves the same function as Jim Crow and slavery served in their time: to isolate one, ostensibly discrete, segment of our nation's population as deserving of negative sanction and degradation to the extent that we do not question the structural forms of inequality and stratification that have resulted in a disproportionate number of black Americans living in poverty. This coupled with the popularity of art forms that valorize violence, vulgarity, and death among black, brown, and white Americans has completely changed our understanding of the media landscape. In short, as Aurin Squire boldly asserts "Hip hop, the black community's widening generational gap, and now [Bill] Cosby's very public demise may have killed BRP [Black Respectability Politics] for good." He further contends that

> in 2014, BRP just may have died of its wounds. From the diminishment of its main spokesman Bill Cosby, to the wholesale discrediting of police murders where BRP buzzwords like "thug" were lobbed at black victims, to even President Obama's gradual abandonment of lecture-y speeches directed at the black community, "respectability" reads as hollow and manipulative to a new generation [Squire].

And it is to this generation that Beyoncé is packaging her images, lyrics, public appearances, and videos for consumption. She is one of them, having grown up in an era where drug dealers are valorized on television series alongside family dramas, police sitcoms, and situation comedies featuring men and women across the spectrum of race, sexuality, age, and ability. She has come to adulthood with an inherent understanding of intersectional identity politics and she, therefore, negotiates them with expedience and rational, albeit, economic, imperative and resolve. Rather than bemoaning the fate of the "black female body" as a commodified entity, Beyoncé, and other performers like her have found a way to become an integral part of this process of commodification and reproduction. They have, as Langston Hughes called for, begun the slow and steady ascent up the artists' "racial mountain."

What remains to be seen, however, is what is to be found on the other side of that mountain. I remain concerned that the politics of self-representation remains fundamentally fraught with peril for black men and women because of the continued prevalence of racial stereotypes in media depictions of black America. To ensure that artists share in the profits and have some voice in the images projected does not change the way in which these racialized media depictions are received. From our current vantage point, it certainly appears that we may redefine the politics of intersectionality in its most simplistic terms yet again, becoming more additive, according to capitalist imperative, than multiplicative and multifaceted. Even as we understand that people, regardless of race, gender, class, etc. have differing life chances for a variety of images, we must continue to question the pervasive presentation of black media images and portrayals that are not multifaceted and nuanced, choosing instead to present black men as animalist and violent and black women as subservient and sexually voracious, no matter who the artist is and what message they are selling.

REFERENCES

Beyoncé. 2003. "Crazy in Love" and "Dangerously in Love." *Dangerously in Love.* New York: Columbia Records.
_____. 2006. "Irreplacable." *B'Day.* New York: Sony.
_____. 2008. "Diva" and "If I Were a Boy." *I Am ... Sasha Fierce.* New York: Columbia Records.
_____. 2013. "Flawless," "Drunk in Love" and "Grown Woman." *Beyoncé.* New York: Columbia Records.
Butler, Octavia. 2003, 1979. *Kindred.* Boston: Beacon Press.
Carmen Jones. 1954. Dir. Otto Preminger. Perf. Harry Belafonte, Dorothy Dandridge, Pearl Bailey. Twentieth Century–Fox. Film.
Combahee River Collective. 2000, 1977. "A Black Feminist Statement" in *The Black Feminist Reader*, edited by Joy James and T. Denean Sharpley-Whiting. Malden, MA: Blackwell Publishers. 261–270.
Dill, Bonnie T., and Marla H. Kohlman. 2012. "Chapter 8: Intersectionality: A Transformative Paradigm in Feminist Theory and Social Justice" in *Handbook of Feminist Research, Second Edition*, edited by Sharlene Hesse-Biber. Los Angeles: Sage. 154–174.
Ferguson, Roderick A. 2003. *Aberrations in Black: Toward a Queer of Color Critique.* Minneapolis: University of Minnesota Press.
Gates, Henry Louis, Jr., and Julie Wolfe, 2015. "Dorothy Dandridge: The 1st African American to Get an Oscar Nomination for a Leading Role." *The Root.* Retrieved June 10, 2015. http://www.theroot.com/articles/history/2015/02/dorothy_dandridge_the_1st_african_american_to_get_an_oscar_nomination_for.html.
Gone with the Wind. 1939. Dir. Victor Fleming. Perf. Vivien Leigh, Clark Gable, Hattie McDaniel, and Olivia de Havilland. Metro-Goldwyn Mayer. Film.
Harris, Frederick C. 2014. "The Rise of Respectability Politics." *Dissent* magazine. Retrieved May 28, 2015. https://www.dissentmagazine.org/article/the-rise-of-respectability-politics.
Higginbotham, Evelyn Brooks. 1993. *Righteous Discontent: The Women's Movement in the Black Baptist Church, 1880–1920.* Cambridge: Harvard University Press.

Hughes, Langston. 2001, 1926. "The Negro Artist and the Racial Mountain" in *Doubletake: A Revisionist Harlem Renaissance Anthology*, edited by Venetria K. Patton and Maureen Honey. New Brunswick: Rutgers University Press. 40–44.

King, Deborah K. 1988. "Multiple Jeopardy, Multiple Consciousness: The Context of a Black Feminist Ideology." *Signs* 14: 42–72.

Kohlman, Marla H. 2014. "Chapter 23: The Demography of Sexual Harassment" in *Intersectionality: A Foundations and Frontiers Reader*, edited by Patrick R. Grzanka. Boulder, CO: Westview Press. 175–183.

Lawrence, John. 2015. "Lena Horne: A Great Lady Who Broke the Color Line." *San Diego Free Press*. Retrieved June 10, 2015. http://sandiegofreepress.org/2015/03/lena-horne-a-great-lady-who-broke-the-color-line/.

Lee, Shayne. 2010. *Erotic Revolutionaries: Black Women, Sexuality, and Popular Culture*. Lanham, MD: Rowman & Littlefield.

McGuire, Danielle L. 2010. *At the End of the Dark Street: Black Women, Rape, and Resistance—A New History of the Civil Rights Movement from Rosa Parks to the Rise of Black Power*. New York: Knopf.

Mitchell, Margaret. 1976, 1936. *Gone with the Wind*. New York: Macmillan.

Squire, Aurin. 2015. "The End of Respectability Politics." *Talking Points Memo*. Retrieved April 14. http://talkingpointsmemo.com/theslice/the-end-of-black-respectability-politics.

West, Carolyn M. 2008. "Mammy, Jezebel, Sapphire, and Their Homegirls: Developing an 'Oppositional Gaze' Toward the Images of Black Women" in *Lectures on the Psychology of Women*, 4th ed., edited by J. Chrisler, C. Golden, and P. Rozee. Boston: McGraw Hill. 286–299.

White, E. Frances. 2001. *Dark Continent of Our Bodies: Black Feminism and the Politics of Respectability*. Philadelphia: Temple University Press.

Beyoncé as Aggressive
Black Femme and Informed
Black Female Subject

Anne M. Mitchell

Beyoncé's self-titled album of 2013 has thrown her feminism into relief; it also highlights the complexity and multiplicity of her image. I argue that Beyoncé's public persona is that of a femme who troubles and engages both aggressive and submissive femininity. While she engages both of these personas, she also takes careful measure to subtly critique submissive femininity even as she performs it. Some might wonder why apply these queer identities of femininity to a reading of a heterosexual woman, to that I argue that Black female bodies—even those that are heterosexual—are read as queer in popular culture because heteropatriarchal sexuality is raced as white. Heteropatriarchy is the combination of a male dominated society, and the privileging of heterosexual couplings. This ordering of society anoints masculine men in "traditional" relationship as the "ideal" citizen worthy of all of its right and privileges, while anyone who does not fit this identity is considered of lesser value.

Cathy Cohen's "Punks, Bulldaggers, and Welfare Queens" (1997) argues that the lessons of queer organizing can serve as a cite from which to create a new politics that bonds marginal and non-normative people together, if we are willing think about being othered through racialized and classed lenses. She argues that queer politics could be a place for radical organizing for all non-normative people, if we begin to see anyone outside of heteronormativity as queer. I argue that Beyoncé's 2013 album creates a space to experience non-normative Black femininity and allows its audience to begin to imagine a new politics of being for Black womanhood. Kara Keeling's *The Witches Flight: The Cinematic, the Black Femme, and the Image of Common Sense* is also instructive here because it argues that the Black femme in U.S. cinema is cite of possibility that makes categories of identity unstable and provokes viewers into thinking. I argue that Beyoncé is an aggressive Black femme whose public persona troubles our cultural understandings of the 'proper' place and sexual desires of Black women. Keeling writes that the Black femme

> [c]hallenges each of the primary categories that have been constructed in response to racism, sexism, and homophobia ("Black," "woman," and "lesbian," respectively) to contend with what is excluded from that category in order for it to cohere as such…. [T]he Black femme is a figure that exists on the edge line, that is, the shore line between the visible and the invisible, the thought and the unthought in the critical theories that currently animate film and media studies [Keeling 2007, 1–2].

Exploring Black femme identity as it appears in popular culture is important because it challenges the very definition of categories of identity as they are normatively formed. I place Beyoncé within this category because the iconography of her work places her outside of heteronormativity and, in thinking through Cohen's work, Beyoncé creates a space for queer identities to converge.

　　While some may think that Beyoncé is invested in heteronormativity within her videos, Beyoncé works through and with queer femme identities. The iconography of the videos "Green Light," "Yoncé," and "Flawless" highlight Beyoncé's femme identity and flirtations with kink culture and homoeroticism, which place her image outside of "vanilla" heteronormativity. In the video for "Green Light" Beyoncé appears in fetish gear with an all-female cast and welcomes an unseen man to perform sexual acts on her. Similarly, in the video "Yoncé" Beyoncé appears with an all-female cast, but this time there is a homo-erotic energy between herself and the other women, despite the lyrics of inviting the desire of her partner. Moreover, Beyoncé's image is highly constructed and goes beyond "vanilla" heteronormative feminine performance, therefore I argue that her persona is that of a femme, an aggressive high femme, a person who elevates femininity to the level of theatrical performance, who consciously constructs themselves as a feminine being.

What Is Aggressive Femme Identity?

　　An aggressive femme is an identity and posture that differs from the traditional heteropatriarchal femininity. Traditional femininity demands a feminine performance that accompanies a submissive personality and approach to sexual intercourse. Hegemonic cisgendered femininity demands that women take-it and is indifferent to their pleasure, sexual or otherwise. As Mulvey's "Visual Pleasure and Narrative Cinema" highlights in her discussion of film, women, specifically feminine women are represented as a lack, and only the masculine, cisgendered male can be represented as whole and complete. Although it is the 21st century, and many kinds of gender performances are acknowledged as existing, there is still a premium on, and preference for, representations of cisgendered heteropatriarchal femininity in popular culture, which is why Beyoncé's most recent break with this performance is important.

Aggressive femme identity is rarely articulated in mainstream media, but it has a home in queer culture, specifically Black and Latino queer communities. A film that captures butch/ stud aggressive identity, aptly titled *The Aggressives* (2005) chronicles the lives of masculine-of-center women from the African American lesbian community, but does not explore the lives of femme aggressives. The aggressive femme identity is multiplicitous, but can be characterized as a gender identity or presentation that takes charge, tops, actively initiates and participates in sexual intercourse. She takes no shit, appreciates the female body, and wants to please it. This is precisely where she breaks with hegemonic femme identity, she takes her sexual pleasure and other women's sexual pleasure seriously. Beyoncé's early foray into displaying a kinky pleasure is illustrated in the "Green Light" video (2010).

Beyoncé's video for "Green Light" demonstrates her adherence and defiance of submissive femininity. This video is definitely a visual homage to Madonna's "Human Nature" (1994). Beyoncé's "Green Light" details the story of a woman who finds out that her partner is cheating on her. What these songs have in common is that their music videos play with images of BDSM. Whereas Madonna plays the role of the dominant who doles out pleasurable punishment. Visually, Beyoncé takes the role of the submissive, who gives the "Green Light" to her unseen dominant, while donning multiple sexy latex outfits and seven-inch high fetish ballerina pointe boots, but the lyrics point to her being the dominant because she is telling her cheating lover to leave.

The video for "Green Light" is one of Beyoncé's early breaks with heteronormative femininity. She troubles what it means to be submissive because she plays the non-dominant partner a Bondage Domination/Sadism Masochism (BDSM) version, while singing from a subject position that is moves between dominant and submissive. A Submissive with a BDSM relationship is someone who has agreed to be the non-dominant partner. BDSM is both a lifestyle choice and relationship style. Within a sexual relationship the style involves pleasure and play that involves fantasy styled scenes that may include costumes and props along with roleplay. The difference between BDSM and traditional heteropatriarchal relationships is that each person comes into the relationship with negotiating power, rather than relying on the assumption that men have all the power and women must submit. Moreover, the submissive partner gets to choose how and when they want to acquiesce to their partner and can renegotiate the terms.

Beyoncé is telling her lover that his actions lead her to the decision to end the relationship. Again, there are no men in this video, just Beyoncé, her all female band, and female backup dancers. The band members vary in their adherence to heteropatriarchal femininity, but the dancer present as traditionally feminine. But when Beyoncé and the backup dancers are seen without the band they wear fetish gear and beckon an unseen dominant. They tempt as the lyrics dismiss their dominant, this is an example of troubling submissive femininity. Within traditional heteropatriarchal relationships, the submission is understood as a given and the woman is not supposed to occupy her place in a powerful way. Here Beyoncé troubles that tradition, by illustrating the power of submissive femininity by demonstrating that she has the power to dismiss her dominant and still display her sexuality. His cheating has not diminished her love for herself. She remains confident. Beyoncé is an enigma because to be perceived as traditionally feminine one must give credence to the idea that proper femininity means submitting to the heteropatriarchy. The aggressive femme does not submit, unless it is by her own choosing and on her own terms, and it most often includes her partner doing some of the submitting too.

Another example of Beyoncé engaging an aggressive femininity occurs in the "Yonce" video. The video begins with a close-up on red lips and then cuts to a shot of Joan Smalls' buttocks and thighs as she walks down the street. The camera then cuts to Channel Iman and Jourdan Dunn. These three women, Smalls, Iman, and Dunn, are high fashion models of African descent. As the song continues, Joan Smalls mouths the lyrics of the song while wearing red lip gloss and gold fake teeth that are made in a vampire style that features enlarged canine teeth. By centering Joan Smalls the featured model, Beyoncé effectively decenters herself and shines a light on the beauty of other Black women. Throughout the two-minute video, the models seduce Beyoncé, and each other. At one point Joan Smalls licks Beyoncé's breast. Later, while sucking on a lollypop, Beyoncé looks at Jourdan Dunn as if she is sizing her up for a sexual encounter. Though the lyrics are partially concerned with Beyoncé's desirability to her male partner, she also brags about her femininity, how she writes hit songs, and how much her partner desires her.

There are no men in this video, but it definitely has the male gaze built in; however when Smalls licks Beyoncé décolletage there is a definite shift to a woman-on-woman sexuality. The woman gaze upon each other in a way that signals a female gaze is also present (Mayne 1993). Not only does the iconography enunciating a new female power, so does Beyoncé's new moniker, Yonce. She used to be called "Bey," now she is announcing that a new woman is emerging over a hard baseline and almost Go-Go groove. Femme identity within hegemonic heterosexuality is constructed as weak, but within queer culture femme identity is thought of as a complex mixture of desire, presentation, and longing. Jewelle Gomez describes being a femme as a re-invention of femininity in an interview with Heather Findlay as,

> I think that's what being femme really means. It means to take things that you appreciate from historical feminine traits, and to repackage them, redesign them for your own practical as well as psychological use. For example, I always carry a handkerchief. When I was a kid, my grandmother—who was a high femme, the incredibly glamorous type—always carried a handkerchief…. It means something to me because it's very utilitarian, and it reminds me of my grandmother [Findlay 1997, 149].

Gomez goes on to argue that anyone who thinks that being a femme means being passive, does not understand the exchange of power between butch and femme women.

> What do people mean by passive? That would be my question. Do they mean receptive, which is one of the reasons why butches find femmes attractive? If they mean receptive, then I would say, "Oh, yes we are!" If they mean we don't initiate, I don't know who they're thinking of [Findlay 1997, 151–152].

Similarly, people do not see the ways that femmes and femininity can be powerful when utilized outside of heteropatriarchy. What Gomez is describing is the commencement of doing femininity different. And I argue that Beyoncé's work demonstrates that she also is interested in revisioning the feminine and the femme as sites of power. Beyoncé is not just an aggressive femme, but her presentation is that of a High Femme, which is complicated by race.

"Why Don't You Love Me": Submissive Femininity and High Femme Presentation

High Femme refers to a style of feminine performance often seen in drag shows, where the performer adheres to all of the standards of femininity in a way that draws attention to its constructedness, and gives dramatic flair to the performance. This style of performance is recognized in the gay club scene, and is often performed by cisgender and transwomen, though they perform in this style, it is not common to see people adhering to this style outside of the clubs. High Femme gender performance is not limited to transwomen and cisgendered men, within queer communities it is also performed by lesbian, bisexual, and queer femmes. Where High Femme can readily be seen in mainstream media is in the performance of pop stars. Tina Turner, Diana Ross, Mariah Carey, Britney Spears, Jennifer Lopez, Katy Perry, and Beyoncé subscribe to High Femme presentation. I argue that the performance of High Femme on a Black female body is resistant to the stereotypical constructions of Black womanhood.

Her representation of High Femme identity and troubling of submissive femininity is present in song "Why Don't You Love Me" (Knowles 2010). This video opens with a title sequence and tells the view that Beyoncé will be playing the part of "B.B. Homemaker." Beyoncé comes into view wearing a sexy Rosie the Riveter outfit with her shirt tied up, short jean shorts, and high heels on while attempting to fix a car. As the video continues, Beyoncé appears in multiple 1950s housewife garbs while attempting various housework tasks, but continuously failing at them. B.B. Homemaker is shown crying in vintage lingerie while smoking and calling her lover to tell him that she might be leaving him. She continues her household tasks, such as mopping, making dinner, gardening, and washing dishes in High Femme attire. She is fully made-up, wearing high heels, and fake nails. Though she moves through multiple iterations of this character, one of which is Beyoncé's version of Bettie Page. The video continues to cut to B.B. crying, falling down, and possibly adding drugs to her drink, in full drag. Her makeup runs down her face during multiple shots.

The visual images of "Why Don't You Love Me" speak to the impossibility of being a perfect femme within heteropatriarchal culture. As the video shows B.B. Homemaker failing in her attempts at perfection, the lyrics discuss her intelligence, class, and the fact that her lover does not notice any of it. When B.B. dusts Beyoncé's actual Grammy Awards, the song breaks and elevator music plays. When B.B. finishes dusting the evidence of her accomplishments while wearing a French Maid's uniform, she flops down into the chair presumably from exhaustion.

The viewer is led to question, why should one do all of this labor if it does not guarantee you a faithful lover? Though the video pays homage to 1950s glamour, it troubles the notion that being a submissive partner is troubling and impossible to achieve while having a life of one's own. While there is definitely an appreciation of the labor that goes into being a submissive femme and the identity in general, within the iconography of the video, the lyrics question it as a strategy for maintaining a relationship. The High Femme Beyoncé plays, B.B. Homemaker is needy and constantly failing at her gender identity. As Judith Butler theorizes in *Gender Trouble* (1999), gender is constant failure. There is no such things as perfection in regard to gender, cultures are constantly constructing and re-constructing their ideas of sex and gender based on an original that does not exist. Beyoncé is playing with this idea that no one can be perfect at gender performance. And as the title states, why don't you love me—is a question that cannot be answered by one's genitals or performance at household tasks.

What Beyoncé demonstrates through her lyrics and visual iconography within her music videos that she is "knowing" Black female subject. Here I use "knowing" in the Foucauldian sense, meaning that her image is agenic and a maker of meaning rather than a "known" subject, which is a person whom society constructs as a being that must be examined by experts who explain meaning to the "known" subject (Foucault 1976). The known subject can be agenic in the everyday interactions and form social movements, but in the current moment most "known" subjects are enacted upon by forces of domination and surveillance. What Beyoncé's star image presents is a powerful form of resistance that simultaneously conforms to the forces of domination: blond hair, thin body, conventional attractiveness; while resisting the conventional and hegemonic subject position reserved for Black female bodies, whom are often characterized as unattractive, undesirable, unruly, and lacking feminine grace. She is an aggressive femme, who is serving High Femme glamour, which allows her to occupy the public sphere, but she has made a 180 and made that space one to revere the power of womanhood, in general, and worship the Black female body, in particular.

Beyoncé's place in world popular culture is one that has been occupied by very few Black women before her, namely, Josephine Baker, Diana Ross, and Janet Jackson. What is different about Beyoncé's occupation of this space is that she as she has risen in the pop ranks, her star has shifted and I argue that she has positioned herself as a representation of aggressive femininity.

Josephine Baker and Beyoncé: The Terms of Engagement

It is clear from her participation in Fashion Rocks 2006 that Beyoncé understands that her work is in dialog with the legacy of Josephine Baker The purpose of Fashion Rocks is to honor fashion designers, while musical icons perform a concert wearing items from the honored designers, and a portion of the proceeds go to charity. During this event, Beyoncé, Jay-Z, Christina Aguilera, Fergie, and Nelly Furtado performed. Though it is implied that the artists will honor a specific fashion designer, Beyoncé honored Josephine Baker. I am writing about how her new embrace of sexuality and feminism creates a space to imagine Black womanhood in new ways. She is carrying on Josephine Baker's legacy, but explicitly making it feminist.

She performed "Crazy in Love" with Jay-Z. He wore a tuxedo with a white jacket and black lapels, Beyoncé opted for a banana skirt, designed by Tina Knowles, her mother. Not only did Beyoncé wear the banana skirt, her female backup dancers wore complimentary yellow skirts, and the male backup dancers were adorned in body paint and shorts that fit the motif. The background image contained Beyoncé's name in large print, but as the curtain lifted it revealed three screens, the center screen contained an artist's rendering of a headshot of Josephine Baker, the left and right sides screens projected a rendition of Baker dancing in the banana skirt. As the performance progressed, the images changed into color melding yellow and black, then the center screen projects multiple iconic images of Baker, while the two side screens contain a large image of a honey bee, which is Beyoncé's nickname and the name she has given to her fans. Toward the end of the performance, Jay-Z leaves after his verse is done and more female background dancers enter the stage wearing banana skirts and bedazzled bra-tops to match Beyoncé's. When the song came to its finale, Beyoncé and her female background dancers to into high gear doing a dance that was homage to Baker's famous Banana Dance.

In a moment where most artists were honoring Tom Ford, Donatella Versace, and Karl Lagerfeld, Beyoncé chose to honor the fashion designs of her mother, Tina Knowles, and the career of Josephine Baker. This moment is very important for a few reasons: Beyoncé was thumbing her nose at the event, placing Black women's work at the center rather than the periphery, and placing herself and her career in dialog with Josephine Baker's legacy. Beyoncé was not playing by the rules, but because of her status as a pop icon she can sometimes do as she pleases. This was clearly one of those times. No one else did a historical reference like this Josephine Baker tribute. She puts the work and career of Josephine Baker front and center, and the fashion creations of her own mother. Here is a Black woman honoring the current work of a Black woman, and the life and legacy of deceased Black woman at an event that mainly honors the work of white men (and a minority of women) who occupy the upper echelon of the fashion world of the early 2000s. What does it mean for a Black woman who has "crossed-over" to mainstream, read: is popular with white audiences, to not play by the rules and honor the work of other Black women? I argue that it means that Beyoncé is conscious of what, and who, created her—namely Black women. Beyoncé does not owe her success to the white fashion industry, nor to a benevolent white record executive. There is no Clive Davis or Tommy Mottola behind her pulling the strings. Her work and looks are products of Black womanhood. More importantly, her performance brings back the ghost of Baker to haunt the fashion elite and fellow pop-stars in the audience, and places Beyoncé's career directly within Baker's legacy.

By wearing the banana skirt, and doing the Banana Dance, Beyoncé enunciates that she understands that the demands on her career and stardom are intertwined with Baker's. In this two-step, she pays homage and makes the live and television audiences have to deal with the fact that a Black lady is dancing around in a banana skirt that Black women have had to dance in banana skirts to capture mainstream attention. Beyoncé is saying with her dance moves that mimic Bakers, this is what you want. This is what you want, a Black woman playing into stereotypes about the Black female body being hypersexual and animalistic. This is what you want? This is what you desire. As a whole troupe of Black women come to the stage with matching banana skirts and bedazzled bra tops, the viewers have to ask themselves, is this what I want?

In 2006, 100 years after Josephine Baker's birth, are these still the terms that Black women in popular culture have to contend with? The answer is obviously yes, while there are many artists that actively reject the racist and sexist terms of engagement for Black women in the public sphere, for example: Janelle Monae, Erykah Badu, and Lalah Hathaway, but those who want to achieve and maintain mainstream success, read: popularity with white audiences, must still engage with ideas that they inhabit a world of hypersexuality and animality. The performance is telling the audience that this is what they want, but it does so by honoring the legacy and creativity of Josephine Baker, all while butts are shaking for wealthy white audiences in banana skirts. This performance, both challenges and conforms to racist and sexist visions of Black womanhood. But most importantly, it demonstrates that Beyoncé knows the terms of engagement.

I argue that Beyoncé's career both mirrors and exceeds, the career of Josephine Baker. Each woman has used sexuality in ways that both cater to the basest desires and yet, challenge these notions of Black female sexuality. Lisa Collins's "Economies of the Flesh: Representing the Black Female Body in Art" is instructive in thinking through the connection between Baker and Beyoncé's careers. She argues that Black women's representations in fine art have moved between a hypervisibility and invisibility that is imbued with racist and sexist understandings. To counter the malignant understandings of the Black female body, Black women visual artists are creating spaces for people to contemplate the ways that these bodies have been used, exploited, and reclaimed.

Looking to fine art and its visual representations, Collins finds that there is an absence of Black female nudes during the 19th century. She concludes that this lack can be attributed to the ways that the Black female body was constructed in the popular imaginary. Nudes are supposed to represent beauty, longing, desire; what would it have meant for white male artists to create such works that featured Black women's bodies? When the Black female body does begin to appear in nudes, it is either as a noble slave yearning for emancipation or as a symbol of servitude. Collins demonstrates that the Black female body nude, evoked for viewers and artists libidinal desires or the memory of Black bodies for sale. It is not until the late 1900s, when the work of Black women artists gets more recognition that complex representations of the Black female body enter the public sphere. Collins argues that the works of these female artist both trouble previous understandings and create space for new ways of seeing Black women's bodies on display. I argue that both Beyoncé and Josephine challenge the terms but they have circumscribed agency.

Lisa Collins's exploration of Baker's career is of particular significance here because of its influence on Beyoncé's career. She argues that Baker and Baartman both trafficked in exotica and erotica, and trouble how we think about Black women's agency and influence. Baartman's story has been thoroughly examined in feminist literature. Baker's career has not received enough feminist analysis and critique as Baartman's life. Within film studies, Baker's work has been taken up as both capitulation and resistant to white supremacy. This work rarely examines what Black women of her time period thought of Baker's work. Lisa Collins reminds us that at the same time that Baker was baring it all, Black clubwomen were challenging malicious notions of Black women's sexuality through encouraging a culture of dissemblance. She writes,

> Challenging all conventions of prudity and propriety, Josephine Baker was a visual predicament. When the clubwomen were advocating discretion in the United States, she appeared nude in France. While they were downplaying their sexuality, she was flouting hers. When the clubwomen were seeking venues for "dignified" work, she became rich and powerful as a scandalous dancer. And most important, while they encouraged imposed invisibility, she craved visible exposure. And she got it…. The history of the traffic in the Black female body causes a crisis of representation, particularly for artists who have inherited the culture of dissemblance [Collins 2002, 110–113].

Josephine Baker presented a very public problem for Black clubwomen. As they were advocating for a de-sexualization of Black women's public lives, Baker was publicly reveling in her sexuality. This culture of dissemblance remains with Black women today, despite the ubiquitous images of sexualized Black women in popular culture, but the difference is that there are multiple efforts to change it. I posit that Beyoncé is one of the forces of change in this culture of dissemblance, which negatively affects Black women's lives. Moreover, I argue that the same phenomenon is happening with feminist theorizing of Beyoncé's career.

Beyoncé's career is starting to be theorized, but for many using a Black feminist lens can lead to dichotomous thinking, which is why using a queer theory lens is so important because her career is complex and the work it does affects many groups. Using a queer of color critique lens, I am able to think through the ways that Beyoncé's career works through femme representation to enunciate new ways to understand Black femininity. Moreover, online people are theorizing and examining Beyoncé's career, identity as a feminist, and latest album through new lenses. Michelle Jackson, names one of these new lenses Ratchet Feminism. This kind of feminism refers to "ratchet music" or "ratchet rap" which is music that usually discusses drug-dealing, stripping, committing crimes, or general non-respectable behavior. Though Beyoncé's music only flirts with the "ratchet" genre, I argue that thinking of this music as a part of one's feminism is a direct result of Black women engaging feminism on the web and more women in popular culture identifying themselves as feminists. Jackson writes,

> For me, I am a loud-mouthed, opinionated, progressive, liberal feminist committed to social justice … who also loves swinging her ass around to a trap beat. The two are not mutually exclusive. But of course, there will always be those individuals who hear me sing along to Ty Dolla $ign's "Paranoid" or Tyga's "Rack City B*tch," and ask, "But how can you be a feminist and listen to these lyrics?" Well, because feminism is not a monolith, and no singular interpretation of feminism is perfect. These people fail to understand that (a) there are multiple ways to encounter ratchet music as a woman; and (b) there are also multiple ways to engage with and embody feminist principles. I reject the idea that to be a feminist, my life cannot be messy. I reject the idea that to be a feminist, I cannot engage with—and sometimes enjoy—"un-feminist-y" things. I reject any prescription of feminism that does not allow for a complex intersectionality [Jackson 2014].

Jackson is enunciating a new way to understand music and its place with a complex intersectional feminism. I argue that Beyoncé aids women like Jackson because she is troubling the old notions of Black women's bodies and sexualities and reclaiming them for Black women's pleasure. Her body is constantly on display, but it is not here for the male gaze.

"Flawless"

Beyoncé's "Flawless," featuring Chimamanda Ngozi Adiche, is a feminist anthem writ large. During her recent concerts, Beyoncé would begin this song with "Feminist" on a large screen behind her. The lyrics speak to women about claiming a flawlessness, despite their actual flaws. This song encourages women to embrace their power boldly.

The video opens with Ed McMahon from *Star Search* announcing a competition between two singing groups. Then the video moves to a black and white sequence, featuring Beyoncé sitting on a leather couch between two Skinheads. According to Jake Nava, the director, scene morphs into a Two-Tone Party that includes Skinheads, Punks, and Rudeboys partying together in a setting that is reminiscent of the 1980s scene in London (Nava 2014). The use of this scene where Beyoncé is dressed in a flannel shirt, thong jean shorts that have netting covering her buttocks, a necklace with a single bullet as the pendant, and high-heeled combat boots complete with chains, visually demonstrates that Beyoncé is in dangerous territory. A Black woman in a party of Skinheads is not safe. She is definitely taking a risk with her life, which parallels the risk of coming out as a Feminist female pop star today. In a genre that asks career driven women to pretend to be submissive femmes at all times, Beyoncé is taking a risk with her career, popularity, and future. To become political in any way can damage a Hollywood persona, especially in a woman's career because much of women's popularity is based on their sexual availability, conventional attractiveness, and lack of opinion. To venture out of this persona, is to invite the wrath and scorn of the public for getting out of "one's place."

Beyoncé places a portion of Chimamanda Ngozi Adichie's Ted Talk on feminism in the middle of the song, where she defines feminism as working for the social, political, economic, and social equality between the sexes. She is clearly aligning herself with feminism. Moreover, she is giving everyone who listens to this song a mini-lesson on feminism. Although the lyrics tell other women to bow down to Beyoncé's greatness, which can be viewed as anti-feminist, I argue that Beyoncé is enunciating a complex feminist manifesto that does not deny challenges that exist between some women, but engages the audience to think about their strength. For Beyoncé, her strength comes from her family, learning from failure, and lyrically challenging standards of female beauty. As the song ends, Ed McMahon announces that Beyoncé's group, *Girls Time*, has lost to the reigning champions, Skeleton Crew. This ending is instructive because it changes how one hears the beginning of the song. Where one might be lulled into thinking that the song begins with a triumph, when it actually starts and ends with failure. The audience is lead to question, where would Beyoncé be if she stopped with that failure on *Star Search*?

There are some problems within this manifesto that point to some shortsightedness on Beyoncé's part. First is the calling other women bitches, and telling them to bow down to Beyoncé because she is a bigger star. This is plainly problematic and relies on a hierarchal view of the world which feminism works to undo. The second problem is the praising of capitalism and wealth (Rock Flawless). And finally, I would be remiss if I did not mention that throughout the visual album, Beyoncé appeared to be conforming more closely to Western beauty standards throughout the videos for the self-titled album. When the 2013 album was released, without promotion, the public got a new version of Beyoncé's physical self. She appeared with hair that had brown roots, and platinum blonde strands. And she was very thin, this is not to police her body, but to emphasize that Beyoncé re-emerged in the public eye with messages of "Pretty Hurts," "No Angel," and defining feminism for young fans with a body that appeared to be more adherent to hegemonic and racist standards of beauty.

There is an inherent contradiction that speaks to the old adage, do as I say, not as I do. How can anyone looking at her believe her messages? As I have argued previously, for Black women the terms of engagement in the public sphere are set by a standard of beauty that does not include us. The terms of engagement are set around a white submissive femininity that honors the gendered boundaries of heteropatriarchy. Though it is problematic, another way of thinking about this issue is to ask, if Beyoncé was not conventionally attractive, with a light complexion, and willing to lose weight by any means necessary, would anyone be listening to what she says? Would feminism be part of a national discussion that includes young women, non-academics, and non-activists without this album? There is a growing body of feminist work that is aimed at popular audiences, but "Flawless" made discussions of feminism much easier and moved the discourse away from the derailing "Femin-Nazi" discourse of conservative pundits. Beyoncé did not do it alone, but she gave the discourse a much needed push into the public consciousness beyond the usual stereotypes and misconceptions.

"Flawless" is a dangerous song, that contains dangerous imagery, and the voice of feminist theory and politics is a Nigerian intellectual, Chimamanda Ngozi Adichie. Beyoncé made some very bold choices here because she could have left this song off of the album or made it a hidden bonus track. Women have taken serious hits to their careers for taking up political causes, especially within an American popular culture that trades in women's bodies as commodities and makes money on our feelings of inadequacy based on unachievable beauty standards. And to make the voice of reason come from a Black woman, and a Nigerian woman with a Nigerian accent was a very bold choice. For a Black woman to choose another Black woman as an intellectual mentor is to disrupt white supremacy. In the 21st century, ideas of Black inferiority still loom large, so for Beyoncé to choose another Black woman was important. On the self-titled album, Beyoncé has chosen to center Black womanhood as a site of beauty and knowledge, for a world audience. And throughout this project she takes on a complex Black femininity that is sexual, intelligent, seductive, manipulative, and feminist.

Conclusion

Beyoncé's work in "Green Light," "Why Don't You Love Me," "Yonce," and "Flawless" point to a move away from heteropatriarchal femininity and towards a kinky, aggressive femme persona. Her new work on the 2013 self-titled album, specifically "Yonce" and "Flawless" enunciate a Black woman centered femme sensuality and feminist surety.

Though her work is not perfect it definitely opens a space in the popular imaginary to rethink Black womanhood and femme identity. Being an aggressive femme is not about weakness, it is a position of power that is rarely praised by popular culture. And when the woman is Black, it can easily fall into stereotypical depictions. Beyoncé has avoided this in her new embodiment of femme-ness. She manages a two-step of fulfilling conventional desires and enunciating a kinky queer subjectivity, simultaneously.

Contrary to the belief that women need to be more masculine to gain and possess power, femme-ness shows us that this conception is false. And for Black women, we do not need to avoid aggressiveness because of Western stereotypes about our womanhood. We need to embrace both queer femininity and masculinity to allow for complex expressions of our racial identities.

REFERENCES

The Aggressives. 2005. Directed by Daniel Peddle. DVD.

Butler, Judith. 1990. *Gender Trouble: Feminism and the Subversion of Identity*. New York: Routledge.

Cohen, Cathy J. 1997. "Punks, Bulldaggers, and Welfare Queens: The Radical Potential of Queer Politics?" *GLQ: A Journal of Lesbian and Gay Studies* 3.4 (May): 437–465.

Collins, Lisa. 2002. "Economies of the Flesh: Representing the Black Female Body in Art." In *Skin Deep, Spirit Strong: The Black Female Body in American Culture*, ed. Kimberly Wallace-Sanders, 99–127. Ann Arbor: University of Michigan Press.

Collins, Patricia Hill. 2000. *Black Feminist Thought: Knowledge, Consciousness, and the Politics of Empowerment, 2nd Edition*. New York: Routledge.

Ferguson, Roderick A. 2004. *Aberrations in Black: Toward a Queer of Color Critique*. Minneapolis: University of Minnesota.

Findlay, Heather. 1997. "Fishes in a Pond: An Interview with Jewelle Gomez." *Femme: Feminist Lesbians and Bad Girls*, eds. Laura Harris and Elizabeth Crocker, 145–159. New York: Routledge.

Foucault, Michel. [1976] 1980. *The History of Sexuality, Volume 1*. New York: Vintage Books.

_____. [1977] 1995. *Discipline and Punish: The Birth of the Prison*. New York: Vintage Books.

Jackson, Michelle Denise. 2014. "Yes, My Feminism Is Ratchet." *For Harriet*. Nov. 8. www.forharriet.com/2014/11/yes-my-feminism-is-ratchet-reflections.html.

Johnson, E. Patrick, and Mae Henderson, eds. 2005. *Black Queer Studies: A Critical Anthology*. Durham: Duke University Press.

Keeling, Kara. *The Witches Flight: The Cinematic, the Black Femme, and the Image of Common Sense*. Durham: Duke University Press.

Knowles, Beyoncé. 2009. "Green Light." Last Modified: Oct. 3, 2009. https://www.youtube.com/watch?v=bOXvqkC3W4M. Sony Music.

_____. 2010. "Why Don't You Love Me." Last Modified: May 18, 2010. https://www.youtube.com/watch?v=QczgvUDskk0. Sony Music.

_____. 2013a. "Flawless" featuring Chimamanda Ngozi Adichie. https://www.youtube.com/watch?v=jcF5HtGvX5I. Directed by Jake Nava. 2013. Sony Music.

_____. 2013b. "Yonce." Last Modified: Dec. 13, 2013. https://www.youtube.com/watch?v=jcF5HtGvX5I. Sony Music.

Madonna. 1994. "Human Nature." Last Modified: Oct. 16, 2013. https://www.youtube.com/watch?v=XTSrV_0vG-4.

Mulvey, Laura. 1975. "Visual Pleasure and Narrative Cinema." *Screen* 16.3: 6–18.

Muñoz, José Esteban. 1999. *Disidentifications: Queers of Color and the Performance of Politics.* Minneapolis: University of Minnesota Press.

Nava, Jake. 2014. "Behind the Scenes." https://www.youtube.com/watch?v=ryQlrfVU QfQ. Last Modified: 2014. Sony Music.

Perry, Jade. 2005. "Why I Liberated Myself from Traditional, Respectable Relationships." Last Modified: June 17, 2015. http://www.forharriet.com/2015/06/why-i-liberated-myself-from-respectable.html#axzz3dL0LPSoJ. *For Harriet.*

Policing Beyoncé's Body
"Whose Body Is This Anyway?"

NOEL SIQI DUAN

On the cover of August 2015 issue of American *Vogue*, shot by Mario Testino, Beyoncé leans against—or rather pushes into—a cream-colored piece of upholstery, forming a clearly delineated S-curve with her body. She granted the fashion publication use of her image (A-list actresses grovel for months to be considered for the cover) but the accompanying cover story, which usually consists of an effusive profile, didn't include a single interview from Beyoncé. *Vogue* had hired Pulitzer Prize–winning writer Margo Jefferson, who recently wrote the memoir *Negroland* about growing up in upper-class African American society, to do a write-around—an examination of the power of the Beyoncé's cult of personality without actually speaking to the subject about it. "The most powerful thing about her persona is the unabashed pleasure she takes in her own body: its beauty, its power, its versatility," she wrote (Jefferson 2015).

Beyoncé is notorious for speaking few words to the media, but she is not passive, especially when her persona is linked to her corporeal body. Some leading feminist scholars—most prominently bell hooks—have critiqued Beyoncé as a figure of female empowerment and success within a patriarchal capitalist system: she is attractive (and while she does not have a stick-thin high-fashion model's body, she works hard on her hard-to-achieve body), wealthy, light-skinned as a Black American, and though she sings about sexuality and sex, she sings about them in the context of a committed heterosexual marriage (Harris 2013a). Beyoncé is the perfect example of how to succeed in capitalism. In her book, *Black Looks: Race and Representation* (2015), the only mention that hooks gives Beyoncé is in the following disparaging description:

On the cover of *Time* magazine as one of the one hundred most influential people in the world she dons her long bone-straight blonde hairdo. In keeping with
this affirmation of whiteness she, clothed in bra and panties on the cover, continues the stereotype that black females are more sexually active and loose than
other groups of women" [under "Preface to the New Edition"].

Beyoncé's devoted fans, the BeyHive, claim that her brand of "fierce feminism," in which she is unabashedly sexy, is empowering and aspirational
because she stringently controls her own image (Harris 2013a, Jones 2014).
Indeed, the condemnation of her body, her choice of dress, and provocative
performance on stage is an aggressive effort to eradicate difference—and
consequently ignoring the historical narratives of slavery and forces of
oppression that limit one's choices and ownership of capital: by regulating
the bodies of non-white women. Beyoncé, therefore, resists against fetishistic
and oppressive narratives about her body by hyper-exaggerating them—the
curves, the hair, the legs—while enforcing the dialog around her body at the
same time, telling her audience why Black women's bodies matter: they are
not props and they are not passive sites.

Legacies of Black Women's Bodies

The control of Beyoncé's body by herself and the dialog in the media
(offline and online) is situated in the legacies of colonialism and imperial-
ism—institutions of domination, slavery, and commodification. In the early
nineteenth century, for example, white bodies sexualized black bodies while
simultaneously dissociating themselves from these bodies—they were able
to project their sexual desires without making it a part of themselves and
part of whiteness (Gilman 1985, 205). The Black female body, eventually
became an "icon" for black sexuality, male and female, in opposition to white
purity, such as Edouard Manet's *Olympia* painted in 1862 (Gilman 1985, 207).
One of the most famous and cited examples of the projections of primitivism and sexuality on black female bodies is Saartjie Baartman, also known
as Sara Bartmann and the "Hottentot Venus" (hooks 2015, 62). In 1810, she,
an indentured servant, was put on display to show off her genitalia and pro-
truding buttocks; black women's "primitive" sexuality was externally represented through their "different" genitalia and body parts (hooks 2015, 62).
After her death in 1815, her body—including her genitalia—was dissected,
preserved, and put on display for eternity (hooks 2015, under "Pussy: Representations of Black Female Sexuality in the Cultural Marketplace"). Her
body cast was on display until 1976 in the Musée de l'Homme of Paris, when
feminists complained of it as a degrading representation of women (Gilman
1985, 213). Historian Sander L. Gilman notes that when black male bodies

were dissected in the same time period, the research records did not indicate any discussion of the male genitalia (1985, 218). hooks also points that internationally-acclaimed dancer Josephine Baker capitalized on the sexualization of her body, in particular, to her buttocks (2015, 63). "Many of Baker's dance moves highlighting the 'butt' prefigure movements popular in contemporary black dance," hooks notes (2015, 63).

Beyoncé has, in fact, not only paid homage to Baker's dancing, but has also cited Baker as an inspiration in interviews. On September 7, 2006, Beyoncé sat down with Diane Sawyer on *Good Morning America* to promote her *B'Day* album and to express her similarities to Baker. The segment was composed of Beyoncé's early performing days, Sawyer's narration, the sit-down interview, and black-and-white clips of Baker dancing (*Good Morning America*, 2006). Researcher Terri Francis interpreted Beyoncé's intentions as one of "a performer claiming a history of audacious black female creativity, exemplified—we'd all agree—by Baker, the original Diva" (2008). The singer explained to Sawyer (and the American public watching the segment):

> I wanted to be more like Josephine Baker because she didn't—she seemed like she was just possessed and it seemed like she just danced from her heart, and everything was so free.... This record sounds like a woman possessed. It sounds like a woman that is kind of desperate, and I wanted it to come from the soul. I just did whatever happened there.

Francis calls this "self-possession"—Beyoncé's liberation of her body comes from, ironically, a possession of it (2008). "Beyoncé sought to capture Baker's dance practice, which is characterized by total movement, a sense of possession (see the music-hall party sequence in *Princess Tam Tam*) and unpredictability, controlled with her own bodily intelligence," she wrote (Francis 2008).

And so, at the 2006 Fashion Rocks concert, Beyoncé came full-circle with her Baker statements: she re-imagined Baker's infamous banana-skirt dance, a dance and ensemble that capitalized on the West's romanticized imaginings of what primitivism was, and a key component to Baker's international fame (Francis 2008). The opening of the performance, with Beyoncé's name highlighted in gothic lettering on the backdrop, was a "direct quotation" of Baker's original dance (Francis 2008). Later on in the performance, in backdrop of Beyoncé's Fashion Rocks performance, there is a giant image of Baker (2006). "The historical reference contextualizes Beyoncé's erotic dancing, which includes thrusting her derriere powerfully and circling her hips slowly while she tosses her hair and, adding a comic touch, clicks her neck from side to side," Francis describes the tribute to Baker (2008). It is important to make the distinction that Beyoncé sampled Baker without costuming herself as Baker—she sees herself as a performer who evokes Baker and owes much of her identity to Baker, but her hair, voice, music, and many of her dance moves are still on-brand with Beyoncé (Francis 2008). Francis explains Baker's greatest legacy as creative the space and possibility for black women to be creative within a commoditized mass culture that sexualizes black bodies without paying them for them for it: "This space for black women to make the erotic a space of power and pleasure, not merely humiliation and control, is the paradise Josephine Baker cleared out of fallow, hostile cultural fields in which they were not meant to survive, much less be independent and important," she writes (Francis 2008). The enslavement of the black female body in colonial society has also had ramifications on representation—including in pop culture. Susan Bordo outlines the three body associations of the black female that have resulted from enslavement and indentured servitude:

> A "breeder" to the slaveowner, often depicted in jungle scenes in contemporary advertisements, the black woman carries a triple burden of negative bodily associations. By virtue of her sex, she represents the temptations of the flesh and the source of man's moral downfall. By virtue of her race, she is instinctually animal, undeserving of privacy and undemanding of respect. She does not tease and then resist (as in the stereotype of the European temptress); she merely goes "into heat." But the legacy of slavery has added an additional element to effacements of black women's humanity. For in slavery her body is not only treated as an animal body but is property, to be "taken" and used at will. Such a body is denied even the dignity accorded a wild animal; its status approaches that of mere matter, thing-hood [2003, 11].

Black women in American history, through slavery and servitude, have not been in ownership of their own bodies or capital. They are seen as undesirable or hypersexual. Beyoncé's body, consequently, is undeniably linked to her success as a capitalist, as a woman who has succeeded within the current structures of patriarchy and who herself espouses an ableist, neoliberal view of self-determination. As seen in her 2013 HBO documentary, *Beyoncé: Life Is but a Dream*, in which she was the executive producer, co-director, and co-writer, Beyoncé controls the views (she was even credited for additional camerawork). You, the viewer, are consuming her as a commodity but you are consuming her in the exact manner that she wants you to worship her, buy her songs, and attend her concerts.

Feminism and Beyoncé's Body

Criticism of Beyoncé for her body's sexuality in performance and in public isn't just from stereotypical pearl-clutching scolds and sexist men—they come from self-identifying feminists, too, who find her body offensive. In her performance both on-and off-stage, Beyoncé reverses the panoptic vision of the male gaze—you, the viewer, are self-conscious in her presence, and she is commanding your attention.

When she performed at the halftime show at Super Bowl XLVII in February 2013, wearing a tight leather body suit by little-known designer Rubin Singer and knee-high stiletto boots, she used a popular performance device of hers on stage: rows of mirror images of herself to create the illusion that there are many copies of herself on stages (Chernikoff 2013). She danced with her legs akimbo, gyrating to hits like "Crazy in Love" and "Baby Boy." This was moments before Destiny's Child—with Kelly Rowland and Michelle Williams—reunited onstage (Super Bowl XLVII, 2013). At the time, it was the second most watched show in Super Bowl history with 110.8 million viewers (Collins 2013).

It was a "sexy" performance by any traditional definition of the word: the clothes were tight and the dancing was provocative. But it was self-fashion sexualization that she commanded with her own body, unlike the sexist and sexualized commercials during the Super Bowl that capitalized on traditional ideas of masculine chauvinism—not that many self-identified feminists agreed with her online. Tweets such as "Hello @Beyonce—Dressing provocatively does NOT 'empower' women. It objectifies+teaches that physical appearance=self worth. So plz STOP!" began appearing, prompting actress Jada Pinkett-Smith to ask on Facebook, "Whose body is it anyway?" (Dionne 2013). Pinkett-Smith explained, "Here is the problem I see, a woman's body is too much power for one woman to have, even Beyoncé [sic]" (Facebook, Inc. 2013).

In a roundtable discussion on *Racialicious*, writers Tamara Winfrey Harris and Andrea Plaid compared and contrasted the responses to Beyoncé and Jennifer Lopez's performances to those of Britney Spears' performances—noting that all three performers were known for gyrating their hips and wearing minimal clothing (Harris 2013b). Beyoncé's expression of her sexual agency through her objectively sexy moves is seen as a social taboo: "I can touch you, but you can't touch yourself," which is rooted in a history of the enslavement of the bodies of women of color (Harris 2013b). Harris also pointed out that "Unrestrained fleshiness and jiggle reads differently than hard and trim; Physical abundance is often mistaken for wantonness" (Harris 2013b). In 1920s bourgeois American society in cities, for example, black American dance halls and nightclubs were targeted for reform as sites of "the production of vice" in slums (Carby 1992). Dance venues where black women performed for white audiences, both men and women, however, were of particular concern to reformists because they threatened acceptable interracial experiences (Carby 1992). African American scholar Hazel Carby asks, "What are the consequences of the female self-determination evident in such a journey for the establishment of a socially acceptable moral order that defines the boundaries of respectable sexual relations?" (1992).

Historically, then, the policing of black women's bodies in American culture has always been thinly veiled as an issue of morality (Carby 1992). When Beyoncé performed at the Super Bowl in 2013, accompanied by her all-female band and dancers, during one of the most objectifying and panoptic four hours in modern pop culture, she was not only claiming ownership of her body, but also demonstrating that black women, who are haunted by a long history of being perceived to have either animalistic sexual desires or be desexualized "mammy" figures, can be admired for the very characteristics that have been considered negative race and sex traits. After all, black women in music videos have especially been portrayed with a pornographic gaze as "hoodrats," "chickenheads," or "bitches and hoes" (Hunter and Soto 2009). In the '90s, the so-called "video hoe" became—and still exists as—a socially acceptable excuse for male hip hop artists to degrade women, especially black women who were subject to both racial and gender stigmatizations, in order to align themselves with profit and power (Hunter and Soto 2009).

Therefore, when self-described feminists rail against Beyoncé for not being feminist enough for a variety of reasons, they are policing her body for daring to transgress proper social relations—it may be expected for black women's bodies to be sexual, but it is considered a transgression for them to be celebrating the sexuality. "I'm not always confident. Just tired. Black women influence pop culture so much but are rarely rewarded for it," fellow pop star (and much more outspoken individual) Nicki Minaj wrote on Twitter on July 21, 2015. In *Black Looks*, hooks observed that most black American women are "more concerned with projecting images of respectability than with the idea of female sexual agency and transgression, do not often feel we have the 'freedom' to act in rebellious ways in regards to sexuality without being punished" (160).

Beyoncé has branded herself as a feminist and has made deliberate attempts to align herself with feminism even though many feminists, as seen on reactions on the internet, have not accepted her as one due to how she uses and displays her body. At the 2014 Video Music Awards, the words "FEMINIST" were emblazoned across the stage while the dark silhouette of her body stood in front, closing out the show. The show consisted of a medley of songs including "Partition" performed with pole dancing and "Flawless" sampled with Chimamanda Ngozi Adichie's words (2014). Many media outlets, such as *Time*, called the performance "empowering," and it was without a question at this point that Beyoncé was officially a self-described feminist—even without uttering the words in public herself (Bennett 2014, Dockterman 2014).

That is the great spectacle of Beyoncé's performativity: while she does not make many politicized or polarizing statements, not even daring the possibility of making one by granting in-person interviews, her declaration of feminism at the 2014 Video Music Awards was flashy, flawlessly produced, and widely publicized. It was also widely criticized. In an article for British newspaper *The Telegraph*, Emma Gannon asked, "If we accept that Lena Dunham likes to take her clothes off and celebrate her body (with the majority of the media giving her a firm thumbs up), then how come Beyoncé is branded 'not a feminist' for doing the same?" (2013). When the Gloria Steinem–founded feminist magazine *Ms.* dedicated their Spring 2013 issue to "Beyoncé's Fierce Feminism," with a photograph of the smiling performer with honey-gold locks on the cover, outrage erupted on the publication's Facebook page, calling her a "whore" and a "stripper" and "disgusting," among other names (Hobson 2013a). Janell Hobson, an associate professor at the University of Albany who wrote the cover story, responded online in June 2013, comparing the outrage over Beyoncé's exposure of her body with outrage over the "oppression" of Muslim women who wear the hijab:

> What certain feminists clearly want is to regulate the bodies of women of color in order to *eradicate difference*. Since when did feminism reinforce dress codes instead of women's autonomy and solidarity with other women, in which we support all of our choices while also recognizing how those choices are sometimes limited by intersectional oppressions (*and no one is immune from this*)? [2013a].

In her 2014 eponymous album, which debuted at top of the U.S. Billboard 200 charts, Beyoncé sampled Nigerian writer Chimamanda Ngozi Adichie's TED talk "We Should All Be Feminists" in the song "Flawless," addressing the criticism that she was not a feminist because she did not tick off certain criteria. Mikki Kendall of *The Guardian* praised her:

> It's clear that like a lot of black American women, the mainstream middle class white feminist narratives with which we are so familiar aren't necessarily compatible with Beyonce's view of herself. This album makes it clear that her feminism isn't academic; isn't about waves, or labels. It simply is a part of her as much as anything else in her life [2013].

Maintaining Control Over Beyoncé's Body

Beyoncé's control over her image is notorious to anyone who follows the dialog around her on the Internet—and this attempt to control the representation of her body is necessary to present herself as an effortlessly flawless woman. The pre-approved images from her performances, like her record-breaking Super Bowl halftime show, come from Parkwood Entertainment, a management company she founded in 2008 (Gensler 2013). As noted by feminist media site *Jezebel*, the credits for the approved Super Bowl images read, "Photo by Frank Micelotta/Invision for Parkwood Entertainment/AP Images" (Stewart 2013). On February 4, 2013, *BuzzFeed* had assembled a fawning listicle called "The 33 Fiercest Moments from Beyoncé's Halftime Show," which published images of Beyoncé in mid-performance (Yapalater). Judging from the headline of the story, *BuzzFeed* meant no malice against the performer—it was meant to be a collection of photos that only solidified her larger-than-life persona as "fierce" (Yapalater 2013). The captions included, "Basically every moment was fierce, "Because she's Queen B.," and "AND SHE RUNS THE WORLD" (Yapalater 2013).

Beyoncé is a photogenic person, as proven by her being named the World's Most Beautiful Woman by *People* in 2012. But even attractive and talented individuals will grimace in exertion when doing something as physically and mentally intense as dancing and singing onstage in high heels (Chiu). The next day on February 5, *BuzzFeed* claimed that her representative, Yvette Noel-Schure of Schure Media, emailed the online media site with a request to delete some of the photos: "As discussed, there are some unflattering photos on your current feed that we are respectfully asking you to change. I am certain you will be able to find some better photos" (BuzzFeed-Celeb 2013). She named seven photos from the listicle that were the "worst" (BuzzFeedCeleb 2013). BuzzFeed did not take down the photos.

Beyoncé is neither the first nor the only celebrity to request that images of herself to be taken from the Internet, of course—Kanye West successfully forced Getty Images to erase photos of himself performing in a skirt at the 12/12/12 Concert for Hurricane Sandy relief in December 2012 (Juzwiak 2013). Unfortunately for Beyoncé and her public relations team, their efforts backfired: as with all viral scandals on the Internet, memes were created and shared. One just has to Google "Beyoncé ugly face" to find them (Stewart 2013).

To avoid this issue happening twice during the Mrs. Carter World Tour two months after the Super Bowl performance, Noel-Schure banned outside photographers altogether from shooting the show (Galai 2013). The "2013 World Tour guidelines for photography and TV crews" reads: "There are no photo credentials for this show. Local news outlets, including print and online will be given a link to download photos from every show. They will need to register to access the photos" (Galai 2013). And so, after the first show in her highly publicized world tour, there were only photos officially released by her management company (Galai 2013). "Featuring her in a backlit demure, feminine pose, the images are a stark contrast to the unfortunate split second shot caught in New Orleans, which spawned a thousand memes," Sara C Nelson of *The Huffington Post UK* described the photos (2013). But this is not a perfect solution for Beyoncé's attempt at flawless image control: Noam Galai of *Fstoppers* also noted that "[i]f [the media] can't send a photographer to give them original photos, the next best thing they can do is buy photos from fans in the front rows in the arena (cameras were not allowed, but no one can take away phones)" (2013).

One may wonder why Beyoncé goes through such exhausting lengths to appear immaculate, never tired, always glowing. After all, other A-list female celebrities like Jennifer Lawrence and Emma Stone base at least part of their appeal on being slightly awkward, relatable, and essentially the celebrity best friend some women wish they had—the real-life equivalent of the rom-com trope of a conventionally attractive woman whose only flaw is her clumsiness (Dobbins 2012). Between 2013 and 2014, Beyoncé didn't give any face-to-face interviews (Schneier 2015). In 2013, she told *GQ* in one of the last interviews she did, "I'm more powerful than my mind can even digest and understand" (Wallace). Jefferson, the writer who wrote the thinkpiece in *Vogue* without speaking to her (or her close relations), told the *New York Times* in August 2015, "She has to be studying how effective her interviews have been so far. She may have decided that they do not contribute as dazzlingly to the portrait of Beyoncé as the other stuff. It's a perfectly reasonable decision" (Schneier 2015).

However, while the Beyoncé persona as the perfect woman—glowing skin, confident stance, long hair, wealth—is achieved through strenuous hard work, the message that she conveys is not that Beyoncé does not work hard, but that working hard is easy for Beyoncé. It comes naturally to her—and she'll even share some information on how she does it all, if you have the willpower to plunge into your lifestyle. Hence, the invention of the popular (and slightly chiding) phrase, "You have as many hours in the day as Beyoncé" (Dahl 2014). The "ease" of being hardworking is the codified framework of being elite in American society. In his 2010 book *Privilege*, about prestigious American boarding school, sociologist and alumnus Shamus Khan writes,

> Though everyone claimed an enormous amount of work, they displayed an ease or indifference to it. The work didn't matter. The difficulty of getting it done was not displayed. Instead, achievements seemed to almost passively "happen"—as if the students themselves hadn't done it or that doing it was not really very hard for them.... Hard work was a frame ... that students mobilized to code their advancement within hierarchies, but this frame did involve an attendant corporeal display of effort. They displays were meant to be just the opposite: full of ease. Why did these students get ahead? Because hard work comes easy—they are naturals [Khan 2010, 120].

This concept of ease, which connotes that people who are elite have the predisposition of being hardworking, can be seen in the few opportunities in which Beyoncé does speak about her diet and workout regiment. "I can't eat what I want, and I can't not go to the gym," she told *Self* in an interview in 2009. "The truth is it's a lot of sacrifice. It's more about your mental strength than physical strength. You have to push yourself" (Marquina 2015)." To *Teen People* in 2002, as a young member of Destiny's Child, she said, "Us sisters have padding back there. Being bootylicious is about being comfortable with your body" (Bordo 2004, xxii).

But Susan Bordo, author of *Unbearable Weight: Feminism, Western Culture, and the Body*, points out: "Beyonce [sic] is comfortable with her body because she works on it constantly" (2004, xxii). Beyoncé told *Teen People* that she did 500 sit-ups every night while on the road touring (Bordo 2004, xxii). *Marie Claire UK* noted in 2008 that she requested "no chips, no candy, no desserts, no junk food, no fried food" as her catering needs on set. She explained to the publication that she had to gain 20 pounds to play Etta James in the musical biopic, *Cadillac Records* (*Marie Claire UK* 2008). "Putting on the pounds was so much fun" she told *Marie Claire UK* (2008). "But I had to lose it. I was so angry with myself. I was like, 'Doh! Why do you have to go through this?' You can't blame a girl for wishing to avoid temptation, particularly one whose living is partly dependent on her looks" (*Marie Claire UK* 2008). On June 8, 2015, she officially announced her vegan diet on the morning show, *Good Morning America*: "I am not naturally the thinnest woman. I have curves—I'm proud of my curves," she said in a pre-recorded video. "And I have struggled since a young age with diets. And finding something that actually works and actually keeps the weight off has been difficult for me" (*Good Morning America* 2015). The plant-based diet that she was advocating for was not just a simple list of guidelines that anyone could download for free off the internet—it was attached to a new diet plan book and home delivery meal program, *The 22-Day Revolution*, by her trainer nutritionist, Marco Borges, who also trains her husband Jay-Z and Pharrell: "I felt like my skin was really firm, a lot tighter than when I deprived myself of food and got the weight off fast. And the weight stayed off," she claimed (*Good Morning America* 2015). Both Beyoncé and Jay-Z were active shareholders of the diet program upon launch in 2015 (Parkwood Entertainment 2015). A press release quoted Beyoncé:

> I am so grateful that I took the challenge and credit Marco with leading by example. He is the most energetic person I know and it's all because of his decision to live a healthy lifestyle. He came up with a great program to get people motivated to make better nutritional choices. All you have to do is try. If I can do it, anyone can [Parkwood Entertainment 2015].

You have as many hours in the day as Beyoncé. The performer's own body maintenance through diet and exercise is exalted because the public sees just how hard she works for it. Beyoncé's reclaims her body by not allowing it to rest; while labor, especially considering the history of humiliation and enslavement of the black female body, can make a body docile and submissive, Beyoncé's body labor is marketed as freedom—the lesson gained from her body is that hard work on the body is liberating and worthy of celebration.

On May 6, 2014, hooks went viral in the mainstream media—with audiences that weren't familiar with hooks but were very familiar with the singer—for calling Beyoncé a terrorist (hooks, Mock, and Blackman 2014). hooks was a speaker at the "Are You Still a Slave?" public dialogue at New York City's New School, in conversation with Janet Mock and Marci Blackman (hooks, Mock, and Blackman 2014). "I see a part of Beyoncé that is in fact anti-feminist—that is a terrorist, especially in terms of the impact on young girls," hooks had said (hooks, Mock, and Blackman 2014). They were discussing Beyoncé, with straight blonde hair, being scantily clad in a pair of white underwear on the cover of *Time*'s 2014 "100 Most Influential People" (hooks, Mock, and Blackman 2014). "In keeping with this affirmation of whiteness she, clothed in bra and panties on the cover, continues the stereotype that black females are more sexually active and loose than other groups of women," hooks had written about this cover in *Black Looks*, also noting that Laverne Cox was, too, photographed with long blonde hair and a "hypersexualized body" on the cover of *Time* (2015, x). Blackman claimed that the cover infantilized Beyoncé into a "little girl," conveying the message that 'black women are supposed to be child-like and children" (hooks, Mock, and Blackman 2014). hooks agreed, adding that Beyoncé was not only photographed as a little girl, but a sexualized little girl to add insult to injury (hooks, Mock, and Blackman 2014). "Let's take the image of this super rich, very powerful Black female and let's use it in the service of imperialist, white supremacist capitalist patriarchy because she probably had very little control over that cover—that image," she said (hooks, Mock, and Blackman 2014). Mock disagreed, arguing that in this discussion of Beyoncé, her own agency, apart from her own marketing team and the marketing team at *Time*, should be dismissed—she has final say over the image, after all, and she brings her own stylist (hooks, Mock, and Blackman 2014). While hooks argued that she is colluding with the "imperialist, white supremacist, capitalist patriarchy," Blackman asked us to consider that she is re-claiming this image, even if there is some collusion involved (hooks, Mock, and Blackman 2014). It was here that hooks said it didn't matter if Beyoncé had a stake in choosing, and making, the image for the cover, because she's only interesting and worth talking about because of her financial assets: "Here is a young black woman who is so incredibly wealthy, and wealthy is what so many young people fantasize, dream about, sexualize, eroticize, and one could argue that even more than her body, it's what that body stands for" (hooks, Mock, and Blackman 2014). No one would care about Beyoncé if she were homeless, argued hooks, even if she looked the same way (hooks, Mock, and Blackman 2014). But hooks overlooks—or neglects to mention—in the livestreamed discussion in front of The New School's academic community that Beyoncé would not look the way she does without her wealth and prioritization of beauty maintenance as a pre-condition to maintaining that wealth.

As we've seen previously through her stringent dieting, intensive fitness regime, and professionally-coordinated hair and makeup routine, Beyoncé is able to look the way she does because she has the time and money to invest in her looks—it is part of her full-time job. As noted by phenomenologist Jean Grimshaw in "Working Out with Merleau-Ponty," the contemporary myth that we can choose our bodies effaces the "inequalities of privilege, money, and time to engage in these practices" (1999). Body parts are part of a celebrity's capital; that's why Dolly Parton insured her bosom for $600,000 and Heidi Klum insured her legs for $2 million (Acuna 2012).

Beyoncé, private as usual, has not spoken about the insurance of her body parts, but it would follow precedent if she did. Thus, hooks was correct that Beyoncé's body is undeniably tied to the capitalist class system, but her interpretation of Beyoncé's body neglects to give Beyoncé any agency of her own. Beyoncé is proud and confident in her idealized body, which has been shaped by dieting and exercise, but this particular body is also outside of the norm of traditionally celebrated upper-class bodies, which are white, tall, and thin—indeed, Beyoncé is not fighting class oppression, but she has transformed the enslaved body of the black women, either desexualized or hypersexualized and always in ownership, and made it a figure of class aspiration, female empowerment, and liberation (Bordo 2003, 11). Ideal body types have changed throughout the years, but what has remained the same is that these idealized bodies, from curvaceous Marilyn Monroe of the 1950s to androgynous Twiggy of the 1960s, have largely been the bodies of white women. Women still want a "normalized" body—but now this body can be a black one that doesn't look like a high-end fashion model. If hooks is correct and Beyoncé's body is still colonized by white patriarchy, she has, at least, reversed the control of the panoptic gaze. Foucault wrote, "A body is docile that can be subjected, used, transferred and improved" (1975, 136). A docile body is not necessarily passive—it is constantly in motion and being led by the oppressor into body transformations. In her ethnographic research, model-turned sociologist Mears provides a direct quotation from a New York–based fashion stylist who worked with models:

Basically, high-end ethnic means, the only thing that is not white about you is that you are black. Everything else, you are totally white. You have the same body as a white girl. You have the same aura, you have the same the old, aristocratic atmosphere about you, but your skin is dark [2010, 39].

Black supermodel Iman, for example, received worldwide acclaim as a universally celebrated beauty because she fit into the requirements of a "white ice goddess beauty"—she just happened to have darker skin and, regardless of her skin color, her hair was as sleek and straight as any other white fashion model's (hooks 2015,72). Mears adds, "Because ethnic is automatically distanced from the high end, and this relegated to the commercial realm, editorial producers much search for a model of color who can embody an air of rarity, no easy feat given the entrenched construction of non-white ethnicity as vulgar" (2010, 39). Consequently, cultural producers assume that non-white bodies have negative implications, making them undesirable for working with luxury fashion designers and for aspirational imagery (Mears 2010, 40). But on the contrary to Mear's observations, prestigious designers clamor to clothe Beyoncé onstage (Muller 2014). She's not begging for the social capital that comes from wearing the right designer—they want to be associated with her and they want the social capital from Queen Bey wearing their designs (Muller 2014). Wardrobe for her 2014 On the Run tour included custom-made pieces from labels like Givenchy, Alexander Wang, Versace, Diesel, and Elie Saab, all created with at least two-and-half-months' notice (Muller 2014). Beyoncé's body, thus, is desirable far beyond the sexual appetite and the male gaze—and in its desirability, there is an act of resistance against the colonizer's ideal. She's not leading a gender and racial revolution by a rejection of standards of beauty, but she has achieved a monumental resistance against the white male gaze: Beyoncé directs our gaze to exactly how and when she wants to be seen.

Looking at Beyoncé's Weave Closet

Beyoncé's high-maintenance body routine also extends to her hair, and the preoccupation with her hair, by both herself and the media, also draws upon a long history of black female performers wearing faux hair and a long history of the stigmatization of "natural" hair. As early as the 1950s and 1960s, across class lines, having straight or sleekly wavy hair was considered "good" hair and having kinky or very curly hair was considered "bad" in black American communities (Walker 2000, 538). In very simplistic terms, straight hair represented femininity, and femininity was represented by whiteness (Walker 2000, 539). It is a well-known fact that Beyoncé wears a weave—or many weaves, in actuality (Madison III 2015). In the September 2015 issue of *Flaunt*, she told the fashion publication about her "over-populated" hair closet through a fill-in word-association chart. (Once again, as for that same month's issue of American *Vogue*, she did not grant an actual interview.) "It is ironically appropriate that much of this hair is synthetic and man-made, artificially constructed as is the sexualized image it is meant to evoke," hooks notes, also referencing Tina Turner and Diana Ross for their highlighting their sexualized hair—almost in replacement of the rest of the body—in promotional imagery (2015, 70).

Beyoncé is neither the first nor the only black women with influence and wealth in popular culture to have oftentimes opted for blonde and straightened wigs, hair extensions, and weaves. British supermodel Naomi Campbell, for example, has been heralded as the "black Brigitte Bardot" by fashion critics (hooks 2015, 73). hooks argues that the hair is not Beyoncé's true hair—that she is buying into the image of the oppressor (hooks, Mock, and Blackman 2014).

But even if one agrees with hooks' argument that straight blonde hair on a black women is a relic of colonialism and complicity with the oppressor (hooks, Mock, and Blackman 2014), a black woman wearing her hair "naturally," as is considered a form of African American pride, isn't without its instances and implications of commoditization, either. In 1994, activist Angela Davis decried the Afro as a nostalgic "hairdo" that "reduces a politics of liberation to a politics of fashion"—she cited a fashion magazine spread in *Vibe* in which the model dressed up as Angela Davis, circa 1969 (42). Davis notes that in 1969, when the FBI was investigating her and she was actually trying to avoid looking like a communist revolutionary, she wore a wig of long straight black hair, long eyelashes, and more makeup that she had ever worn in public before (1994, 41). "[I]t seemed to me that glamour was the only look that might annul the likelihood of being perceived as a revolutionary," she wrote, surprised that the very "revolutionary" look she was trying to avoid was seen as glamorous a few decades later (Davis 1994, 41). For many women, the aesthetics of an "Afro" is seen as an act of personal and political revolution—a rejection of a "white" aesthetic and an abandonment of beauty commodification tied to returning to "authenticity" (Walker 2000, 541). The beauty industry of the 1960s responded to the Afro movement by insisting that "natural" hair required specialized products and treatments, just as relaxing, braiding, or straightening one's hair would (Walker 2000, 547).

Fast-forward about 50 years and, in 2015, "natural" hair is still heralded as both a personal and political statement about confidence and celebrating Afrocentric beauty. In March 2015, Cipriana Quann, co-founder of a popular natural hair blog called *Urban Bush Babes* told online beauty publication *Into the Gloss*:

> Now, young girls see images of women of all colors and shapes and hair textures, and I think it's really inspiring everyone to be braver. It's not just about hair—it's also about feeling comfortable and being yourself and saying to the world, "Here I am. If you don't like it, tough luck." Quann also spoke frankly about maintaining "natural" hair: "Natural hair is work and the longer your hair is, the more work it is. I'm not saying that it's difficult to manage, but it is work—especially detangling" [*Into the Gloss* 2015].

Beyoncé, consequently, couldn't be inclined to forgo her wigs and weaves for "natural" hair out of pure convenience—there's nothing low-maintenance about any of these hairstyles. But while Beyoncé's choice to wear a weave or wig may garner criticism for "whiteness," one could theorize that wearing these extensions would actually be less controversial. For many black women, even those out of the paparazzi-hounded limelight, straight and sleekly styled hair is a shield of protection in a society that attaches negative connotations to traditionally African features (Williams 2012). In 2014, for example, a Change.org petition received over 5,000 signatures, urging Beyoncé to comb her daughter Blue Ivy's hair. The petition read:

As a woman who understands the importance of hair care. It's disturbing to watch a child suffering from the lack of hair moisture. The parents of Blue Ivy. Sean Carter a.k.a. Jay-Z and Beyoncé has failed at numerous attempts of doing Blue Ivy Hair. This matter has escalated to the child developing matted dreads and lint balls" (2014). One signee, Nancy Kondo from Toronto, Canada, wrote, "Because no child who's [sic] mom spends thousands on her hair (monthly) should live life looking like a sheep! (2014)." The policing of Blue Ivy's hair, which consists of kinky curls much like her mother's natural hair (seen in the early days of as a member of Destiny's Child), is reminiscent of the criticism of United States Olympic Games gymnast Gabrielle Douglas, the first black woman to win the Olympic gymnastics women's individual all-around competition—with a few stray hairs (Williams 2012). "gabby douglas gotta do something with this hair! these clips and this brown gel residue aint it?" wrote one person on Twitter (Williams 2012). "Why hasn't anyone tried to fix Gabby Douglas' hair?" asked another person online (Williams 2012). Douglas, unfortunately, even by making world history as the first woman of color of any nationality to win the event, was not able to avoid the criticism of her hair (Macur 2012). Consequently, Beyoncé's decision to completely obfuscate her own hair with manufactured heads of honey-colored locks cannot simply be read as a desire to be more "white." If one presumes that she is protecting her image to avoid criticism as much as possible—as evidenced by her attempt to delete "unflattering" photos off the internet and avoidance of face-to-face interviews—then wearing a wig becomes a solution to a practical, not a political problem for Beyoncé.

If we view Beyoncé's flowing, expensively-designed, smooth locks as empowering in any way, it is because we know that Beyoncé has achieved the aspirations of many black American women, as evidenced by the $684 million black hair industry: the dream is to have the financial capital and resources to always have a socially-acceptable hairstyle (Susan 2014).

Black Womanhood in Performance

Given that black American women's bodies have a continuous historical trajectory of being policed, enslaved, and disciplined, it may appear that

Beyoncé's discipline and control of her own body, from how it looks to how we look at it, can be furthermore oppressed and made subservient for white patriarchal appetites. Beauty—and the pursuit of it—as a normalizing discipline works in different ways for different bodies. hooks wrote:

> The general tyranny of fashion—perpetual, elusive, and instructing the female body in a pedagogy of personal inadequacy and lack—is a powerful discipline for the normalization of all women in this culture.... [W]hen Oprah Winfrey admitted on her show that all her life she has desperately longed to have "hair that swings from side to side" when she shakes her head, she revealed the power of racial as well as gender normalization, normalization not only to "femininity," but to the Caucasian standards of beauty that still dominate on television, in movies, in popular magazines [2015, 255].

Non-white female bodies must be shaped and formed into acceptable standards of feminine beauty in order to be worthy of acceptance. These accepted notions of feminine beauty, of course, discipline white and other non-white female bodies, too—but black female bodies have the additional burden of bearing postcolonial and racist attitudes that are so embedded within society that visual productions coming from privileged cultural producers—like fashion magazines or Super Bowl halftime shows—usually do not realize these oppressions and calls for resistance. But while Beyoncé becomes a larger-than-life body when she is in performance, her off-camera "performances" have been considered banal. In 2013, Jody Rosen of *The New Yorker* noted that much of Beyoncé's self-produced HBO documentary was full of platitudes and clichés—somewhat surprising coming from a woman known at various points in her career as "America's Sweetheart, National Bombshell, and Entertainer-in-Chief." However, ultimately, Beyoncé claims individual agency against the panoptic patriarchal disciplining gazes because she controls when and how we see her—usually in performance. We must therefore, consider Beyoncé's body in performance, in motion, as the standard in understanding her personal agency. "Why do we have to take a backseat?" Beyoncé asks in her 2013 HBO documentary, *Beyoncé: Life Is but a Dream*, which starts with her 2011 decision to sever relations with her father. "I truly believe that women should be financially independent from their men. And let's face it: money gives men the power to run the show. It gives men the power to define value. They define what's sexy. And men define what's feminine. It's ridiculous." By using her financial capital to make the black female body visible—the main object of admiration, in fact—in some of the most public spaces in the American society, Beyoncé's painstakingly designed performativity becomes a celebratory ode to both the liberating and oppressive experiences of black American womanhood.

References

Acuna, Kirsten. 2012. "20 Celebrities Who Insured Their Body Parts for Millions." *Business Insider*, March 5. http://www.businessinsider.com/20-celebrities-who-insured-their-bodies-for-millions-2012–3?op=1.

Bennett, Jessica. 2014. "How to Reclaim the F-Word? Just Call Beyoncé." *Time*, August 26. http://time.com/3181644/beyonce-reclaim-feminism-pop-star/.

"Beyoncé Interview." 2008. *Marie Claire UK*, September 3. http://www.marieclaire.co.uk/news/celebrity/272366/beyonce-interview.html.

Beyoncé: Life Is but a Dream. Directed by Ed Burke, Beyoncé Knowles, and Ilan Y. Benatar. HBO, 2013.

"Beyoncé Reveals Secrets Behind Vegan Diet." 2015. *Good Morning America*, ABC, June 8.

"Beyoncé: We Built a City, We Enthroned a Queen, and She Provided the Words, in Her Own Hand." 2015. *Flaunt*, September 9. http://flaunt.com/people/beyonce-califuk/.

Bordo, Susan. 2003. *Unbearable Weight: Feminism, Western Culture and the Body.* Berkeley: University of California Press.

BuzzFeedCeleb. 2013. "The 'Unflattering' Photos Beyoncé's Publicist Doesn't Want You to See." *BuzzFeed*, February 5. http://www.buzzfeed.com/buzzfeedceleb/the-unflattering-photos-beyonces-publicist-doesnt-want-you-t#.kkMZVvykB.

Carby, Hazel V. 1992. "Policing the Black Woman's Body in an Urban Context." *Critical Inquiry* 18:4 (Summer): 738–55.

Chernikoff, Leah. 2013. "Beyoncé Wears Little-Known Designer Rubin Singer for Her Super Bowl Halftime Show." *Fashionista*, February 2. http://fashionista.com/2013/02/beyonce-wears-rubin-singer-super-bowl-halftime-sho.

Chiu, Alexis. 2012. "Motherhood Makes Beyoncé Feel 'More Beautiful Than Ever.'" *People*, April 25. http://www.people.com/people/package/article/0,,20360857_20589758,00.html.

"Cipriana & TK Quann, Urban Bush Babes." 2015. *Into the Gloss*, March 27. https://intothegloss.com/2015/06/cipriana-tk-quann/.

Collins, Scott. 2013. "Super Bowl Ratings Dip Slightly from Last Year." *Los Angeles Times*, February 5. http://articles.latimes.com/2013/feb/05/entertainment/la-et-st-0205-super-bowl-ratings-20130205.

Dahl, Melissa. 2014. "You Absolutely Do Not Have as Many Hours in the Day as Beyoncé." *Science of Us*, November 4. http://nymag.com/scienceofus/2014/11/powerful-people-think-they-control-time.html.

Davis, Angela Y. 1994. "Afro Images: Politics, Fashion, and Nostalgia." *Critical Inquiry* 21:1 (Autumn): 37–9, 41–3, 45.

Dionne, Evette. 2013. "Jada Pinkett-Smith Sets Body-Shaming Critics Straight." *Clutch*, June 5. http://www.clutchmagonline.com/2013/06/jada-pinkett-smith-sets-body-shaming-critics-straight/.

Dobbins, Amanda. 2012. "Celebrity BFF of the Year: Jennifer Lawrence." *Vulture*, December 5. http://www.vulture.com/2012/12/celebrity-bff-of-the-year-jennifer-lawrence.html.

Dockterman, Eliana. 2014. "This Year's VMAs Were All About Empowered Women." *Time*, August 25. http://time.com/3172050/vmas-2014-beyonce-nicki-minaj-female-performances-feminism/.

Facebook, Inc. "Jada Pinkett-Smith's Facebook Page." Last modified February 4, 2013. Accessed November 1, 2015. https://www.facebook.com/photo.php?fbid=10151710945141320.

Fashion Rocks Live Concert. 2006. Radio City Music Hall, New York, September 7.

Foucault, Michel. 1975. *Discipline and Punish: The Birth of the Prison*. New York: Vintage Books.

Francis, Terri. 2008. "What Does Beyoncé See in Josephine Baker? A Brief Film History of Sampling La Diva, La Bakaire." *The Scholar and Feminist Online* 6:2 (Spring). http://sfonline.barnard.edu/baker/print_francis.htm.

Galai, Noam. 2013. "Beyoncé Bans All Pro Photographers from Her Concerts." *Fstoppers*, April 22. https://fstoppers.com/pictures/beyonce-bans-all-pro-photographers-her-concerts-3410.

Gannon, Emma. 2013. "Why Beyoncé Is My Kind of Feminist." *The Telegraph*, February 4. http://www.telegraph.co.uk/women/womens-life/9847710/Beyonce-is-my-kind-of-feminist.html.

Gensler, Andy. 2013. "Beyonce on Self-Management, Following Madonna's Footsteps, Developing Other Artists." *Billboard*, December 22. http://www.billboard.com/biz/articles/news/legal-and-management/5847820/beyonce-on-self-management-following-madonnas.

Gilman, Sander L. 1985. "Black Bodies, White Bodies: Toward an Iconography of Female Sexuality in Late Nineteenth-Century Art, Medicine, and Literature." *Critical Inquiry* 12:1 (Autumn): 204–42.

Good Morning America. 2006. ABC, September 6.

Grimshaw, Jean. 1999. "Working Out with Merleau-Ponty." *Women's Bodies: Discipline and Transgression*, ed. Jane Arthurs and Jean Grimshaw, 91–116. London: Cassell.

Harris, Tamara Winfrey. 2013a. "All Hail the Queen? What Do Our Perceptions of Beyoncé's Feminism Say About Us?" *Bitch*, May 20. https://bitchmedia.org/article/all-hail-the-queen-beyonce-feminism.

_____. 2013b. "Racialized Performances in Pop Music or Why Are Beyoncé and JLo So Scandalous?" *Racialicious*, June 4. http://www.racialicious.com/2013/06/04/racialized-performances-in-pop-music-or-why-are-beyonce-and-jlo-so-scandalous/.

Hobson, Janell. 2013. "Policing Feminism: Regulating the Bodies of Women of Color." *Ms.*, June 10. http://msmagazine.com/blog/2013/06/10/policing-feminism-regulating-the-bodies-of-women-of-color/.

hooks, bell. 2015. *Black Looks: Race and Representation*. New York: Routledge. Kindle Edition.

hooks, bell, Janet Mock, and Marci Blackman. 2014. "Are You Still a Slave? Liberating the Black Female Body." Public Dialog, bell hooks Conversations and Dialogs, New York, May 6.

Hunter, Margaret, and Kathleen Soto. 2009. "Women of Color in Hip Hop: The Pornographic Gaze." *Race, Gender & Class* 16:1/2: 170–91. http://www.jstor.org/stable/41658866.

Khan, Shamus. 2010. *Privilege: The Making of an Adolescent Elite at St. Paul's School*. Princeton: Princeton University Press.

Jefferson, Margo. 2015. "The Reign of Beyoncé." *Vogue*, August 13. http://www.vogue.com/projects/13293183/beyonce-september-2015-cover/.

Jones, Nate. 2014. "From 'Boof-Boof' to 'Surfbort': The Complete Beyoncé Dictionary." *People*, March 4. http://www.people.com/people/article/0,,20793540,00.html.

Juzwiak, Rich. 2013. "Kanye West Is the 'Pioneer of This Queer Shit,' Says Homophobe Rapper." *Gawker*, February 4. http://gawker.com/5981601/kanye-west-is-the-pioneer-of-this-queer-shit-says-homophobe-rapper.

Kendall, Mikki. 2013. "Beyoncé's New Album Should Silence Her Feminist Critics." *The Guardian*, December 13. http://www.theguardian.com/commentisfree/2013/dec/13/beyonce-album-flawless-feminism.

Macur, Juliet. 2012. "A Very Long Journey Was Very Swift." *New York Times*, August 2. http://www.nytimes.com/2012/08/03/sports/olympics/gabby-douglas-of-united-states-wins-gymnastics-all-around.html.

Madison, Ira, III. 2015. "PSA: Beyoncé Wears a Weave." *BuzzFeed*, August 13. http://www.buzzfeed.com/iramadison/stop-the-track-let-me-state-fact#.nfLomB5y6.

Marquina, Sierra. 2015. "Beyonce Shares Her Intense Workout Routine in Sped-Up Instagram Video—Learn Her Moves Here!" *Us Weekly*, February 25. http://www.usmagazine.com/celebrity-body/news/beyonce-shares-her-intense-workout-routine-watch-2015252.

Mears, Ashley. 2010. "Size Zero High-End Ethnic: Cultural Production and the Reproduction of Culture in Fashion Modeling." *Poetics* 38: 21–46.

Minaj, Nicki. 2015. Twitter post, July 21, 6:14 p.m. https://twitter.com/nickiminaj/status/623617003153035264.

MTV Video Music Awards. 2014. The Forum, Inglewood, CA, August 24.

Muller, Marissa G. 2014. "Dressing the Queen: Beyoncé's Stylist Breaks Down Her On the Run Tour Looks." *Vogue*, September 20. http://www.vogue.com/13280694/beyonce-on-the-run-tour-stylist-interview/.

Nelson, Sara C. 2013. "Beyoncé Avoids 'Muscly' Picture Repeat by Issuing Just Two Flattering Snaps at Start of Mrs Carter World Tour." *The Huffington Post UK*, April 16. http://www.huffingtonpost.co.uk/2013/04/16/beyonce-muscly-flattering-mrs-carter-world-tour_n_3090064.html.

Parkwood Entertainment. 2015. "Beyonce Teams Up with Exercise Physiologist Marco Borges for 22 Days Nutrition." *PR Newswire*, January 28. http://www.prnewswire.com/news-releases/beyonce-teams-up-with-exercise-physiologist-marco-borges-for-22-days-nutrition-300027297.html.

Rosen, Jody. 2013. "Her Highness." *The New Yorker*, February 20. http://www.newyorker.com/culture/culture-desk/her-highness.

Schneier, Matthew. 2015. "Beyoncé Is Seen but Not Heard." *New York Times*, August 19. http://www.nytimes.com/2015/08/20/fashion/beyonce-is-seen-but-not-heard.html.

Stewart, Dodai. 2013. "Beyoncé Solves Unflattering Photo Problem by Banning Photogs." *Jezebel*. April 22. http://jezebel.com/beyonce-solves-unflattering-photo-problem-by-banning-ph-477260832.

Susan, Trudy. 2014. "It's Time: Black Women Need to Take Back the Hair Industry." *Ebony*, July 14. http://www.ebony.com/style/black-women-need-to-take-back-the-hair-industry-887#axzz3s5uBhKL3.

Super Bowl XLVII. 2013. CBS, February 3.

T, J. 2014. "Petitioning Blue Ivy: Comb Her Hair." Petition. *Change.org*. https://www.change.org/p/blue-ivy-comb-her-hair.

Walker, Susannah. 2000. "Black Is Profitable: The Commodification of the Afro, 1960–1975." *Enterprise & Society* 1:3 (September): 536–64. http://www.jstor.org/stable/23699596.

Wallace, Amy. 2013. "Miss Millennium: Beyoncé." *GQ*, January 10. http://www.gq.com/story/beyonce-cover-story-interview-gq-february-2013.

Williams, Vanessa. 2012. "Gabby Douglas's Hair Sets Off Twitter Debate, but Some Ask: 'What's the Fuss?'" *Washington Post*, August 3. https://www.washingtonpost.com/lifestyle/style/gabby-douglass-hair-sets-off-twitter-debate-but-some-ask-whats-the-fuss/2012/08/03/38548064-ddaf-11e1–9ff9–1dcd8858ad02_story. html.

Yapalater, Lauren. 2013. "The 33 Fiercest Moments From Beyoncé's Halftime Show." *BuzzFeed*, February 4. http://www.buzzfeed.com/lyapalater/the-fiercest-moments-from-beyonces-halftime-show#.pjqwB1rjA.

I'm Not Myself Lately
The Erosion of the Beyoncé Brand

Kristin Lieb

Throughout most of Beyoncé's career, her power has come from playing her own distinctive game. Beyoncé did Beyoncé, and it worked. In brand terms, Beyoncé was strong, meaningfully differentiated from competitors, resonant with diverse audiences, and, frankly, untouchable. This was a remarkable accomplishment in an industry where female pop stars are created and managed to be interchangeably "sexy," short-term person-brands, not individualized or distinguished career artists (Lieb 2013).

Up through the release of *I Am ... Sasha Fierce*, writers described Beyoncé as polite but guarded during interviews (Petridis 2008), which kept her elegant diva/songstress brand intact and her audiences at arm's length. It's possible that Beyoncé's reputation as a classy, dignified R&B diva actually derived from all the things she *didn't* say, and all of the things people projected onto her from the little they actually knew about her.

Beyoncé was regal, independent and elegant, an accomplished singer, dancer, and actor, whose entertainment credentials and charisma generated opportunities to perform for the Obamas numerous times. She performed Etta James' "At Last" at the inaugural ball in 2009, the National Anthem at Barack Obama's second Presidential Inauguration in 2013, and then a 30-minute set for Michelle Obama's 50th birthday party in 2014 (Samuels 2013; Daily Mail Reporter 2014; Saad 2014). Beyoncé didn't worry about what contemporaries were doing, because she didn't have to. Nobody could really compete with Beyoncé.

But, as a person and a brand, which come together in the form of an integrated person-brand, Beyoncé has experienced three potentially identity-changing events in the past seven years: marrying Jay-Z, firing her father as manager, and birthing her first child, Blue Ivy Carter. Any one of these events in isolation could represent an identity game-changer. But taken together, they have, at a minimum, disrupted Beyoncé's carefully cultivated commercial brand. As Beyoncé became "independent" in her personal life, marrying Jay-Z and establishing her own management company, Parkwood Entertainment, in 2008, and severing ties with her manager/father in 2011, her public persona and brand began to disintegrate (Knowles 2013). She spoke publicly about how these events empowered her, but in exchange for this stated empowerment in her personal context, she sacrificed a considerable amount of professional coherence. Is she musical royalty (The Queen) or is she Bootylicious? Is she the Perfect Wife and Mother or is she a Smoking Hot Sex Machine? It's as if her narratives are fighting with one another to establish dominance within her brand.

Clearly, Beyoncé is trying to have her cake and eat it too. She has been called groundbreaking, a perfect example of feminism in our complicated modern times. But her powerful platform draws shamelessly on the safest and most conservative forms of pleasing men—playing the virgin figure, who evolves into the good mother as she ages, and the whore figure, who will do anything to please her powerful man, in part to show others that she deserves him. By walking the same impossible tightrope so many others have walked before her in order to cash in on the two most normative, lucrative, and ultimately disempowering ways of performing femininity publicly, Beyoncé is arguably playing it safe, not going revolutionary. Beyoncé's male-gaze-ready performances may look a little different from her predecessors, but that's a marketplace imperative. She needs to show audiences that she can reflect the cultural values and tastes of the moment, as other pop stars have before her. Madonna did it differently than Britney, who did it differently than Christina, who did it differently than Miley. But all had the same basic audience, and the same basic commercial interests in mind. All pursued the easiest and most effective methods to be validated, celebrated, and paid in contemporary U.S. culture as female performers.

As Beyoncé began diverging from her classy, elegant, untouchable-in-a-good-way diva persona, and turning up her sex appeal and sexual focus on songs like "Partition" and "Cherry," she shrugged off the very meanings that made her distinctive. With Sasha Fierce, Beyoncé appeared to be executing a strategy of multivocality—or speaking to different target markets using different voices or personas to broaden her appeal (Fournier, Solomon, and Englis 2008). But somewhere along the way, she began sacrificing her core brand values, and at this point Beyoncé's expanded and incoherent brand meanings are at war with one another, resulting in a highly confused, and confusing, brand.

Since 2013, Beyoncé has been blurring "Beyoncé the person" into and out of the Beyoncé brand with impunity. This is not advisable, unless there's a sound strategy and sound boundaries embedded in the approach of expanding a brand's meanings (e.g., you are trying to replace outdated or undesirable meanings with newer, better ones). Erratic boundary blurring between the person and the person brand can have catastrophic consequences. (When a brand gets confusing, people check out of it, and the brand loses followers and revenue.) Person brands should be personal, but not *too* personal.

Person Brand and Celebrity Brands

In personifying brands, those engineering and positioning them must make them be likable; have a voice; exhibit diversity; be memorable; experience conflict; and appear deviant, but not too deviant (Rindova, Pollock, and Hayward 2007). These tactics were initially suggested for businesses wanting to personify or celebratize their brands (even before the companies-are-people movement) but certainly apply directly to person brands, which function as business empires unto themselves. Beyoncé and her legions of handlers have orchestrated these steps several times in her solo career, changing the specifics of her messaging and dress to reflect the cultural climate of the time (e.g., moving from glittery gowns and diva posturing to leotards, leather and hyper-sexualized routines). Other academics have focused more exclusively on person-brand development cycles, indicating that the person (here Beyoncé): births a brand; inserts herself into the brand; becomes equal to the brand; becomes greater than the brand, and ultimately becomes less than the brand (Fournier and Herman 2006). In 2013, Beyoncé was larger than her brand, but two years later, Beyoncé is less than her brand, a slew of disconnected hashtags and contradictory rhetorical moments that fail to sum to anything coherent or meaningful. She went for broke in 2013 playing every pop star game in the book—good girl, temptress, whore, diva, exotic, and provocateur, among others—simultaneously, presumably to garner mass appeal. Beyoncé capitalized on this approach in the short-term, but shortchanged herself in the long term by trading away what made her special, different, like no other pop star. In brand terms, and in terms of a long-term career view, this was reckless, not wise.

Marital Brand Meanings and
Related Brand Erosion

As stated earlier, the beginning of Beyoncé's brand experimentation was *I Am … Sasha Fierce* in 2008. On this effort, Beyoncé split her brand into two distinct characters, her so-called real self, the timeless-but-potentially-boring married, straight, domesticated Beyoncé, and her emerging bad-girl, leotard-wearing persona, Sasha Fierce. It's vital to note that Jay-Z—whom Beyoncé married six months before revealing her Sasha Fierce side—may have influenced Beyoncé's transition into more bootylicious—a term created by Beyoncé that now resides in the Oxford English Dictionary—edgier territory. (In some ways, Beyoncé's marriage enabled her to be more risqué without consequence—as a married woman, her antics read as performances for Jay). As an entrepreneur, rapper, producer, and songwriter, Jay-Z is a powerful brand in his own right, embodying the myth of the American dream, with his rags-to-riches story of cocaine dealer-turned rapper-turned-Def Jam-label president (A&E Television Networks 2014; *Jay Z on His Rags-to-Riches Story* 2014). One documentary noted: "To some, the urban savvy rapper, known for his lyrics about crime and drinking pricey champagne, was an unlikely match for the R&B churchgoing southern girl" (Kennedy 2013).

Beyoncé gained new brand meanings through her marriage to Jay-Z, in part for becoming a "wife," which carries heavy social connotations, and in part from marrying the crafty entertainment mogul whose victories include founding Rocawear and discovering Rihanna. Jay-Z provided Beyoncé with a dash of street credibility, while she provided him with associations of class and elegance. Together, they built a family brand—Bey-Z for the purposes of this essay—which many aspired to, admiring the couple's good looks, prodigious power, and bottomless bank accounts. As Beyoncé became a cross-capitalized music industry entrepreneur herself—founding Parkwood Entertainment in the same year she married Jay-Z and revealed Sasha Fierce—her brand began to encompass power and influence, autonomy, and entrepreneurship. As her relationship with Jay-Z intensified, and her business empire expanded, her relationship with her father/ business manager disintegrated. This "break-up" resulted in new associations for the Beyoncé brand, making it more sympathetic, introducing meanings of vulnerability to it for the first time. Then, with the birth of Blue Ivy Carter in 2012, the Beyoncé brand acquired new associations—such as compassion and accessibility—related to motherhood. She also began migrating her brand toward her husband's, in terms of dress, swagger, style, and performance.

Complicated People Versus Complicated Brands

From a personal psychological perspective, Beyoncé's growing brand complexity may be a good thing. Living inside of cultural scripts is difficult for anyone, and exponentially more difficult for pop stars, who feel intense pressure to meet industry and audience expectations. The music industry guides stars to live inside of elaborately constructed narratives designed to sell culturally desirable stories. This often ends badly, especially for women of color, whose popular music scripts are even more restrictive and regulatory than those penned for white peers, sometimes with devastating consequences (e.g., Whitney Houston). The cultural scripts of the music industry are mostly written for white people by white people, with a single/monolithic white beauty ideal and standard of behavior in mind. As impossible as they are for white women to perform, they are even more difficult for women of color to enact convincingly because of the ways in which they're predicated on looking white (Lieb 2013).

Overarching Brand Themes, Multivocality, and Meaning Management

Some might speculate that since *Sasha Fierce*, Beyoncé has been deliberately using different voices to connect more engagingly and convincingly with diverse audiences. Brands used to speak with unified voices, communicating the same qualities in the same words *consistently*, to maximize brand awareness and brand strength while minimizing brand confusion. This worked with mass markets, but became less effective as a fragmented media landscape gave rise to niche marketing, which required more nuanced communication. Multivocality works best when there is a dominant voice that runs throughout all conversations, what I call an "overarching brand theme" (Lieb 2013, 14). This theme remains consistent, but the *communication of it* varies by audience. The trick for professionals using multivocality as a strategy is to engineer brands that are open enough to encourage the audience's meaningful co-creation with them, but established enough to carry some essential, unassailable meanings that persist regardless of target market. Without an overarching brand theme, the brand doesn't really stand for anything—it has no meaning at its core. Without a center, brands speaking to audiences in different voices can confuse and confound audiences, especially if the voices and messages are interpreted as contradictory, or schizophrenic, as they ultimately become on Beyoncé, which will be discussed later in this essay.

Multivocality (Fournier, Solomon, and Englis 2008) is so common many of us use it unwittingly, even in our personal communications. Most people use at least slightly different words, tones, and approaches when they address different groups of people (e.g., parents, kids, colleagues, romantic partners, strangers). The same is true with commercial brands, such as Beyoncé, with respect to cultural environments—she plays up different elements of her brand to reinforce certain meanings at certain points in time—and downplays others to move away from meanings that may not be as beneficial. For example, Beyoncé might not perform "Drunk in Love" at a NAACP fundraiser (due to its glib treatment of domestic violence) or "Partition" at Michelle Obama's birthday party for its explicit accounting of sexual acts between a woman and her husband.

Increasingly, brand management has become about meaning management (Allen, Fournier, and Miller 2008) and Beyoncé is creating new meanings faster than she can properly explain them, much less manage them. Her overarching brand theme (Lieb 2013) of classy, empowered fun is fracturing, splitting into incoherent, incompatible sub brands. We no longer know what Beyoncé really stands for, because she's so busy trying to convince us of her complexity, and that she's every woman—a star, wife, mother, temptress, lover, hoodrat, egomaniac, winner, loser—and the list goes on. The strategy suggests she wants every type of fan to have a point of entry into her brand (through the various versions of it she offers) in order to generate the most revenue possible. It's as though she's trying on different identities—and using different costumes and props—to ask audience members "which version of me works best for YOU?"

In some ways, Beyonce's brand complexity could be viewed as an interesting feminist or postmodern experiment, with Beyoncé showing us she has earned the right to do exactly as she pleases, blurring "Beyoncé the person" into and out of the Beyoncé brand as she wishes. The message may be that we shouldn't pigeon-hole Beyoncé, because she's human, and thus, complicated. But branding is about making the complex coherent, not revealing complicated inconsistencies and contradictions. As Alexis Petridis of *The Guardian* observed: "In pop, honesty isn't always the best policy" (2008, par. 6).

Why? Because when we live in the real world and we use too many voices, people call us schizophrenic. When there are too many brands-within-the-brand for people to reasonably keep track of, people simply stop trying. Beyoncé is abusing multivocality by playing every game in the book simultaneously, acquiring so many new and contradictory meanings, that each one effectively becomes meaningless. There is no overarching brand theme, so there is no brand coherence. Excessive brand meanings overextend the brand, depleting its portfolio of meaning, rather than enhancing it.

From a professional standpoint, personal diversification writ large in the public eye probably isn't the best business model for Beyoncé. People rely on brands for all kinds of reasons—to help reduce buying risk, to show others their preferences or affiliations, to help establish an identity or resolve identity issues (e.g., bridge the gap between who they are and who they want to be—or be seen as). So while it is advantageous for brands to be dynamic, changing or evolving over time to reflect cultural changes, it is not advantageous for brands to change at their core, in their overarching brand theme, disturbing the things that are meaningful about them, that distinguish them from others and make them genuinely matter to people. If they do, they risk alienating their followers, who feel betrayed by such radical departures. Such followers trusted the brand, became loyal to the brand, and expected that it would retain the meanings they held dear. Celebrity person brands such as Beyoncé should contain carefully selected, authentic meanings, but should not blur the lines of the personal and the professional too aggressively, or too often, or the brands develop so many meanings, they can't be successfully explained or managed. In Grant McCracken's "Who Is the Celebrity Endorser?" (1989), he indicates that if choosing between Meryl Streep and Bruce Willis, a company would be wise to choose Willis as an endorser for his coherent, if typecast, meanings, while Streep would be trickier to integrate because she's such a good actor she disappears into her roles, leaving consumers to wonder which of her characters is endorsing this product and what that means.

Beyoncé, Product Endorsements, and Brand Extensions

The historical strength of Beyoncé's brand enables its easy extension into other dimensions of popular culture. In 2013, she inked a multi-year, $50 million celebrity endorsement deal with Pepsi (Davies 2013) and launched a new song ("Standing On the Sun") through an H&M commercial (Powers 2013). She's also extended her brand into realms of fashion and fragrance. Since 2010, Beyoncé has released three core fragrance brands, Pulse, Heat, and Rise, and various line extensions within those brands. But Beyoncé's brand extensions encompass the same contradictions inherent in her brand, and arguably in herself. Rise, Beyoncé's third core fragrance line, was released approximately two months after her self-titled CD hit the market in 2013. Its marketing collateral described the product as "intoxicating, addictive, luminous, [and] floral" (Mau 2013, par. 3). Beyoncé herself declared that the fragrance "encourages women to be all that we are" (Mau 2013, par. 2). If all women amount to is a store-bought commodity, a fragrance to be put on and washed off mainly for the pleasure of others, that's problematic. The marketing for all of these lines taken together suggest that empowerment comes in a phallus-shaped bottle, and that it can be bought and sold.

Another illuminating example of Beyoncé's splintering brand can be found in computer simulation games in which fans can interact with her likeness. Basic simulation games related to celebrities are popular and offer young fans the opportunity to custom-create the pop star—in this case the Beyoncé—of their dreams. A quick Google search will lead a casual observer to more than 10 Beyoncé-related makeover and beauty simulations. The target market for the games appears to be young girls, given the language used, the names of the games, and design elements in the games, such as fonts and illustrations. Within the rigid parameters of the games, participants may change Beyoncé's hair color, weave, eye color, eye shadow, eye lashes—yes, you can give her falsies—blush, lipstick, clothes, shoes—and even her skin tone in some of them—to make her over the way they like her best.

Such games are a "lawless frontier" in terms of licensing right now, according to Todd Harper, who teaches in the University of Baltimore's program in Simulation and Digital Entertainment and completed a postdoctoral research position at MIT's Game Lab in 2014. "Rip offs, clones, and unauthorized IP [internet protocol] use are pretty rampant; it's often hard to tell what's authorized and what isn't" (2015). Although Beyoncé may not have authorized her likeness for this use, the brand metaphor is clear: Fans can turn her into whatever they want her to be.

Beyoncé's charity, BeyGood, is as open-ended as her 2015 brand. A visit to the charity's web site reveals that there is no vision statement or mission statement—there's not even a contextualizing "about" section. As the site encourages volunteers to sign up for the site, it effectively asks them to define its purpose. Co-creating meaning with audiences can be powerful, but the brand needs to know and communicate the basics of what it stands for before attempting to collaborate with others about its most important or valuable meanings.

Beyoncé and Boundaries

In 2013, Beyoncé created a self-produced documentary, distributed by HBO, titled *Beyoncé: Life Is but a Dream* (Knowles 2013). In it, she invites her fans to see the real her, without make-up or pretense. She talks about her estrangement from her father, her miscarriage, and other personal and career difficulties and disappointments. But Beyoncé fails to clearly communicate who she is to audiences, because she seems to be figuring that out for herself in real-time. In combination with the array of shape-shifting performances and priorities on *Beyoncé*—released later the same year—these efforts make her seem somewhat lost, as a person and a brand, and ready to inhabit any personae promising to complete her identity.

In the film, she explained:

> I'm feeling very empty because of my relationship with my dad. I'm so fragile at this point. I feel like my soul has been tarnished. Life is unpredictable, but I feel like I had to move on and not work with my dad. I don't care if I don't sell one record. It's bigger than the record. It's bigger than my career [2013].

Even this part of Beyoncé's narrative is familiar, age-old, and hegemonically supported. As Boose put it in "The Father and the Bride in Shakespeare (1982, 326):

> Following this expressly physical symbolic transfer, the father's role in his daughter's life is ended; custom dictates that he now leave the stage, resign his active part in the rite, and become a mere observer.

Beyoncé clearly stated she needed "boundaries," noting that her father did too. "It's really easy to get confused with this world that's your job that you live and breathe every day and then you don't know when to turn it off," she said. "You need a break. I needed a break" (2013). But the dissolving bonds with her father have been "memorialized and thus, paradoxically, reasserted" (Boose 1982, 326) in her relationship with Jay-Z, presumably curbing her "independence."

Beyoncé: The Surprise Visual Album

Beyoncé has been heralded as an unmitigated success, and along numerous industry benchmarks for success, it clearly was. Beyoncé and her handlers spent a small fortune and nearly two decades building a brand powerful enough to enable her to drop a secret release, *Beyoncé*, with no advance music or publicity, and compel 1.3 million people to buy it in its first several weeks, making it the #8 best-selling release of 2013 (Caulfield 2013, Caulfield 2014). But people were buying the Beyoncé brand they had come to love, with no expectation they would be getting the Beyoncé-as-shapeshifter spectacle they found on the album.

On *Beyoncé*, released in December 2013, her personalities multiplied, with most of them playing like extensions of her Sasha Fierce side. With this "I'm-Every-Woman" strategy, Beyoncé took an unfortunate step back into the pack of pop stars who use their looks and sexuality to fight for attention in a crowded field. This tactic effectively erased Beyoncé's pre-existing points of difference—her class, elegance, and untouchable diva status—rather than amplifying them. It also brought Beyoncé into competition with virtually every other top-level female pop star—at a time in her career lifecycle when this was unnecessary and unwise.

For every old-school-Beyoncé track on *Beyoncé*—such as "Pretty Hurts," a moving anthem about fixing society, not our physical imperfections—there's a "Rocket," a soft-core-porn-inspired, Janet-Jackson-esque video which begins with a suggestive offer involving an "ass"; and a Rihanna-evoking "Partition," in which she asks the driver to roll up the partition in the limo so nobody sees Beyoncé on her knees in the back orally pleasuring Jay-Z.

Beyoncé performed "Drunk in Love" at the 56th Annual Grammys in 2014 in stripper gear, performing a male-gaze-ready dance of submission for her husband—who guests on the song—and the millions of viewers watching. The decision to write and perform "Drunk in Love" was itself off-brand, with its playful reference to a well-known act of domestic violence depicted in Tina Turner biopic, *What's Love Go to Do with It?* (Mokoena 2014). In the scene, Tina Turner refused to eat her dessert and Ike Turner smashed it in her face. (Some radio stations edited the line out of the song for airplay due to its poor taste.) In "Drunk in Love," Jay commands Bey to eat the cake, and later compares his bedroom moves to rapist Mike Tyson, noting that he boxes and bites. This hardly sounds like the aspirational marriage so many fans celebrate. And the physical dynamics between the couple in the performance were cringe-worthy, with Beyoncé clearly performing to and for Jay, at times gazing lovingly at him, while Jay looked beyond and through her, clearly in his own world. Jay-Z's swagger has long depended on him casting himself as the center of the universe. He still does, and Beyoncé seems happy to revolve around him, making him the center of her universe, even during *her* performance at the Grammys, where she is now the most nominated female performer in history (McIntyre 2014).

The lyrics on *Beyoncé* are so sexual, and often so dysfunctional, that they should perhaps provoke genuine concern about what is happening to Beyoncé in this union and in the Bey-Z family brand.

The Family Brand of Bey-Z

Both Jay-Z and Beyoncé had strong, differentiated brands before joining forces. But now, as a power couple, they pass existing meanings and associations from their own brands onto the other's brand through affiliation, marriage, and, perhaps most powerfully, their daughter, Blue Ivy Carter. Beyoncé confers class, elegance, maternity and safety, while Jay-Z contributes mystery, street smarts, and hustle to the shared brand. They create opportunities and threats for each other in the process. They invite new audiences into the family brand, and escort others out.

Blue Ivy (aka B.I.C.) also contributes to the brand family by providing a human brand extension for the power couple—not surprisingly, her life began with her parents' failed attempt to trademark her name (O'Connor 2012). B.I.C. is acknowledged as being the youngest person ever credited on a *Billboard*-charting-song—at two days old, on Jay-Z's "Glory" (Bronson 2012). *Billboard* points out that B.I.C. displaces the previous record holder, Stevie Wonder's daughter, Aisha, who appears on "Isn't She Lovely" (Locker 2012).

So far, in the new brand family, sometimes dubbed Bey-Z, the Jay-Z brand is taking more than it is giving, and the Beyoncé brand is giving more than it is taking. One indicator of this is that when Beyoncé and others talk about *her* brand, they have a tendency to make Jay central to Beyoncé's narrative. When Jay and others talk about *his* brand, Beyoncé is more of an afterthought. Sometimes, Beyoncé isn't even named in Jay's interviews. In one of his interviews with Oprah, he elected to talk about his favorite pizza joints rather than mention his famous wife by name (*Oprah Talks to Jay-Z* 2009).

The once powerful and distinctive Beyoncé brand is being raided for its assets for the sake of building the family brand. It is being absorbed, changed, and essentially reclassified as a sub brand that has become subservient to the family brand. In 2013, Beyoncé told Winfrey: "I would not be the woman I am if I did not go home to that man," causing some outrage among commentators who believed she was neutralizing her own power by talking at length about what Jay does for her, and not what she does for herself, or for him. "Wouldn't you like to believe she'd be amazing whether or not she went home to a man?" *Jezebel*'s Dodai Stewart wrote. "(She would be.) It's a much better message when she talks about how powerful she is as a woman and what a woman can do—without mentioning Mr. Carter" (2013, par. 4).

Meanwhile, Jay-Z's brand associations appreciated in value—all due to his association with Beyoncé. While standing still as her brand moves toward his, Jay-Z inherits meanings related to being married to a strong, sexy, aspirational woman, having a beautiful child with her, and still being the gender-normative, heteronormative "man" in the relationship. Beyoncé's a "feminist," but not when Jay's around. She seems willing to go to all sorts of lengths just to be likable to him, and us, as she sings on "Partition." Far from being progressive, Beyoncé is appealing to the oldest fantasy in the book, performing the lady-in-the-street-but-whore-in-the-sheets act. In marriage, she's sacrificing the most distinctive parts of her brand to the family brand, which is regressive, not progressive, at least if viewed through a contemporary gender and equality lens.

Beyoncé, Female Empowerment, Feminism, and Bootyliciousness

Beyoncé's original messages of female empowerment, backed up by her talent and beauty, allowed her to claim her own place in the world of female pop stars, but on this effort she loses her overarching brand theme of classy empowerment in exchange for pop-star-as-sex-worker, and pop-star-as-submissive, subservient-wife. In brand terms, she's trading distinctive meanings for reductive points of parity, which is a bad trade. In human terms, she's becoming more like other pop stars, fixing public attention on her physical attributes and sexual prowess at the expense of her identity, which effectively disappears into her dazzling sets and costumes. Recalling Beyoncé's bedazzled, see-through dress at the Met Gala in May 2015, *Washington Post* columnist Robin Givhan noted: "Her legs, her breasts, her torso, her back, and her derriere all looked fabulous. But the woman herself was nowhere to be found" (2015, par. 8).

It's also difficult to discuss Beyoncé's brand without pondering her take on feminism. Arguably, in previous eras, Beyoncé's hashtag, sing-along, "go girl" feminism was one part of her multivocal brand, as evidenced by songs like "Single Ladies (Put a Ring On It)" and "Run the World (Girls)." Despite the patent absurdity of the latter—by no calculable measure do girls or women run the world—these songs became spirited, fun, feminist anthems without Beyoncé ever declaring them as such. This is where Beyoncé is at her best, when she's singing and flowing, not really trying to make a statement, at least not overtly.

Beyoncé does have moments of clear feminism, female empowerment, and patriarchal resistance, which, at times are rich with textual nuance. Her Super Bowl performance in 2013 was one of them. As feminist scholar Janell Hobson observed:

> The spectacle invoked goddess power, represented by Oshun—an African orisha (spirit or deity) known for her self-love, generosity and wealth—and Durga, the Hindu warrior goddess whose multiple hands emerged via digital screen as an extension of Beyoncé's essence. Beyoncé also summoned the collective power of women—representing diverse racial and ethnic backgrounds—by having an all-woman 10-piece backing band (The Sugar Mamas), women back-up singers and 120 women dancers [2015, par. 4].

Some watching got that; others didn't. Of course the spectacle was also full of bootyliciousness for those more inclined to see eye candy than goddess symbolism. In other words, it was a rich, substantive, and intersectionally feminist moment, but one that carried little risk for Beyoncé's brand as the revealing costumes and suggestive dance moves foregrounding the performance made many viewers stop and celebrate the hedonism of the spectacle without ever noticing the more nuanced creative concept behind it.

Where she's less interesting or convincing is when she's writing about her feminism. In 2014, Beyoncé's Open Letter to Feminism was included as part of *The Shriver Report: A Woman's Nation Pushes Back from the Brink*. In it, Beyoncé shared her thoughts about equal pay:

> We need to stop buying into the myth about gender equality. It isn't a reality yet. Today, women make up half of the U.S. workforce, but the average working woman earns only 77 percent of what the average working man makes. But unless women and men both say this is unacceptable, things will not change.

Men have to demand that their wives, daughters, mothers, and sisters earn more—commensurate with their qualifications and not their gender. Equality will be achieved when men and women are granted equal pay and equal respect [Knowles 2014, par. 1].

It was a public validation, but it certainly wasn't groundbreaking in thought or expression. And frankly, it read as if someone might have written it for her, which would not be uncommon in such situations. Seven months later, Beyoncé made a much less predictable move, performing in front of a gigantic sign reading "FEMINIST," at the 2014 VMAs (August 24, 2014). This moment only lasted five seconds—in a performance running 16 minutes and 15 seconds—but it was an important moment nonetheless. As spectators saw the sign—and Beyoncé in front of it—they heard a sample of Nigerian writer Chimamanda Ngozi Adichie's definition of feminist: "a person who believes in the social, political, and economic equality of the sexes." But before the moment could really land and be absorbed by the audience, Beyoncé transitioned, remarking: "I'm having such a great time with y'all, but I'm ready to get grimy." From there, she launched into "Flawless," in which she instructed "bitches" to "bow down" to her.

Throughout the 2014 VMA performance, Beyoncé used different signs and props to promote different parts of her identity and brand. That "feminist" was included in this overall scaffolding is important. There would have been tremendous irony in Beyoncé performing some of her most subservient, submissive lyrics in front of a sign that said "feminism," but she didn't do that. To make her "feminism" palatable to the masses, she used it as a prop, just as she did naked, lubed-up booties of others on "Drunk in Love," stripper poles on "Partition" (while singing about how she just wants to be the kind of girl we like), and "BLOW" and "CHERRY" signs during vignettes from songs sharing the same names. Some audience members may not know which word most accurately speaks Beyoncé's truth—maybe all the words do—but perhaps Beyoncé is simply letting us know she has the power to do as she pleases.

That may be, but the song and video cycle on Beyoncé play like a legitimate brand identity crisis. Beyoncé may be trying to convince herself that she still has it, post-marriage and post-baby, and that she can still play a younger woman's game, perhaps even better than her younger competitors can. By inhabiting their stage personas, Beyoncé attempts to best other pop stars at their own games, in their own styles, on her album. At times, it seems she might be getting her brand confused with Rihanna's, or Nicki Minaj's, or even Jay-Z's. This never would have happened earlier in her career, as these artists never posed any real threat to her brand. By competing down rather than up, Beyoncé appears insecure, as though she has lost faith in her own brand.

Like many female celebrities before her, Beyoncé seems to have concluded that she and her rivals derive most of their power through physicality and sex, so she uses them liberally. On "Blow" she provides a vivid account of giving oral sex, on "Cherry" she gets explicit about her own genital arousal, and in the "Flawless" video, she dons flannel, gets made up like crack-is-whack Whitney Houston, and moshes with Skinheads. She loses her class, telling audiences how "crown" she is and suggesting that they "bow down" to her. This all reads as off-tone, and off-brand, for Beyoncé, and more fitting for say, Nicki Minaj. As *Telegraph* writer Felicity Capon declared: "It seems that overnight we've been transformed from Beyoncé's beloved single ladies, independent women and survivors, into her bitches" (2013, par. 9). By disrespecting pop stars, rappers, and haters, and using a swagger more characteristic of Minaj than herself, Beyoncé began to focus her competitive efforts on lesser brands. But this put her in the fray, not above it, where her brand had existed in its pre–Sasha Fierce years. The Beyoncé who is friends with Michelle Obama, and a named role model for Obama's daughters, is now allowing her own child, Blue Ivy, to watch her highly sexualized VMA performances. This should prove equally terrifying to children and adults alike, albeit for different reasons.

Beyoncé should not be anybody's sub brand, but arguably, as a person brand, she has been consumed by the family brand of Bey-Z. By naming her 2013–2014 tour The Mrs. Carter Show World Tour, she publicly took her husband's name in a way she hadn't in real life (*Celebrity Name Changes* 2013, Hobson 2015). She and Jay both took Knowles-Carter as their shared last name (*Celebrity Name Changes*, Swash 2013, Hobson 2015, Winfrey Harris 2015), and some speculated she was trading her "sexy pop star" title for an updated "sexy mama" moniker (Onstad 2013). Interestingly, she assumed this conservative honorific just prior to singing the filthiest songs of her life, taking her brand more "street" or "urban"—industry terms—in how she addresses her peers and audience, and donning costumes that evoke images of dominatrices and strippers. Her brand, which attempted multivocality, stretched and stretched until it became overextended, confused, and, at times, even contradictory (Blatt 2014).

Beyoncé, Autobiography, and Media Consumption Practices

Beyoncé's person brand dissipation must also be viewed with the awareness that she doesn't take a leadership role in writing her songs—even the ones that appear autobiographical (e.g., her situation with her dad and "Listen"). She is often listed as a fourth author, which typically signals minimal involvement in the writing process. In some cases, songs penned by others have been offered to Katy Perry and Rihanna before becoming Beyoncé's, as was the case with the Sia Furler–penned "Pretty Hurts" (Knopper 2014). It's a fair question, then, to wonder if Beyoncé has taken on all these new roles on her own, or at the urging of her handlers and power brokers. Sia, Pharrell, Justin Timberlake (JT), and Frank Ocean are all listed in the album's writing credits. Shawn Carter (a.k.a. Jay-Z) is listed as one of the writers on "Drunk in Love," which serves as a chilling sequel to "Crazy in Love" and "Single Ladies (Put a Ring On It)," if viewed on a developmental timeline.

Malina Matsoukas, director of Beyoncé's "Pretty Hurts" video, explained that Beyoncé isn't a singles artist, and Beyoncé needs to be consumed as a complete work to deliver maximum impact:

> She's such a diverse artist, and you can't take one side of her without another. And that's why it's so important for you to see the whole thing, for you to hear the whole thing. Because she's so multifaceted. She is a woman and she's a sexual being and she's a mother and she's a feminist; she's emotional and she's vulnerable, but then at the same time she's powerful. And I think that's so important to understand and know about her. Each video cannot stand in isolation, you know? They support each other. So I know it's important to her for people to hear and see the entire body of work at once. And she made you do that. She made you do that. She's gonna force you to do it her way. And you're gonna love it [Greco 2013, par. 3].

But even the most compelling star can't dictate consumption requirements to audiences—that's just not how modern media works. Consumers have more choice about what to consume and how to consume it, and asking them to consume and understand everything at once, as a whole, is naïve, unreasonable, and anachronistic—even if you're Beyoncé. And the few devout fans who might have actually seen and heard all the videos and songs on Beyoncé might be the *most* confused of all about what they mean as a complete work. The fracturing of Beyoncé's brand creates consequences: Audiences no longer know what she stands for, which makes it harder for her to really connect with audiences. As *New York Times* blogger Jody Rosen put it: "What does Beyoncé mean? What doesn't she mean?" (2014, par. 5).

Branding is an expensive, complicated, and dangerous game, and there is a great deal at risk. So the question is, will this brand experiment work, bringing diverse groups into the Beyoncé brand for the first time, while maintaining her current fan base? Or will it fail, confusing everyone, and leaving audiences confused about which Beyoncé they will find on her next release? Either way, Beyoncé, her handlers, and her songwriters need to build a narrative that reasonably and authentically brings her various meanings together to reclaim her distinguished dominance.

Reasonable people can, and do, disagree about Beyoncé's brand meanings, but some don't see Beyoncé as much different, representationally, from some of her other female pop star contemporaries at this point in time. As *Huffington Post* blogger Rose Courteau offered: "After centuries of being objectified, our chief feminist demand, as reflected by the stars we've elevated to celebrity status, is the right to be sexy. This is, to put it bluntly, farcically sad" (2014, par. 6). Feminist scholar bell hooks took that criticism several steps further, declaring Beyoncé a "terrorist, especially in terms of (her) impact on young girls" (The New School 2014; Takeda 2014, par 3).

Feminist scholar Janell Hobson notes there are intersectional issues at play in feminist media critiques of Beyoncé. "Since when did feminism reinforce dress codes instead of women's autonomy and solidarity with other women, in which we support all of our choices while also recognizing how those choices are sometimes limited by intersectional oppression?" she asked (Little 2014 par. 6). hooks offered that a more complete intersectional analysis of Beyoncé's power and resonance should go beyond race and gender and consider class and wealth as important dimensions of Beyoncé's appeal. "Wealthy is what so many young people fantasize, dream about, sexualize, eroticize…" she said, arguing that Beyonce's body stands for "wealth, fame, celebrity—all the things that so many people in our culture are lusting for, wanting" (The New School 2014; Takeda 2014, par. 9).

Conclusion

Beyoncé is celebrated for being an empowered feminist role model who runs the world with her endless power. This power arises from the swagger of her songs and performances, her powerful physique, and her role in a celebrity family that many have called the closest thing to royalty in the United States. Those factors are important, admirable, and deserve recognition. But Beyoncé is also relentlessly conformist, a clear product of patriarchy and what it celebrates. In her own career, she's relied heavily on the men closest to her to help guide her career, exchanging the guiding hand of her father/manger for the marital hand of rap mogul Jay-Z. Her accomplishments are staggering, and her influence is considerable, but her strategy for attaining such success is predictable because it is dictated by the demands of our visual culture, and the norms of the music industry that exists inside of it. Beyoncé deserves credit and praise for adeptly encoding the rules of the music industry game well enough to rise to its highest levels through masterful execution. But what would make Beyoncé a stronger and more legitimately differentiated brand is if she used her global platform and prodigious power to do something really empowered and radical—flip the script on the music industry game for longer than five seconds and demand to be celebrated for her talent first, and for being bootylicious second, or maybe even third.

REFERENCES

A&E Television Networks. 2014. "Jay Z Biography." *Bio*. Accessed May 1, 2015. http://www.biography.com/people/jay-z-507696.

Allen, Chris, Susan Fournier, and Felicia Miller. 2008. "Brands and Their Meaning Makers." In *Handbook of Consumer Psychology*, edited by Curtis Haugvedt, Paul Herr, and Frank Kardes. Mahwah, NJ: Lawrence Erlbaum Associates.

Blatt, Ruth. 2014. "Beyoncé at the Grammys: Brand Confusion or Multivocality?" *Forbes*. Last modified January 28, 2014. http://www.forbes.com/sites/ruthblatt/2014/01/28/beyonce-at-the-grammys-brand-confusion-or-multivocality/.

Boose, Lynda E. 1982. "The Father and the Bride in Shakespeare." *Modern Language Association* 97, no. 3: 325–347.

Capon, Felicity. 2013. "Why I don't want to be Beyoncé's bitch." *The Telegraph*. Last modified March 20, 2013. http://www.telegraph.co.uk/women/womens-life/9942872/Why-I-dont-want-to-be-Beyonces-bitch.html.

Caulfield, Keith. 2013. "'Beyoncé's Sales Grow to 550k-Plus, Set for No. 1." *Billboard*. Last modified December 13, 2013. http://www.billboard.com/articles/news/5839792/beyonce-sales-grow-to-550k-plus-set-for-no-1.

_____. 2014. "Justin Timberlake's '20/20' 2013's Best Selling Album, 'Blurred Lines' Top Song." *Billboard*. Last modified January 2, 2014. https://www.billboard.com/articles/news/5855151/justin-timberlakes-2020-2013s-best-selling-album-blurred-lines-top-song.

Courteau, Rose. 2014. "Straw-Man Feminism: What Beyoncé and Miley Have in Common." *The Huffington Post*. Last modified June 16, 2014. http://www.huffingtonpost.com/rose-courteau/feminism-beyonce-miley_b_5160202.html.

Daily Mail Reporter. 2014. "Beyoncé wowed guests with performance at Michelle Obama's 50th birthday." *Daily Mail*. Last modified January 20, 2014. http://www.dailymail.co.uk/news/article-2542342/Beyonce-looks-crave-BO-pictures-Michelle-Obamas-50th-performed-sparkly-frock.html.

Davies, Catriona. 2013. "Inside Beyoncé's business empire: How she became a global brand." *CNN*. Last modified May 8, 2013. http://edition.cnn.com/2013/05/02/business/beyonce-business-global-brand/.

Fournier, S., M.R. Solomon, and B.G. Englis. 2008. "When Brands Resonate." In *Handbook on Brand and Experience Management*, edited by B.H. Schmidt and D.L. Rogers, 33–57. Northhampton, MA: Edward Elgar.

Fournier, Susan, and Kerry Herman. 2006. "Taking Stock in Martha Stewart: Insights into Person-Brand Building and the Cultural Management of Brands." Unpublished manuscript, Boston University, Boston.

Givhan, Robin. 2015. "Beyoncé Got What She Wanted. She Made Us Look. But What Did We Actually See?" *Washington Post*. Last modified May 5, 2015. http://www.washingtonpost.com/blogs/style-blog/wp/2015/05/05/beyonce-got-what-she-wanted-she-made-us-look-but-what-did-we-actually-see/.

Greco, Patti. 2013. "'Pretty Hurts' Director Melina Matsoukas on Beyoncé's Throwup Scene and Casting Harvey Keitel." *Vulture*. Last modified December 16, 2013. http://www.vulture.com/2013/12/beyonce-pretty-hurts-director-melina-matsoukas-interview.html.

Harper, Todd. 2015. Email interview by the author. July 6.

Harris, Aisha. 2013. "Who Runs the World? Husbands?" *Slate*. Last modified February 4, 2013. http://www.slate.com/blogs/browbeat/2013/02/04/beyonc_s_mrs_carter_show_world_tour_why_use_her_married_name.html.

Hobson, Janell. 2015. "Beyoncé's Fierce Feminism." *Ms.* Blog. Last modified March 7, 2015. http://msmagazine.com/blog/2015/03/07/beyonces-fierce-feminism/.

The Hollywood Reporter. 2011. "Beyoncé Fired Dad amid Accusations of Theft, Legal Documents Show: Report." *Billboard.* Last modified July 12, 2011. http://www.billboard.com/articles/news/469277/beyonce-fired-dad-amid-accusations-of-theft-legal-documents-show-report.

The Huffington Post. 2013. Celebrity Name Changes: 7 Husbands Who Took Their Wives' Last Names." *The Huffington Post.* Last modified February 7, 2013. http://www.huffingtonpost.com/2013/02/06/celebrity-name-changes_n_2631803.html.

Jay, Smith. 2014. "Beyoncé & Jay Z Are 'On the Run.'" *Pollstar.* Last modified April 28, 2014. http://www.pollstar.com/news_article.aspx?ID=810958.

"Jay Z on His Rags-to-Riches Story, Wooing Beyoncé, and How Blue Ivy Is His 'Biggest Fan.'" 2013. *Vanity Fair.* Last modified October 1, 2013. http://www.vanityfair.com/culture/2013/10/jay-z-beyonce-blue-ivy-story.

Juergen, Michelle. 2013. "Celebrity Feminists Are Hurting Feminism." *Mic.* Last modified November 20, 2013. http://mic.com/articles/74211/celebrity-feminists-are-hurting-feminism.

Kennedy, Iain, dir. 2013. *Unauthorized Biography* Beyoncé: *Baby and Beyond.* Performed by Jonathan Cook, Anthony Brigham, and George Thomas. N.p.: Vertical Ascent. DVD.

Knopper, Steve. 2014. "How a Song Written by Sia Furler Becomes a Hit." *New York Times.* Last modified April 21, 2014. http://6thfloor.blogs.nytimes.com/2014/04/21/how-a-song-written-by-sia-furler-becomes-a-hit/?.

Knowles, Beyoncé. 2013. *Beyoncé: Life Is but a Dream.* Directed by Ed Burke, Beyoncé Knowles, and Ilan Y. Benatar. N.p.: Parkwood Entertainment. DVD.

Knowles-Carter, Beyoncé. 2014. "Gender Equality Is a Myth!" *The Shriver Report.* Last modified January 12, 2014. http://shriverreport.org/gender-equality-is-a-myth-beyonce/.

Little, Anita. 2014. "Beyonce at the VMAs: Feminist and Flawless." *Ms.* Magazine. Last modified August 25, 2014. http://msmagazine.com/blog/2014/08/25/ beyonce-at-the-vmas-feminist-and-flawless/.

Mau, Dhari. 2013. "Beyonce Has Sold $400 Million in Fragrances—And Is About to Launch a Third." *Fashionista.* Last modified December 20, 2013. http://fashionista.com/2013/12/beyonce-fragrance-rise.

McCracken, Grant. 1989. "Who Is the Celebrity Endorser? Cultural Foundations of the Endorsement Process." *Journal of Consumer Research* 16, no. 3: 310–321.

McIntyre, Hugh. 2014. "Beyoncé Is Now the Most Nominated Woman in Grammy History." *Forbes.* Last modified June 12, 2014. http://www.forbes.com/sites/hughmcintyre/2014/12/06/beyonce-is-now-the-most-nominated-woman-in-grammy-history/.

Mokoena, Tshepo. 2014. "Beyoncé's Drunk in Love: Should we have a problem with it?" *The Guardian.* Last modified January 28, 2014. http://www.theguardian.com/music/musicblog/2014/jan/28/beyonce-drunk-in-love-problem-lyrics.

The New School. "2014. Are You Still a Slave?" *The New School Livestream.* Last modified May 6, 2014. http://livestream.com/TheNewSchool/Slave/videos/50178872.

O'Connor, Emma. 2012. "Blue Ivy Denied: Beyoncé and Jay-Z Can't Trademark Daughter's Name, Court Rules." *Time* Magazine. Last modified October 22, 2012. http://newsfeed.time.com/2012/10/22/blue-ivy-denied-bey-and-jay-cant-trademark-the-name/.

Onstad, Katrina. 2013. "Beyoncé Rebranded: Why Calling Herself Mrs. Carter Is Her

Most Daring Persona Yet." *The Globe And Mail*. Last modified February 8, 2013. http://www.theglobeandmail.com/life/relationships/beyonce-rebranded-why-calling-herself-mrs-carter-is-her-most-daring-persona-yet/article8353173/.

"Oprah Talks to Jay-Z." 2009. *O, the Oprah Magazine*. Last modified October 2009. http://www.oprah.com/omagazine/Oprah-Interviews-Jay-Z-October-2009-Issue-of-O-Magazine

Petridis, Alexis. 2008. "Pop Review: Beyoncé, I Am … Sasha Fierce." *The Guardian*. Last modified November 13, 2008. http://www.theguardian.com/music/2008/nov/14/beyonce-i-am-sasha-fierce.

Powers, Ann. 2013. "The Beyoncé Experiment: How Far Can She Go?" *NPR Music*. Last modified May 3, 2013. http://www.npr.org/blogs/therecord/2013/05/03/1806 35294/the-beyonce-experiment-how-far-can-she-go.

Rindova, V.P., T.G. Pollock, M.L. Hayward. 2007. "Celebrity Firms: The Social Construction of Popularity." *Academy of Management Review* 31, no. 1: 50–71.

Rosen, Jody. 2014. "The Woman on Top of the World." *T Magazine Blog*. Last modified June 3, 2014. http://tmagazine.blogs.nytimes.com/2014/06/03/beyonce-the-woman-on-top-of-the-world/?_php=true&_type=blogs&_r=1.

Saad, Nardine. 2014. "Beyoncé performs at Michelle Obama's 50th birthday, shares pics." *LA Times*. Last modified January 20, 2014. http://www.latimes.com/enter tainment/gossip/la-et-mg-beyonce-michelle-obama-birthday-50–20140120-story.html.

Samuels, Allison. 2013. "Why Beyoncé Is a Tough Friend for Michelle Obama." *The Daily Beast*. Last modified May 1, 2013. http://www.thedailybeast.com/articles/2013/05/01/why-beyonce-is-a-tough-friend-for-michelle-obama.html.

Silman, Anna. 2014. "A Comprehensive History of Jay Z and Beyoncé's Relationship." *Vulture*. Last modified September 19, 2014. http://www.vulture.com/2014/07/jay-z-beyonce-relationship-history.html.

Stewart, Dodai. 2013. "Beyoncé Tells Oprah Jay-Z Is Her 'Foundation,' Kinda Makes It Sound Like She'd Be Nothing Without Him." *Jezebel*. Last modified February 12, 2013. http://jezebel.com/5984549/beyonce-tells-oprah-jay-z-is-her-foun dation-kinda-makes-it-sound-like-shed-be-nothing-without-him.

Swash, Rosie. 2013. "Why is Beyoncé calling herself Mrs. Carter?" *The Guardian*. Last modified February 5, 2013. http://www.theguardian.com/lifeandstyle/the-womens-blog-with-jane-martinson/2013/feb/05/beyonce-calling-herself-mrs-carter.

Takeda, Allison. 2014. "Beyoncé Branded as 'Anti-Feminist,' a 'Terrorist' by Scholar bell hooks." *US* Magazine. Last modified May 9, 2014. http://www.usmagazine.com/celebrity-news/news/beyonce-branded-as-anti-feminist-a-terrorist-by-bell-hooks-201495.

Willoughby, Vanessa. 2014. "Applauding the Bootylicious Feminism of Beyoncé and Josephine Baker." *Bitch* Magazine. Last modified March 10, 2014. http://bitch magazine.org/post/the-bootylicious-feminism-of-beyonce-and-josephine-baker.

Winfrey Harris, Tamara. 2015. "All Hail the Queen?" *Bitch Media*. Accessed April 26, 2015. http://bitchmagazine.org/article/all-hail-the-queen-beyonce-feminism.

The Visual Album
Beyoncé, Feminism and Digital Spaces

JAMILA A. CUPID *and*
NICOLE FILES-THOMPSON

The year following the release of singer Beyoncé's self-titled album, *Beyoncé*, on December 13, 2013, was dubbed the "Year of Beyoncé." With annually consecutive album releases between 2006 and 2013, Beyoncé climbed her way to the title "Queen Bey." This was achieved by remaining in the spotlight, and prompting a media storm for the greater part of a decade. What made 2014 undeniably hers, was her shaping, claiming, and perfecting her brand. Throughout the year, she well defined Beyoncé as: a mega-star, wife, mother, feminist, and anything that she wanted to be. While she had described herself as a feminist in prior years, dating back to 2010 (Gordon 2015), the strategic ways in which she communicated her feminist identity were through her social media accounts, tours, appearances, and interviews on various platforms. Thus, the sporadic discussions of Beyoncé feminism that was presented in scholarly circles, on and offline in years prior, propelled to a hypervisible discussion in popular culture. Beyoncé feminism remained a constant subject of social media chatter, blogosphere gossip, feminist criticism, the content for academic discourse, and prominent popular culture fodder.

By taking Beyoncé's self-definition as a feminist to mean that Beyoncé *IS* a feminist, the authors address the role of new media as a space for Beyoncé to engage in a feminist strategic communication with the release of *Beyoncé (The Visual Album)*. Also by the extension of her brand in the following ways: new media empowered Beyoncé to exercise a new level of autonomy in relation to her cultural production; new media empowered Beyoncé by providing a platform for fandom; new media empowered Beyoncé to *BE* feminist. The discussion concludes with the implications that *Beyoncé (The Visual Album)*'s success is strategically for other artists and feminists, and goes in-depth in regards to the practical relationship of Bey's feminism and commodity.

Music, Branding, and Feminism in Digital Media

Armed with a far reaching, dynamic, loyal, and vocal fan base reflective of the maturation of Beyoncé's mega stardom, on December 13, 2013, singer Beyoncé shocked a worldwide audience when she released her self-titled visual album, *Beyoncé*. The album appeared exclusively on iTunes at midnight, sans prior promotion or official forewarning. A video clip announcing the album was then posted to her Instagram account, accompanied by the caption reading, "Surprise." The music artist's fans, in a massively ecstatic response, spun into an online frenzy to purchase and spread the news of the artist's newest 14-song compilation. Donned *The Visual Album*, it was released as a set of 17 music videos. In addition to the singer's lauded vocals, Beyoncé's fifth album featured collaborations with Jay-Z, Drake, and Frank Ocean, as well as songs written by Pharrell Williams, The-Dream, Ryan Tedder, and more (Danton 2014). An overview of music, branding, and feminism in digital spaces is offered as the pretext to the discussion of relationship between new media and Beyoncé, the feminist, in the case of *Beyoncé (The Visual Album)*.

Music Realms in Digital Spaces

Music consumers have been able to use social media to seek and share information about the music and artists of interest to them. Peer-to-peer file sharing sites like LimeWire and Napster made it possible for users to download as many songs as they desired without having to pay for the individual songs. Although such access was controversial because it fed music piracy, and caused huge dips in song sales, Internet radio and music streaming sites like Pandora, iHeartRadio, Last.fm, and Spotify are now rather common. On these platforms users cannot download unlimited songs as with peer-to-peer file sharing, however; they are still tuning in to hear full songs without paying the artists or record labels. Most music streaming sites also enable the listener to customize playlists and avoid lengthy commercial breaks that come with traditional radio. Video sharing sites, such as YouTube and Vimeo, add another component to online music access, in which users are able to watch and share music videos at no cost.

It has been suggested that the increased access to songs and albums on social media impacts music sales, with sites like Napster affording users the ability to sample and share music without purchasing it. A 2014 study showed evidence of free online sampling off-setting the positive effects word of mouth has on sales (Ramaprasad and Dewan 2014). Global record industry revenue trends have been unstable over the last few years, rising by 0.3 percent in 2012, falling by 3.9 percent to $15 billion in 2013 (Dredge 2015). Then only decreasing by 0.4 percent to $14.97 billion in 2014 (Ingham 2015). iTunes, the Apple brand that functions as a media store, media library, media player and more, is a one-stop solution for basic music consumer needs. However, music artists voiced discontent with the amount of revenue they see compared to how much goes to iTunes. The company enjoyed its profitable position in the market until most recent years, when it also began to experience 2.1 percent decrease in 2013, followed by a whopping 14 percent decline in 2014. Jay-Z, Beyoncé's husband, purchased Tidal, the subscription-based music streaming and music cataloging service that is developed by music journalists and curated by music artists. When the transaction occurred in March 2015, it was widely publicized that this digital platform was meant to be Jay-Z's answer to empowering artists and consumers. Positioned to provide artists with compensation, as well as control over the sharing of their music and musical preferences, Tidal would give consumers more direct access to their favorite music and artists. Similarly, Apple Music, with a launch date set in late June 2015, will offer a global radio station, music streaming, and more direct access to artists and music recommendations from aficionados. These platforms are in their early transitional, developmental stages, so it unclear whether they will thrive, but they are likely to usher in a new thought surrounding best practices for the music industry on social media.

Branding in Digital Spaces

Today, since just about any goods, services, or public personalities must develop and promote a distinguishable, relevant, and recognizable brand in order to survive in the market, brand strategists work to develop the most effective strategic communication plan. That often involves using a combination of suitable and innovative communication strategies for their brands. Generally, a mixture of marketing, public relations, and advertising is executed to attract consumers to the brand. Even in the instances where one would have a difficult time finding paid advertisements, like television commercials or Internet banners, for certain well established brands, the companies still take great measures to differentiate themselves from their competitors. For example, many brands now focus on some forms of marketing, like placement and word of mouth. Or aspects of public relations, like media outreach and event planning.

The determinant of whether or not social media platforms will assist artists in successfully expanding their brands and selling their music lies in how capable the site is in facilitating relationships between the artists and their audiences. Connectivity on social media platforms allows these artist-to-audience or consumer-brand relationships to form. Alliances or communities grow in connection to an artist's brand and help to shape target audiences, hence reaching consumers (van Dijck 2013).

The goal is not simply to establish a connection, but to build committed relationships that sprout from a consumer's emotion based attachment to the brand (Turri, Kemp & Smith 2013). Considering the concept of social relevance, brands benefit significantly when they make themselves relevant enough that the consumer wants a continued relationship with the brand. Directly related to the music industry, implications found in a 2013 study suggest strong commitment was positively related to consumers' greater purchase loyalty and brand advocacy, while lowered tolerance for digital piracy of music (Mulhern 2009).

It was revealed in the study that in order to bring consumers to that level of commitment, they must perceive a certain authenticity about the brand. They must feel they can trust the brand will deliver that which it promises. Then, consumers become more willing to pay for information they can retrieve for little to no cost. The artist and management team at the record label design a social media presence on media streaming, video sharing, media cataloging, and social networking sites to promote the artist's brand via official and fan pages, online groups, and communities, and tantalizing content, in an effort to draw their target audiences and instill trust. Out of the relationships built with target audiences and loyal consumers, the artist's fan base and online community are birthed.

Feminism in Digital Spaces

Advances in digital technology have resulted in new forms of community building and interpersonal communication. The ability for people with common interests to connect in cyberspace has presented as one of the most advantageous aspects of digital technology.

Digital spaces have also enhanced the ability for feminist scholars and activists to join together and create feminist communities. Additionally, it has enhanced the ability for feminism to reach the level of the everyday, to be removed from small circles of highly educated and/or highly socially engaged feminists, by affording the space for all people interested in engaging the dialog of feminism to participate in and be a part of it.

In the context of feminism in digital spaces, despite the socially transformative aspects of new media, "political activists may use new media to challenge hegemonic forms of communication, while simultaneously appropriating these in a largely uncritical way" (Hamilton 2009, 88). Thus, the democratized spaces even in feminist communities do not inherently suggest that all feminisms, or feminists, are afforded a seat at the table. Moreover, it does not suggest that digital spaces are transformative in the way of a large, united feminist community. What digital spaces do afford feminism is a platform for a variety of feminist voices to connect and create communities. As in the instance of hip hop feminists' communities that flourish in the virtual sphere (Durham, Cooper and Morris, 2013). The visibility of feminism is credited to the work of feminists work online. Feminist bloggers note that blogosphere via social media in particular, has created a "digital public forum for feminist-consciousness raising" (Durham et al. 2013, 731). More broadly, digital spaces and the use of blogs, video blogging, and micro blogging, in addition to platforms such as Twitter, Facebook and Instagram have made feminism hypervisible (Martin and Valenti 2012). The technological advances have led to the phenomenon of online feminism. Touted as the "new engine for contemporary feminism" (Martin and Valenti 2012, 6), online feminism ignites activism in a revolutionary way:

> No other form of activism in history has empowered one individual to prompt tens of thousands to take action on a singular issue—within minutes. Its influence is colossal and its potential is even greater. Feminists today, young and old, use the Internet to share their stories and analysis, raise awareness and organize collective actions, and discuss difficult issues [Martin and Valenti 2012, 6].

The report #FemFuture: Online Revolution, as the title suggests, details the ways in which the collection of online feminists which consists of Feminist Bloggers, The "Twitterati," Activists & Thought Leaders, Organizations, and Petition Websites represent a distinct moment in feminism as a social movement, a revolutionary moment where the potential for impactful dialog can reach the widest and most varied audience in history. Online feminism, then, ushers in new era of feminism where the personal being political means that the importance and relevance of popular culture to structural disenfranchisement to feminism and gender equality meet an audience.

New Heights Feminist Strategy: The Case of The Visual Album

Strategic communication planning, relationship building, and generation of online community are emphasized because it is highly unlikely that the record-breaking bar of The Visual Album would have been set without them. Sure, it is unknown exactly what equation makes most internet sensations go viral. However, the launch of *Beyoncé* was not left to chance with hopes that consumers would like it enough to buy it in mass. In addition to all of Beyoncé's branding and promotion since she became a celebrity, there were measured steps taken throughout the year 2013 to further enhance and heighten her brand, and bolster her fame. In that year, she solidified the vastness of her global brand, her committed consumer-brand relationships, consumers' brand loyalty, and fans' brand advocacy, then cashed in one staged media event after the other.

Beyoncé secured the halftime spot at Super Bowl XLVII in early February 2013. She delivered a blowout show, performing a medley of her most popular songs as a solo artist, and she brought her former Destiny's Child members on stage for a reminiscent performance. The show ended with an unforgettable black out that momentarily shut down the electricity in the stadium. Whether intentional or not, it indicated that she pulled all of the stops for this show, either employing a major staged event or short circuiting the electrical system. By mid–February, the performer, wife, and mother dared to expose the multiple facets of her life in her self-filmed, autobiographical documentary *Life Is but a Dream*. The film, with home videos, baby photos, and behind the scene shots, was used to reveal the authentic, vulnerable side of the celebrity, and stir a sense of intimacy with her fans. She then released the surprise visual album in April of that year. Soon to follow, Beyoncé gave a cover story interview that was published in the May 2013 issue of *Vogue UK*, titled "Mrs. Carter Uncut," in which she declared herself a modern-day feminist who believes in equality; but is also happily married. With this claim she distanced herself from any feminist ideology that may be considered "extreme," and aligned her brand with women of the younger generations who identify with their own notions of female empowerment. She rounded out the year with *Beyoncé (The Visual Album)*, and leapt in to the "Year of Beyoncé."

The artist and her team continued to ride the intensive global media coverage she was receiving. *The Visual Album* soared in popularity and sales. Beyoncé landed the cover of *Time* magazine in April 2014. She announced, in conjunction with Jay-Z, the 2014 "On the Run Tour" via a mock movie trailer on social media that May. The international tour ran from June to September 2014, and then aired on HBO in September. Two new songs were leaked during the late holiday season of 2014, a few weeks before releasing the *Platinum Edition Box Set* that included the *Beyoncé* album from the previous year, an additional CD of music, DVD of the album, and a portion of the Mrs. Carter Show World Tour (Krepts 2014).

The following discussion will nuance the strategic communication planning and relationship building of Beyoncé as a feminist in the age of new media. It will explore how testing the bound's traditional methods of branding and promotion in moving to the digital realm can be understood as a feminist branding strategy.

Beyoncé as Commodity: Driving the Brand

During a panel discussion in 2014, while panelists discussed Beyoncé's agency, and her taking control of her brand in her promotion of *The Visual Album*, well known feminist scholar and activist bell hooks disagreed with viewing her imagery as liberatory. She described the agency found in Beyoncé's construction of her mediated image as being collusive with "imperialist white supremacist capitalist patriarchy" (hooks 2014). For hooks, Beyoncé's reclamation of the visual oppression of Black women in popular culture is not agency even when it serves to make a profit.

Taking a step back to Beyoncé's 2006 album titled *B-Day*, the production of which was done with her exacting total creative control, inviting a reading of *B-Day* as a "black feminism surrogation," an "embodied cultural act" (Brooks 2008, 183) representative of Black womanhood in the zeitgeist of its release.

> Equally concerned with work (romantic, sexual, and physical, as well as monetary), as it is with questions of black women's access to property, ownership, and modes of production, *B-Day* is the post–Hurricane Katrina answer to southern black women's spectacular disenfranchisement in the wake of that natural disaster. It is a record that documents the sheer virtuosic mastery of a singer-songwriter-performer's claims to owning and controlling her own work, property, and much-lauded body [Brooks 2008, 183–184].

Given this alternative context, in this discussion we can come to understand Beyoncé's agency in relation to feminism and commodity in another way. Reading Beyoncé's production of *B-Day* in secrecy from her manager and record label, in addition to the content, this was perhaps Beyoncé's first exercise of agency and control within the confines of the music industry and society. Moreover, it implies Beyoncé's acute awareness of Beyoncé as a commodity.

As a shift in her relationship to the mode of production, by controlling the production of her product and brand, even if it was eventually turned over to her record label, represented empowerment, at a minimum, as a matter of personal agency. Continuing her efforts in personal and professional development, Beyoncé *being* a feminist supported *her* commodification. When hip-hop feminists "insist on living with contradictions, because failure to do so relegates feminism to an academic project that is not politically sustainable beyond the ivory tower" (Durham et al. 2013, 723). It must be considered that agency lies not solely in the theoretical examination of feminism, but in the practical exercise of personal agency operating within the bounds of imperialist, white supremacist, capitalist patriarchy. Where theory and practice are often at odds with one another, the everyday lives of women living in global capitalism must find some level of compromise between ideals and reality.

A *Bitch* magazine article, argues that the criticisms of Beyoncé "the limited choices available to women in the entertainment industry and the limited ways Beyoncé is allowed to express her sexuality, because of her gender and her race" (Winfrey 2013). In this, there are instances where we can measure the agency with the options. In reaching success as an artist within a capitalist system, Beyoncé inherently is beholden to the confines of it. The case of *The Visual Album*'s release is an effort in a continuum of Beyoncé as a feminist woman that enjoys her work, and acknowledges her artistry as commodity. New media, then, presented the moment where her small triumphs of personal agency as a feminist worker, reached a new level of autonomy. Self-titling this album is representative of Beyoncé's access to a new level of autonomy in the coupling of this digital album release to her brand strategy.

The Release of Beyoncé (The Visual Album)

The unadvertised launch of the *Beyoncé* was a noted game-changer in today's music industry. Although neither worldwide social media campaigns for music album, nor unexpected album releases, can be viewed as unique to Beyoncé, her nuanced combination of the two marketing tools made a larger statement than prior instances. Jill Scott surprised fans with her live concert release of *Experience 826+* in November 2001. In the same year as Beyoncé, her husband Jay-Z first stirred excitement, even if initially accompanied by media illiteracy for this sort of promotional experience, across a global audience with a Samsung advertising collaboration that was used to announce his new album *Magna Carta … Holy Grail*. That announcement was in June 2013, and was released with no music track leaks in July 2013. David Bowie's fans were more than pleased with his shocking, but long-awaited announcement of a new album when he brought them *The Next Day* in March 2013.

Yet, Beyoncé's album launch was able to map out unchartered territory due to a well-orchestrated, airtight production plan, and code name system within the management team. No songs or videos from the visual album were leaked. Leading up to the album release, no press outreach, public appearances, interviews, corporate sponsors, album-specific teasers, or social media posts were tied into the visual album. Despite casual mention of an upcoming album, there was no announcement of album details prior to the release.

"The Beygency" accomplished what was previously impossible. As the comedic authority amongst television shows, *Saturday Night Live* suggested in a humorous, yet eerily accurate sketch, "The Beygency" controls all things Beyoncé. As much as the satirical piece was a poke at the megastar and her highly efficient management team, it was also a relevant social commentary on the perceived power that this one entity holds across popular culture. It also points towards an explanation of how Beyoncé was able to pull off the entire plan in secrecy, and was empowered to engage a new strategy in the album launch. Where sisterhood, loyalty, respect, empowerment, and agency serve as core principles in feminism, Beyoncé, a feminist, was empowered not only by the support of her handlers, but also by her network of fans.

Critical to whichever strategic communication plan a brand leads with are the relationships in which the brand builds with its stakeholders, particularly its target audience. Consumers make decisions about brands based on what they understand to be the brand's social relevance. (Klososky 2014) In a world that exposes people to an abundance of options on convenient digital platforms, including social media and applications, they want to cut through the noise and be informed on how a brand serves their needs before they are willing pay or show support.

As critical as Beyoncé's aforementioned management team was to the success of the album release and sales, it is plausible that of equal or greater importance was her enormous and ferociously loyal fan base, commonly termed as the "Beyhive" (Ghansah 2014). This network acted as a support system for her exercise in autonomy as an artist through the digital release of *The Visual Album*. On the day the album appeared online; Beyoncé had 53 million likes on Facebook, gained 500,000 subscribers on YouTube, and released the short announcement video to her nearly eight million followers on Instagram. Her super fans engaged in immediate e-word of mouth (along with traditional word of mouth), marketing of the album across social media sites like Twitter, Tumblr, and Instagram. On Twitter alone, the album trended with 1.2 million tweets in twelve hours. They created a reverberating buzz around the album, capturing the attention of others and the media, and presumably playing an instrumental role in rapidly increasing sales (Huba 2014). According to a December 2013 *New York Times* article, 365,000 copies of the album were sold in the United States alone within the first day (Sisario 2013). *The Wall Street Journal* reported that the album broke Apple's record for iTunes global sales, with the album selling 828,773 copies in the first three days (Little 2013).

Another feature that enhances the uniqueness of the album release of *Beyoncé* was that it defied the trend of parceling albums into singles available for purchase by consumers that dominated album releases. Particularly in the digital age, and in downloading trends, consumers were able to select what they wanted from albums instead of having to purchase entire albums (David 2014). However, when Beyoncé was released, consumers were given only one option from iTunes—all or nothing. The fact that consumers had to purchase the entire *Beyoncé* album, and could not select only specific songs can be viewed as a strategy that supported her agency and control of her product as a commodity. Indeed, Beyoncé exercised a level of control of her brand and its messaging via creative production by maintaining its integrity as a total package. One of the charges of feminism is for women to be viewed in a holistic manner. As full human beings, that encompasses a dynamic identity, and is not viewed through an objectified lens that denies wholeness, and undermines an entire picture. With that, in making it a requirement to consume "Beyoncé," as a package becomes more significant. The consumer had to purchase all of the aspects, performances, offerings of Beyoncé. They had to consume a complete package and a holistic view of the creative project.

The multiple risks that Columbia Records took on this album release can be seen as an affirmation of the power of Beyoncé the brand, as a commodity. Not only did they exclude traditional retailers in favor of a release in the digital realm, they saw this as an opportunity to use the power of Beyoncé. It was financially advantageous to force consumers to purchase the entire album versus purchasing singles (David 2014). There were high stakes for Columbia Records in this album release, and ultimately, the risk was worth the reward as the fandom of the "Beyhive," efficiently worked as a support network of advocacy across new media platforms, making not only the *Beyoncé (The Visual Album)*, but Beyoncé the brand, Beyoncé the feminist, Beyoncé Feminism, and feminism(s) hypervisible. As a commodity, Beyoncé, broke records for iTunes album sales, defied previous trends in marketing and distribution, and as a successful endeavor for Beyoncé, Columbia Records, and iTunes, created conversations and opportunities in the music industry, academia, and new media.

Beyoncé Feminism and New Media

Though *Beyoncé* came to be known as *The Visual Album* due to it having a music video for every track, the name of the album speaks to the implications of digital strategy. In the year that followed the album release, Beyoncé continued to identify herself as a feminist, making feminism hypervisible. In a literal sense, there is the instance that she instagrammed a photo of herself as Rosie the Riveter. In doing so, she introduced feminist iconography in to the lexicon of a generation that ponders post-feminism as reality. In a figurative sense, existence of new media creating a space for feminist voices has created a space for feminist voices to demand that second wave feminists to stop policing feminists.

Following Beyoncé's performance at the MTV Video Music awards of a compilation from *The Visual Album*, on a set that featured the word "feminist" as her backdrop, the headline on mtv.com read: "Beyoncé's 2014 VMA Performance: Fearless, Feminist, Flawless, Family Time" (Nadeska 2014). A few weeks later, singer Annie Lennox called the performance "feminist lite" and hinted at feminism being commodified saying, "I see a lot of it as them taking the word hostage and using it to promote themselves, but I don't think they necessarily represent wholeheartedly the depths of feminism" (Azzopardi 2014).

With the wide spread availability of digital platforms for feminist voices to be heard, these contentions challenge the theory and practice of feminism(s). A feminist blogger who asserts, "yes, my feminism is ratchet" (Jackson 2014), ponders the inclusivity of feminism, and the availability of spaces to which her theory and activism are not judged against her tastes in music. The critique of Beyoncé, her identity as a feminist, and her feminism, in the context of continuous discussions of alienation from feminism(s) is a reminder that exclusion and invisibility continue to be problematic in self-defining feminism. Lamenting in the critique of Beyoncé,

> Black women are, it seems, damned if we do and damned if we don't. Our collective singleness, independence, and unsanctioned mothering are an affront to mainstream womanhood. But a high-profile married black woman who uses her husband's name (if only for purposes of showbiz), or admits the influence her male partner has had on her life is an affront to feminism [Winfrey 2013].

The outpouring of the debate in the blogosphere suggests that deregulating feminism may be a key issue on the agenda, not only for women of color, but for all women. An analysis of the value of testimony to feminism and its reception in online feminist communities concluded that despite the increased availability of feminism in the blogosphere, these communities often serve to reinforce the hierarchies and "recreate older forms of privilege, divisions, and exclusions" (Hamilton 2009, 86–101). In reaction to the policing of feminism, have come calls for dismantling this hierarchy. The article "6 Things That Definitely Don't Make You a Bad Feminist (No Matter What Anyone Says)," starting the list with a .gif of Beyoncé and her husband to visualize the first item "1. Changing your last name when you get married" and ending the list with "6. Disagreeing with something 'feminist' someone said" (George, 2015), expresses the anxieties stimulated by many of the criticisms launched about women, including Beyoncé, that the "Beyhive" has spent consuming and processing as a matter their place as well as Beyoncé's place in the feminist movement. With the call for accessibility coming from blogs posts in non-feminist communities, and communities specifically created for accessibility such as *Everyday Feminism*, it is clear that Beyoncé feminism represents larger contexts at the intersections of generation, theory and practice.

The historical alienation of Black women from feminism, begged the question: In the 21st century "is feminism on the agenda for women of color?" (Marbley Year, 611). Answering that question made yet another case for sharing in definitions of feminism and agenda setting in the feminist community. Conversations defining feminism(s), contentions of the boundaries, and feelings of alienation and rejection from a critical feminist community have expanded through new media. Blogs in reaction to the commentary offered as to all that is wrong, anti, and problematic with Beyoncé's feminism has also led to feminist challenges that make feminism accessible to a new generation of feminists. If "the Internet can keep an issue visible, alive, and evolving in a way to always be relevant" (Syfret 2015) connotes the optimism of online feminism, Beyoncé, as a commodity and as a feminist, minimally, served to maintain feminism as hypervisible in the year following the release of the *Beyoncé* album.

Conclusion

Beyoncé's self-titled visual album debuted at number one on the Billboard 200 chart. Beyoncé not only set a new record for iTunes sales, but also for female artists and for her own career. She became the first woman to have her first five studio albums place at the top spot on the chart. The *Beyoncé* visual album also proved to deliver the best first week of sales for the singer, topping her *B'Day* album sales of 541,000 copies in 2006 (Caulfield 2013). The momentum of Beyoncé's new media success is now spilling over and taking on new forms. For example, her digital strategy has proven to be a massive success, and her networks continue to expand. Beyoncé's social media following has drastically increased to 40.6 million Instagram followers, nearly 8 million VEVO subscribers, approximately 14 million Twitter followers (despite the fact that she has not tweeted in nearly two years), and a following of over 63 million on Facebook as of July 2015. In the years to come there is little doubt that those numbers will continue to soar.

As another example of the extension of her feminism in practice, we can look to her support of another Black female artist, Nicki Minaj. In mid–May 2015, Nicki Minaj stunned the music world by premiering her new single "Feeling Myself," featuring Beyoncé, with a fun-filled, fashion forward video that was only made available on the Tidal site. Considering the strategy of releasing *Beyoncé The Visual Album*, an exercise of Beyoncé's personal agency, we can view this instance through a feminist lens as her extending her own empowerment to other women. Beyoncé, the feminist, has now used Beyoncé the commodity, to support Nicki Minaj as an artist to employ the same digital strategy for the release of her single. Beyoncé has fortified her platform to the extent that she has not only empowered her own brand and fans, but has also been able to set the elevated stage to empower Minaj and her fan base. The possibility for the ball to keep rolling and extending to uplift other female artists, along with the women who are part of the artists' online communities and audiences, has been set in motion. Beyond singing techniques, dance moves, and fashion, Beyoncé's digital strategy may continue to serve other artists to emulate her exercises of autonomy and self-empowerment.

The continued dominance of Beyoncé's feminism across social media platforms will continue to invite fans and detractors to important feminist conversations. Her digital media strategy represents an intersection and call to action. Where pop culture discussions lead to clicks and to discussions of feminism and the struggles for equality in the everyday lives of women, indeed, googling Beyoncé will serve as a "gateway drug," to online feminism. We learn that Beyoncé, the self-proclaimed feminist mega star, "letting young women know that they can be a feminist and care about pop culture gives them permission to care about equality." The interest in Beyoncé the brand, and Beyoncé the feminist will empower her audiences to have a seat at the table in the discussion of feminism.

While it is not too difficult to see how Beyoncé the Feminist has established herself as a superwoman and super celebrity who has it all and can do it all, the next step is to look forward to the reach and longevity of this feminist branding. There is space for a further discussion of Beyoncé and feminism in practical applications of feminism by women in the entertainment industry. Beyoncé's strategies will continue to be the center of discussions both on and offline, and in the hallways of institutions that continue to be male dominated. Undoubtedly, digital spaces have moved Beyoncé, a Black woman and feminist, from margin to center. Where there is room for optimism in feminism is the degree to which a new generation of women is engaged in feminist discussions. Digital spaces ushered in a new era of feminism, and Beyoncé's digital strategy offers the movement a new diversity of participation. When the "Beyhive" stands in defense from the latest slight to Beyoncé's feminism, there is a refreshing engagement with feminism that takes place amongst many women who were once apathetic and/or disconnected. Forcing the hand of previously established definitions of feminism, both theoretically and practically, will continue to inform new voices, activism, and participation in the feminist movement.

REFERENCES

"Apple Music." 2015. https://www.apple.com/music/ (accessed June 9, 2015).

Azzopardi, Chris. 2014. "Q&A: Annie Lennox on Her Legacy, Why Beyoncé Is 'Feminist Lite.'" September 25. http://www.pridesource.com/article.html?article=68228 (accessed January 5, 2014).

"The Beygency." 2014. *Saturday Night Live.* Alex Buono, Chris Kelly, and Sarah Schneider.

Brooks, Daphne A. 2008. *"All That You Can't Leave Behind": Black Female Soul Singing and the Politics of Surrogation in the Age of Catastrophe.* Indiana University Press.

Caulfield, Keith. 2013. *Billboard.* December 17. http://www.billboard.com/biz/articles/news/5840087/beyonce-makes-billboard-200-history-with-fifth-no-1-album (accessed December 11, 2014).

Danton, Eric R. 2013. *Rolling Stone.* December 13. http://www.rollingstone.com/music/news/beyonce-surprises-with-new-album-release-20131213 (accessed December 11, 2014).

David, Philip. 2014. "Get Classy: Comparing the Massive Marketing of Anchorman 2 to the Non-Marketing of Beyoncé's Beyoncé Album," *MEIEA Journal* 14, no. 1: 219–249. http://search.proquest.com/docview/1650134791?accountid=11091.

Durham, Aisha, Brittany C. Cooper, and Susana M. Morris. 2013. *The Stage Hip-Hop Feminism Built: A New Directions Essay* 38, no. 3: 731.

Dredge, Stuart. 2014. *The Guardian.* March 18. http://www.theguardian.com/technology/2014/mar/18/music-sales-ifpi-2013-spotify-streaming (accessed June 9, 2015).

Ellison, Jo. 2013. "Mrs. Carter Uncut." *Vogue* Magazine. http://www.vogue.co.uk/news/2013/04/04/beyonce-interview-may-vogue (accessed April 4, 2013).

George, Kat. 2015. "6 Things That Definitely Don't Make You a Bad Feminist (No Matter What Anyone Says)." *Bustle.* January 27. http://www.bustle.com/articles/58182–6-things-that-dont-make-you-a-bad-feminist-no-matter-what-anyone-says?utm_source=huffingtonpost.com&utm_medium=referral&utm_campaign=pubexchange_article (accessed February 1, 2015).

Ghansah, Rachel Kaadzi. 2014. *NPR.* March 17. http://www.npr.org/sections/thererecord/2014/03/17/258155902/how-sweet-it-is-to-be-loved-by-you-the-beyhive (accessed December 11, 2014).

Gordon, Jane. 2010. "Beyoncé: The Multi-talented Star Reveals What She Is Planning Next." *You* Magazine. http://www.dailymail.co.uk/home/you/article-1301838/Beyonc--The-multi-talented-star-reveals-planning-next.html (accessed May 27, 2015).

Hamilton, Carrie. 2009. "Feminist Testimony in the Internet Age: Sex Work, Blogging and the Politics of Witnessing." *Journal of Romance Studies* 9, no. 3 *Communication & Mass Media Complete*, EBSC: 86–101.

Hilton, Perez. 2014. "The Year of Beyoncé." http://perezhilton.com/2014-12-31-year-of-beyonce-2014-gallery-gifs#.VXpr3VVhBc (accessed January 7, 2015).

hooks, bell. 2014. Tuesday, May 6, 6:00 p.m. "Are You Still a Slave?" panel discussion, live stream, The New School.

Huba, Jackie. 2013. *Forbes.* December 17. http://www.forbes.com/sites/jackiehuba/2013/12/17/beyonce-uses-only-word-of-mouth-to-market-surprise-new-album/ (accessed December 11, 2014).

Ingham, Tim. 2015. *The Guardian.* April 14. http://www.musicbusinessworldwide.com/global-record-industry-income-drops-below-15bn-for-first-time-in-history/ (accessed June 9, 2015).

Jackson, M.D. 2014. "Yes, My Feminism Is Ratchet: Reflections on Inclusive Feminism." http://www.forharriet.com/2014/11/yes-my-feminism-is-ratchet-reflections.html#axzz3dRWzBXbf (accessed June 10, 2015).

Klososky, Scott. 2012. *Financial Executive*. May. www.financialexecutives.org (accessed December 11, 2014).

Kreps, Daniel. 2014. "Beyoncé to Release Two New Songs on Self Titled Album's Platinum Edition." *Rolling Stone*. November 4. http://www.rollingstone.com/music/news/beyonce-to-release-two-new-songs-on-self-titled-albums-platinum-edition-20141104 (accessed December 10, 2014).

Little, Lyneka. 2013. *Wall Street Journal*. December 16. http://blogs.wsj.com/speakeasy/2013/12/16/beyonces-surprise-album-expected-to-sell-600000-copies-and-land-at-no-1/ (accessed December 9, 2014).

Marbley, A.F. 2005. "African-American Women's Feelings on Alienation from Third Wave Feminism: A Conversation with My Sisters." *The Western Journal of Black Studies* 29, no. 1: 611.

Martin, Courtney E., and Vanessa Valenti. 2012. "#FemFuture: Online Revolution." Banard Research Center for Research on Women.

Mulhern, Frank. 2009. "Integrated Marketing Communications: From Media Channels to Digital Connectivity." *Journal of Marketing Communications* 15, no. 2–3 (April–July): 85–101.

Nadeska, Alexus. 2014. "Beyoncé's 2014 VMA Performance: Fearless, Feminist, Flawless, Family Time." August 25. http://www.mtv.com/news/1910270/-2014-vma-performance/ (accessed January, 5, 2015).

Ramaprasad, Jui, and Sanjeev Dewan. 2014. *Social Media, Traditional Media, and Music Sales*. MIS Quarterly 38, no. 1: 101–121.

Sisario, Ben. 2013. *New York Times*. December 15. http://www.nytimes.com/2013/12/16/business/media/beyonce-rejects-tradition-for-social-medias-power.html?_r=0 (accessed January 5, 2015).

Syfret, Wendy. 2015. "Has The Internet Made Us Better Feminists?" *Think Pieces*. https://i-d.vice.com/en_au/article/has-the-internet-made-us-better-feminists (accessed March 19, 2015).

Turri, Anna M., Karen H. Smith, and Elyria Kemp. 2013. "Developing Affective Brand Commitment Through Social Media." *Journal of Electronic Commerce Research* 14, no. 3: 209–214.

van Dijck, Jose, and Thomas Poell. 2013. "Understanding Social Media Logic." *Media and Communication* 1, no. 1: 2–14.

Winfrey, Tamara Harris. 2013. "All Hail the Queen?" *Bitch Magazine*. May 20. http://bitchmagazine.org/article/all-hail-the-queen-beyonce-feminism (accessed January 7, 2015).

Beyoncé and Social Media
Authenticity and
the Presentation of Self

MELISSA AVDEEFF

On November 12, 2012, Beyoncé joined Instagram by posting a photo of herself, casually dressed in jeans and a shirt that read "Texans for Obama." She joined without fanfare, but it didn't take long for Beyoncé to become the second most followed account on the site, behind the account for Instagram, itself. As of June 15, 2015, Beyoncé has more than 36.3 million followers on Instagram, followed closely by Kim Kardashian, the self-styled queen of social media, with approximately 34 million followers. Whereas Kim Kardashian has become synonymous with the selfie—photos that are taken by the poster of themselves—Beyoncé's Instagram account contains very few selfies, and predominantly allows for fans to have a glimpse into her extraordinary life.

Beyoncé's use of social media is outside the norm for contemporary celebrities who are online. Although she has over 14 million followers on Twitter, she does not post on that platform (beyond 8 Tweets that were posted from 2012–2013), and appears to prefer interacting with her fans through Facebook, her personal site, and Instagram. It is widely accepted that those who engage with celebrities through social media expect a certain degree of authenticity in the form of transparency between the celebrity and their posts. Observations of Beyoncé's Facebook feed show that it is largely maintained by a social media manager, as it is fairly obvious that it is not Beyoncé, herself, posting. The authenticity of the posts is under question; therefor, the Facebook feed may function more as a site for news, information, and media, as opposed to a fan/artist relationship that relies on the perception of reciprocity.

This essay will primarily focus on Beyoncé's Instagram use, as it presents an interesting case study of the use of visual-based social media sites in

109

celebrity branding, and a re-negotiation of the fan/artist relationship. This essay explores different approaches to studying celebrity social media use, including Goffman's presentation of self, parasocial interaction, and the circuit of culture, using Beyoncé as a case study. Superficially, Beyoncé's social media relationship with fans appears to be primarily parasocial, but in examining aspects of follower reception, it is demonstrated that her Instagram use actually incorporates a form of reciprocal relationship with fans, as seen in her choice of thematic material, and presentation of identity.

Social media and fandom is a growing area of research. A field is emerging that examines celebrities and their Twitter use, and this research is generally conducted from the perspective of the celebrity, as opposed to the reception of the fans interacting with these accounts (Dobson 2012, Kapidzic and Herring 2015). An area that has received much less scholarly attention, a problem that I seek to address, is the incorporation, or close examination, of the role of music and musicians within social media use, and, by proxy, the fandoms involved. I question whether there is something inherently different about a musician, as opposed to other forms of celebrity, and if these differences are great enough to warrant special treatment. Pop music, a type of music that we can clearly label Beyoncé's music as, is generally agreed upon to be a visual-heavy media. The importance of the visual aspect of the genre is recognized, and has steadily increased in importance since the advent of music videos in 1981. Pop music is clearly not just about the music, and these visual elements are integral to the artist's brand construction. Instagram therefore becomes an important aspect of this identity and brand creation in pop music. Videos remain an important medium of music consumption, especially amongst youths, and the use of social media and Instagram provides not only a behind-the-scenes look into the perceived "authentic" version of the star, but also serves to strengthen the bond between fan and artist through an engagement with visual texts representing, on the one hand, vulnerability, and, in the case of Beyoncé, glamour.

Musician Authenticity on Instagram

A critical discussion of authenticity is prevalent both within the fields of social media and pop music. In discourses surrounding pop music there is an ongoing dichotomy in the mainstream press, and also within the academy to a certain extent, between pop/rock and inauthentic/authentic which has also permeated the use of social media (Frith 1978, Moore 2002). A carefully curated Instagram profile, in some instances, functions to increase perceived authenticity of the star, but on the other hand, functions to mask the authentic self through the curation process. The addition of the Instagram narrative in musicians' branding complicates the authentic/inauthentic dichotomy, as consumers' expectations of Instagram authenticity are not similarly expected in stage or music video performances.

The use of a persona is quite common for pop musicians, whether implicitly stated by the artist, or not. Pop music has long been considered a "carnivalesque" (Railton 2001) medium whereby the artists, and fans, can participate in a temporary period of identity exploration and sexual liberation, largely outside the norms of society. Beyoncé, herself, has utilized the personas of Sasha Fierce and Yonce in order to separate her "authentic" performance of self from her more sexually aggressive stage performances. The persona, or alter ego, allows stars to separate themselves from behaviors that may garner negative reactions in the press, especially for females who are portraying themselves as overtly sexual, which is often outside the accepted societal conventions, no matter how outdated these stereotypes are. While stage and music video personas can challenge societal norms surrounding gender and sexuality conventions, it is the perceived inauthenticity of the persona that allows them to be accepted and consumed by the masses without *too* much judgment. When an artist presents themselves through social media, however, they are expected to remove themselves from the stage persona in order to present their authentic self to their followers. This has become an unwritten rule within social media use, and one that requires more research and observation.

I argue that the desire for authenticity of pop musicians on Instagram ties into larger notions of music and identity. The idea that music tastes are bound within identity formation adds another layer to the fan/artist relationship. By creating an emotional connection with an artist (persona or otherwise), fans have come to expect a certain degree of authenticity within the relationship that exists on Instagram and other social media platforms. Musical preferences are largely tied to identity formation (Frith 1996), and if consumers feel an emotional and authentic relationship with specific music, it would follow that that relationship would be expected to coincide with the fan's relationship to other aspects of the music's brand, including Instagram.

Perhaps it is the perceived authenticity that is the appeal, as discussed below, of Beyoncé's Instagram photos whereby she is engaged in more private endeavors, such as enjoying time with her daughter or husband. Is this a glimpse into her "authentic" life? Do her fans feel an increased emotional connection to an artist when they can relate on a more personal, albeit mediated, level? David Marshall refers to this as the "public private self" (2010, 44) whereby celebrities present a constructed private version of themselves through social media, which ultimately becomes another version, or layer, in the public presentation of self. With the public private self, according to Marshall, celebrities negotiate their presentation of self through social media in a "recognition of the new notion of a public that implies some sort of further exposer of the individual's life" (2010, 44), enforcing the notion that fans expect a certain degree of interaction and authenticity from the celebrities they follow online. Marshall notes that Twitter has become the primary vehicle for celebrities to demonstrate their public private selves, but it is arguable that Instagram, especially in the way that Beyoncé has used the platform, presents a version of the self that, by utilizing visuals instead of text, removes the possibility for literal misinterpretation. That being said, the intentions behind Beyoncé's Instagram posts are unknown, but if they are considered as both a presentation of self, as well as a form of artwork, they can become subject to subjective interpretation. Marshall's public private self is part of a larger typology of online celebrity presentation of self, which also includes the public self, or the official, industrial version of the self. For Beyoncé, this would be her Facebook account, which largely functions as publicity and promotion. And also the transgressive intimate self, whereby celebrities, often in the heat of the moment, reveal intimate details, or temporary emotion. Beyoncé's strict control over her digital presence negates the presence of a transgressive intimate self (2010, 44–45).

An interview with Beyoncé's digital strategist, Lauren Wirtzer-Seawood, as conducted by Stuart Dredge, has revealed that Beyoncé prefers the visual-based medium to other text-based social media sites, such as Twitter, because it leaves less room for misinterpretation. Instagram functions as a "personal communication" tool for Beyoncé, something "that Beyoncé most of the time uses directly herself: she posts pictures. It's her way of communicating to fans a little bit of what her personal life is like" (Dredge 2013). According to Wirtzer-Seawood, Beyoncé and her digital networking team "don't use Twitter at all. It is a personal choice. I think as an artist, Beyoncé really prefers to communicate in images. It's very hard to say what you want to say in 140 characters" (Dredge 2013). Regardless of how Beyoncé's brand is perceived along the continuum of authenticity, the immense control that Beyoncé exerts over her digital presence represents, on one level, an authenticity of production. The presentation of self is tightly controlled by Beyoncé herself, allowing her to present her public private self, in a carefully curated front stage performance.

Instagramming Beyoncé

As of January 2014, 26 percent of adult internet users, and 21 percent of the entire adult population use Instagram. The Pew Research Centre's research shows that, notably, 53 percent of young adults aged 18–29 use Instagram. The platform has a clear youth preference, as only 11 percent of online adults between the ages of 50–64 use Instagram, and 25 percent of online adults ages 30–49. Since joining Instagram in 2012, Beyoncé has (as of April 18, 2015), posted 991 photos to Instagram. The ephemerality of the platform, however, prevents knowledge of the *actual* amount of photos that have been posted, as photos can be deleted. It is apparent that Beyoncé has deleted many photos from her Instagram feed, as there are photos referenced on older online news sources which do not currently occur in her feed. The ephemerality allows for a continuous curation of identity and brand, taking into account the fact that anything posted on the internet has a certain degree of permanence, as the photos will nevertheless remain online in one form or another. Screen shots of Instagram photos are largely outside the control of the artist, becoming a permanent documentation that, although not posted on "official" sources, are nevertheless a part of the brand of the artist by ultimately contributing to their discourse of identity.

Within the 991 photos, Beyoncé is present in 700 (70.1 percent). Her husband, Jay-Z, is featured in 85 (8.6 percent) of her Instagram photos, and Blue Ivy, their daughter, is present in 38 (3.8 percent). Of the 38 photos of that contain Blue Ivy, only 3 show her face. The choice to originally not show Blue Ivy's face appears to be a conscious effort, most likely to protect the privacy of her daughter (*Huffpost Celebrity* 2013). On February 14, 2015, Beyoncé posted the first full-view face photo of Blue Ivy, alongside herself, in what remains the most "liked" photo in Beyoncé's Instagram feed, with over 1.9 million likes. The photo appears to be a selfie with Beyoncé and her daughter, whereby they have placed small bee ornaments on their faces.

Beyoncé's Instagram photos can be categorized into the following non mutually-exclusive themes: concert, paparazzi, candid, fashion, throwback, holiday, food, scenery, message, and selfie. Concert photos, which account for 16 percent of her feed, are photos which have been taken during a concert. They appear, for the most part, to be taken by professional photographers. There are no concert selfies. Paparazzi photos are professional photos which appear to have been taken by the paparazzi; they include red carpet photos, photos from premieres, and photos from basketball games. They account for 6 percent of the feed. Candid photos (20 percent of the feed) are those that show Beyoncé in her potential "authentic" self. Often, these photos are taken when Beyoncé is looking away from the camera, not working, and/or in what could be construed as her version of everyday activities. Fashion photos make up a large percentage of Beyoncé's Instagram feed at 24 percent, reinforcing the notion that pop music branding is all-encompassing, and not dependent solely on the music itself. Beyoncé's focus on fashion may serve to reflect her own involvement with the world of fashion with her label, House of Dereon, but at the same time, her fashion posts do not make mention of specific brands or labels, leaving this information up to the viewers to determine.

This category features a fair amount of close-up photos of manicures, jewelry, and full-body shots where the emphasis is clearly on the clothing and Beyoncé's body. Bees are an ongoing theme in Beyoncé's jewelry photos. Photos that are from holidays or travels make up 17 percent of the feed, while scenery shots, those which do not feature any people and are largely scenery-based, make up 14 percent. Statistically, the scenery shots are the least "liked" photos on Beyoncé's Instagram account. Food photos, which are a common theme, in general, on Instagram, occur in 2 percent of Beyoncé's feed. Throwback photos, another common Instagram trope, account for 5 percent. Beyoncé does not often directly address her fans. She rarely captions her Instagram photos, and leaves interpretation largely up to the viewer. That being said, 8 percent of her photos are what I call "message" photos, in that the photos contain a form of text, either typed or hand-written, that presumably address her followers. Often, these message posts are promotion for Beyoncé.com, or hand-written lyrics, motivational quotes, or other forms of self-promotion. As with the scenery photos, these receive less "likes" than photos that show Beyoncé's public private self.

Interestingly, selfies only account for 3 percent of Beyoncé's Instagram feed. This is surprising, as this is the genre that has driven the success of Instagram (Saltz 2014), and is in stark comparison to other celebrities that are highly popular on Instragram, such as Kim Kardashian or Taylor Swift. In reiterating that Beyoncé is a unique case study, it should be noted that she is largely *not* reaching out to an imagined audience for a reciprocal relationship. She is predominantly presenting an opportunity for her audience to glimpse into her highly extraordinary life, as opposed to presenting her extraordinary life as something that is ordinary, and relatable to the average viewer/fan.

Beyoncé and the Presentation of Self

There is much discussion about the presentation of self on social media, through a re-interpretation of Erving Goffman's 1959 book, *The Presentation of Self in Everyday Life.* The dramaturgical model posits that human interaction is filtered through a series of social scripts that prescribe situation-based acceptable forms of behavior. But when we move this interaction to the online realm, and in regards to musician celebrities in particular, it goes beyond the presentation of social scripts, towards a complicated balance between self-branding and a desire to "sell" a product which is essentially themselves. A common theme exists amongst musicians desiring to reveal their "common-ness" on Instagram in order to demonstrate similarities between themselves and their fans, presumably to strengthen the consumer bond by incorporating strategic vulnerability. This is common in artists such as Taylor Swift, who regularly posts photos of herself doing everyday activities, such as hanging out with her friends, playing with her cat, and going to the beach. Swift also regularly posts photos of herself with her fans, blurring the boundaries between what is considered a reciprocal relationship, and one that appears as one. With this in mind, Beyoncé's Instagram feed differs from many high-profile musicians. Her photos present a view into life in the 1 percent; highly glamorous, but also built on the foundation of hard work. Labor is represented in the numerous photos of her on stage, in rehearsal, or in the studio. In total, 19.7 percent of her photos have some sort of relation to music and/or the process of creating or performing music. Alice Marwick has found that Instagram users are more likely to "like" photos on Instagram that are aspirational or "reinforce an existing hierarchy of fame, in which the iconography of glamour, luxury, wealth, good looks, and connections is re-inscribed in a visual digital medium" (Marwick 2015, 141). Beyoncé's Instagram feed does not just resemble the "lifestyles of the rich and famous" trope that allows micro-celebrities to become "Instagram famous," rather, she is the epitome of the trope and functions to represent and serve as a model for others seeking online celebrity status. Her glamorous photos do not appear to promote excess for the sake of excess; Beyoncé does not seem to flaunt her wealth and elite lifestyle through Instagram, unlike other Instagram photos that regularly appear on the profile, @richkidsofinstagram. The profile, which originated as a Tumblr account, re-posts photos from wealthy adolescents who flaunt their extravagant lifestyles. The profile of the account reads: "Rich Kids Of Instagram: They have more money than you and this is what they do." Whereas these profile are, in general, flaunting wealth inequality through inheritance (Marwick 2015), Beyoncé's profile balances photos of extravagance with a demonstration of labor.

Goffman's dramaturgical model of the presentation of self—that we engage in a series of performances, determined by the social situation in which we find ourselves—is quite relevant when discussing the curation that occurs on Instagram, but when we consider the prevalence of the persona within pop music, the issue becomes complicated. As discussed, there is an expectation for female pop musicians to perform under a stage persona, but this can become quite confusing for fans/followers, as they have no concrete evidence to determine what is, and is not, a part of the carefully constructed brand. Photos posted on Instagram serve as a "performative practice" (Marwick and boyd 2011, 140) of celebrity. Marwick and boyd note, in an exploration of celebrity practices on Twitter, that celebrities must "constantly navigate complex identity performances" (2011, 140) and manage the disconnect between the public persona and the "authentic" self. Whereas magazines and paparazzi attempt to disclose celebrities for their "true" selves, Instagram gives that power back to the celebrity, in the form of a carefully curated performance of identity. An ongoing performance of celebrity, through Instagram, is crucial for the maintenance of celebrity in digitality, even for a top-tier performer such as Beyoncé. As Marwick and boyd note, "In the broadcast era, celebrity was something a person was; in the Internet era, microcelebrity is something people *do*" (2011, 140). Marwick and boyd often refer to the term microcelebrity as a way to categorize those who are famous online, but I argue that the same holds true for celebrities that are recognizable online and offline, such as Beyoncé. Instagram may allow for new pathways to celebrity status, but it is also a site of fame maintenance.

Where Goffman's theory is most applicable to the discussion surrounding Beyoncé on Instagram, is in the idea of the embodiment of identity; the identity, or persona, by which fans relate to the artist. As musicians disclose personal information through Instagram, they make themselves vulnerable to the public: a vulnerable social performance of identity (Chen 2014). In an investigation of relationship construction through YouTube, Chih-Ping Chen notes that it is this performance of vulnerability that followers identify with. Online relationships and interactions vary vastly from in-person interactions, in that people cannot gauge the reception of their audience and adjust in real time. Instead, artifacts, in this case, photos, are presented to the public and reception comes in the form of "likes" and comments. Hogan refers to social media platforms as exhibition spaces, where photos are presented and processed "when actors are not necessarily present at the same time but still react to each other's data" (Hogan 2010, 344). Therefore, for Hogan, Instagram is still considered a presentation of the self, but outside the time and space constraints of in-person impression management. In examining Beyoncé's Instagram feed, it can be interpreted that, as the curator, she has reacted to the engagement of her followers in order to adapt her impression, outside of real-time engagement. For example, her earlier posts included more "message" photos, but these have subsequently decreased in frequency. These photos received substantially less "likes" than photos from the same time period that featured Beyoncé, or her friends and family. The reduced amount of likes in these earlier message photos cannot solely be attributed to the early adoption of the medium, because fashion photos from the same time period received significantly more likes. To highlight, on November 16, 2012, Beyoncé posted a photo containing a handwritten quote by Anais Nin, "SOME PEOPLE FEEL THE RAIN, OTHERS GET WET," which received approximately 86,600 likes; a fashion photo from two days later received 155,000 likes. Perhaps these message photos decreased in frequency as a reaction to fan engagement and to curate content for maximum appeal. Also from 2012 are a series of photos taken at the Tate Modern Museum. In this series, a photo of the *Slashed Canvas* taken on December 9, 2012, remains the least liked photo in her feed, with approximately 36,8000 likes. This is not to say that almost 37 thousand people liking a photo is trivial, but in comparison to the average amount of likes, which is approximately 532,000, and a median of approximately 491,000, the number is significantly lower.

Beyoncé: Parasocial Interaction or Imagined Reciprocity?

To elaborate on the idea of impression management and the presentation of self through Instagram, I draw on the concepts of parasocial relationship, and parasocial interaction, as originally outlined by Horton and Wohl in their exploring of how fans have extensive information about the celebrity they follow, compared to the celebrity knowing next to nothing about their fans. In the fan/celebrity relationship, fans feel they have "an apparently intimate face-to-face association with a performer" (1956, 228), even though the relationship is highly mediated. Currently, much of the discussion surrounding social networking sites and engagement has occurred around Twitter and YouTube, but much of this discourse is also applicable to the follower/followed relationships on Instagram.

Similar to Twitter, Instagram users can address another profile directly, by tagging that person's profile, either in the photo's caption or in the comments below it. Users are free to reply, or not reply, as there is no expectation of reciprocity built into the platform. Arguably, there is much less of an expectation of reciprocity in Instagram, as compared to Twitter. This is most likely due to the visual nature of the platform. The textual nature of Twitter lends itself more to conversations and the expectations that *maybe* the celebrity will respond to Tweets. Beyoncé has more than 37 million followers on Instagram, but does not follow anyone herself. Her lack of *direct* interaction with her followers appears as parasocial interaction; however, she has, on 11 occasions, tagged other Instagram accounts in photo captions. Notably, four of those tags were the HBO account, @hbo, to promote her HBO *On the Run* tour in 2014. All of the photos with tagged accounts occurred from 2012 to 2014. Apart from the @hbo tags, the remaining seven tagged photos acknowledge specific people, as follows:

12/27/12: @adorabriah tagged in painted portrait of Beyoncé.
2/22/13: @lissyverkade @bootonbootonboots @minimaleanimale @deerdana @classactress tagged in *message* photo for the Beyhive blog.
4/29/13: @maequestoliver @kingkrule @themaccabees tagged in *message* photo about the London Beyhive blog.
8/15/13: @ftolot @nelfarinah @tytryone @lisa_logan tagged as subjects in group photo.

8/20/13: @tytryone tagged in photo with Beyoncé, with birthday shout-out.
12/20/13: @buddyvalastra tagged in photo of Beyoncé celebrating her birthday with a cake made by Buddy Valastra.
1/4/14: @carlizey tagged in a video of the young girl dancing.

Regardless of Beyoncé's limited interaction with her followers on Instagram, users demonstrate a high degree of engagement with her profile. As noted, Beyoncé is one of the most followed accounts on Instagram, and many of her photos receive well over a million likes and her followers comment on her photos in abundance. Beyoncé's fans have come to be known as the Beyhive. Beyoncé exists in the center as Queen Bey and her followers function as the worker drones. Even without the promise of reciprocity, these fans/drones will work tirelessly to serve their Queen. Many of these fans will defend and justify any and all of Beyoncé's actions, or even "attack" other celebrities who criticize her. In 2015 Kid Rock, in an interview with *Rolling Stone*, opined:

> Beyoncé, to me, doesn't have a fucking "Purple Rain," but she's the biggest thing on Earth…. How can you be that big without at least one "Sweet Home Alabama" or "Old Time Rock & Roll"? People are like, "Beyoncé's hot. Got a nice fucking ass." I'm like, "Cool, I like skinny white chicks with big tits." Doesn't really fucking do much for me [Spanos 2015].

Kid Rock's comments prompted Beyoncé's fans to attack his Instagram feed by commenting on every photo he had posted with a slew of bee emoticons—used often by Beyoncé when she does caption her Instagram posts. It has been noted that social media, and Twitter in particular, has great political power, and potential for activism (Bennet 2012). Online protests occur in an environment that is safer that in-person demonstrations, but can still be highly effective. In this Beyoncé and Kid Rock example, fandom is functioning within the established confines of online political protest, with a "silent" visual protest that does not personally attack Kid Rock, but demonstrates celebrity/brand loyalty in a way that is non-destructive. Through parasocial interactions, including those on Instagram, Beyoncé's fans have seemingly formed an emotional bond with the artist, similar to bonds demonstrated in reciprocal relationships. Chen notes that "Just as we form positive or negative attitudes towards other people in 'real life,' media viewers develop positive or negative attitudes about the characters they watch on various media" (5). In this instance, the character is defined as the persona of Beyoncé, and Instagram as the media. Followers are processing the mediated experience in the same manner as "real" experiences. Audiences have become encultured to online relationships and experience no real difference between online and offline relationships. Relationships with celebrities, even highly mediated, become a part of one's identity creating process. Chen notes that "we create a sense of who we are through our consumption" (2014, 11), which extends to the visual branding found on Instagram.

Although Beyoncé does not directly interact with her fans on Instagram, she has utilized the platform to respond to rumors and speculations about her personal life. By considering the Instagram photo as a piece of art, one that allows for multiple interpretations, viewers are left to determine their own understandings. As such, there still remains no expectation for Beyoncé to respond to speculations, as there is no definitive proof that the photos are, indeed, reactionary. When there were rumors that Beyoncé was pregnant with a second child, shortly thereafter a photo was posted with Beyoncé drinking what appears to be wine (Takeda 2013). Many interpreted this as Beyoncé demonstrating that she was not pregnant, without having to directly address the rumors. That photo has since been deleted from Beyoncé's Instagram feed. In addition, after a video was released of a domestic dispute in an elevator between Beyoncé's husband, Jay-Z, and sister, Solange, many Internet reports speculated that there was family tension. Without verbally or literally responding to these reports, Beyoncé began to post many photos of her sister on Instagram, seemingly as a show of support for her sister (Vokes-Dudgeon 2014). Many of these photos have remained on Beyoncé's feed. On the other hand, in January 2015, new pregnancy rumors circulated when Beyoncé posted a photo of herself at the beach, submerged in sand, and what appears to be a pregnant belly made of sand (McRady 2015). Regardless of interpretation, these speculations were revealed as false and the intended meaning of the photo remains obscured.

While Beyoncé may not be directly engaging with her fans on Instagram through @ mentions, tagging, or otherwise, through the above examination of her Instagram feed, it can be argued that she is responding and reacting to fan engagement through the thematic material of her posts and posting photos which address fan and press commentary through open-ended visual narratives.

The Culture of Beyoncé

As a way to include fan reception and celebrity response into an examination of social media, Emily Keats proposes using a circuit of culture theoretical model (Keats 2013). In combination with Goffman's presentation of self, and theories of parasocial interaction, I find that the circuit of culture model is an effective strategy for investigating Beyoncé's Instagram use, and, by proxy, her followers. Drawing from Du Gay et al.'s (1997) application of the circuit of culture in their study of the Sony Walkman, Keats notes that we should include the interactivity of social media platforms as part of the examination therein. In her words, "the freedom and flexibility afforded in such locales identifies a need to more closely examine the roles of consumer and producer and the Circuit provides a strong theoretical framework for doing so" (Keats 2013, 2). Utilizing a circuit of culture allows for an examination of the interconnectedness of social media and the simultaneous articulation of production and consumption. Within the circuit of culture, five processes are examined: production, representation, consumption, identity, and regulation (O'Reilly 2005). We can examine Beyoncé within this model by acknowledging that her brand has reached beyond that of musician, to that of culture. In their study, Du Gay et al. note that "the Sony Walkman is not only part of our culture. It has a distinct 'culture' of its own" (1997, 10). The same can be said about Beyoncé. Her brand has permeated society to the point that it has developed its own culture, which is perpetuated through the consumption and further production of discourse by her fans, especially the Beyhive. While Beyoncé may have total control over how she presents her own image (Harmsworth 2013), the production of Beyoncé-related materials by prosumers contributing to the culture of Beyoncé is largely outside of her control. Instagram allows Beyoncé to maintain a certain degree of control, with a "voice" that is presumably hers and not that of her social media director or manager.

In an interview with *GQ* magazine, it was revealed that Beyoncé has a personal archive in a "temperature-controlled digital-storage facility" (Wallace 2013) that contains almost every piece of media that has been released about her life. This archive includes every photo, interview, concert footage, and diary entry. Since 2005 Beyoncé has employed a "visual director" who records her life for up to 16 hours per day; this footage is also present in the archive. This allows Beyoncé to have full access to her image; she essentially "owns her every likeness," and utilizes this footage to review her past and develop her present and future self into an icon that is both "the aspirational and the unattainable" (Wallace 2013). Beyoncé has developed her own circuit of culture within her everyday life, using the archive and her personal footage to reflect and adapt her performance of self. By posting select photos to Instagram, Beyoncé allows her fans to take part in her personal circuit of culture, and by commenting and "liking" posts, fans' reception has the potential to alter the trajectory of Beyoncé's culture. Production and consumption are not separate spheres of existence, and both contribute to the production of culture.

Conclusion

With the rise of digital media, and digital music dissemination, a dematerialization of consumption has occurred. The dematerialization of musical goods, in the form of MP3s and streaming music platforms such as Spotify,

Pandora, and Rdio, has altered the reception and consumption of music. As the physicality of the music playback technology decreases consumers look for new ways to establish a material connection with music, often in the form of playback technologies, such as vinyl and the turntable. In order to find connections to music and musicians, consumers have also looked online, to digital platforms that provide an aspect of music that is not present in the physical copy: the "self" of the artist. This is not to say that fans did not experience emotional relationships with musicians before the advent of social media and Instagram, but the prevalence of these platforms has created a new space where fans and followers can engage on an emotional level with what they perceive to be a more authentic version of the star. Throughout the development of music playback technology, and subsequent digitalization, a tremendous change in listening and consumption habits has followed. Instagram offers a new visual-based platform for music-related materials. Instagram perpetuates the emphasis that is placed on beauty and the body for female pop musicians, which is reflected in Beyoncé's fashion themed photos. On the other hand, her more candid photos provide a glimpse into her everyday life that can be perceived as vulnerable, even if she is not posting them from a position of vulnerability. Beyoncé's obsessive documentation of her everyday life suggests that her extreme awareness of her brand and performance of self leaves little room for vulnerability, although how followers and consumers interpret such visuals may vary. Beyoncé is notorious for being very selective in which interviews she conducts and with whom she talks to in the press, so, often the only way we can access a version of her authentic self is through her Instagram photos. Crossovers exist between her personal life and her music videos, especially in her 2014 self-titled audiovisual album, which includes locations and dramatic reinterpretations of important moments in her life, but it becomes difficult to separate what is *Beyoncé*, and what is a persona, leaving Instagram to help in that understanding. Beyoncé owns her brand, just as she owns her likeness. In the words of Amy Wallace, *GQ* correspondent,

> There ain't no use being hot as fish grease … if someone else wields the spatula and holds the keys to the cash register. But if you can harness your own power and put it to your own use? Well, then there are no limits. That's what the video camera is all about: owning your own brand, your own face, your own body. Only then, to borrow another Beyoncé lyric, can girls rule the world. And make no mistake, fellas: Queen Bey is comfortable on her throne [Wallace 2013].

Regardless of Beyonce's personal intentions for using the Instagram platform in an ongoing curation of self, a theme has emerged as a constant in her feed: flawless.

REFERENCES

Bennett, Lance. 2012. "The Personalization of Politics: Political Identity, Social Media, and Changing Patterns of Participation." *Annals* 644.

Chen, Chih-Pin. 2014. "Forming the Digital Self and Parasocial Relationships on YouTube." *Journal of Consumer Culture* 16.1: 1–12.

Dobson, Amy Shields. 2012. "Individuality Is Everything: 'Autonomous' Femininity in MySpace Mottos and Self-Description." *Continuum* 26.3: 371–383.

Dredge, Stuart. 2014. "Here's Why Beyoncé Hasn't Used Twitter Since August 2013." *music :) ally*, November 5. Accessed June 2, 2015. http://musically.com/2014/11/05/beyoncé-twitter-facebook-lauren-wirtzer-seawood/.

Du Gay, Paul, Stuart Hall, Linda Janes, Hugh Mackay, and Keith Negus, eds. 1997. *Doing Cultural Studies: The Story of the Walkman*. London: Sage.

Duggan, Maeve, Nicol Ellison, Cliff Lampe, Amanda Lenhart and Mary Madden. 2015. "Social Media Update 2014." *Pew Research Centre*, January 9. Accessed June 15, 2015. http://www.pewinternet.org/2015/01/09/social-media-update-2014/.

Franco, James. 2013. "The Meanings of the Selfie." *New York Times*, December 26. Accessed June 2, 2015. http://www.nytimes.com/2013/12/29/arts/the-meanings-of-the-selfie.html.

Frith, Simon. 1978. *The Sociology of Rock*. London: Constable.

_____. 1996. "Music and Identity." In *Questions of Cultural Identity*, edited by Stuart Hall and Paul du Gay, 108–127. London: Sage.

Goffman, Erving. 1959. *The Presentation of Self in Everyday Life*. Garden City, NY: Doubleday.

Harmsworth, Andrei. 2013. "Beyoncé Knowles Takes Control and 'Bans Photographers from Her Shows and Issues Own Pics.'" *Metro*, April 24. Accessed June 2, 2015. http://metro.co.uk/2013/04/24/beyoncé-knowles-takes-control-and-bans-photographers-from-her-shows-and-issues-own-pics-3664886/.

Hogan, Bernie. 2010. "The Presentation of Self in the Age of Social Media: Distinguishing Performances and Exhibitions Online." *Bulletin of Science, Technology & Society* 30.6: 377.

Horton, Donald, and Richard Wohl. 1956. "Mass Communication and Parasocial Interaction: Observations on Intimacy at a Distance." *Psychiatry* 19: 228.

Huffpost Celebrity. 2013. "Beyoncé Shares Blue Ivy Photo, Still Manages to Keep Her from Prying Eyes." December 20. Accessed June 2, 2015. http://www.huffingtonpost.com/2013/12/10/beyoncé-shares-blue-ivy-photo_n_4420801.html.

Kapidzic, Sanka, and Susan Herring. 2015. "Teens, Gender, and Self-Presentation in Social Media." In *International Encyclopedia of Social and Behavioral Sciences, 2nd Edition*, edited by J.D. Wright. Oxford: Elsevier.

Keats, Emily. 2013. "The Circuit of Culture: A Useful Theoretical Model for Studying Social Media." *Selected Papers of Internet Research 14.0*. Denver.

Marshall, David. 2010. "The Promotion and Presentation of the Self: Celebrity as Marker of Presentational Media." *Celebrity Studies* 1.1: 35–48.

Marwick, Alice. 2015. "Instafame: Luxury Selfies in the Attention Economy." *Public Culture* 1.75: 137–160.

Marwick, Alice, and danah boyd. 2011. "To See and Be Seen: Celebrity Practice on Twitter." *Convergence* 17.2: 139–156.

McRady, Rachel. 2015. "Beyoncé Posts Instagram, Sparks New Pregnancy Rumors: See the Picture!" *Us Weekly*, January 11. Accessed June 2, 2015. http://www.usmagazine.com/celebrity-moms/news/beyoncé-instagram-sparks-pregnancy-rumors-2015111.

Moore, Allen. 2002. "Authenticity as Authentication." *Popular Music* 21.1: 209–223.

O'Reilly, Daragh. 2005. "Cultural Brands/Branding Cultures." *Journal of Marketing Management* 21: 573–588.

Railton, Diane. 2001. "The Gendered Carnival of Pop." *Popular Music* 20.3: 321–331.

Saltz, Jerry. 2014. "Art at Arm's Length: A History of the Selfie." *Vulture*, January 26. Accessed June 2, 2015. http:// www.vulture.com/2014/01/history-of-the-selfie. html.

Spanos, Brittany. 2015. "Beyoncé Fans Attack Kid Rock Online After Derogatory Comments." *Rolling Stone*, February 27. Accessed June 2, 2015. http://www.rolling stone.com/music/news/beyoncé-fans-attack-kid-rock-online-after-derogatory-comments-20150227.

Takeda, Allison. 2013. "Beyoncé Squashes Pregnancy Rumors with Wine-Drinking Picture." *Us Weekly*, May 31. Accessed June 2, 2015. http://www.usmagazine.com/ celebrity-news/news/beyoncé-squashes-pregnancy-rumors-with-wine-drinking-picture-2013315.

Vokes-Dudgeon, Sophie. 2014. "Beyoncé Posts Throwback Pictures with Solange After Jay Z Elevator Fight at Met Gala Party." *Us Weekly*, May 14. Accessed June 2, 2015. http://www.usmagazine.com/celebrity-news/news/beyoncé-posts-solange-pictures-instagram-after-jay-z-fight-2014145.

Wallace, Amy. 2013. "Miss Millennium: Beyonce." *Gq.* Accessed June 2, 2015. http:// www.gq.com/story/beyonce-cover-story-interview-gq-february-2013.

Flawless Feminist or Fallible Freak?

An Analysis of Feminism, Empowerment and Gender in Beyoncé's Lyrics

TIA C.M. TYREE *and* MELVIN L. WILLIAMS

In the 21st century, there is perhaps no other more polarizing figure in discussions of feminism than millionaire actress, pop icon and international music superstar Beyoncé Giselle Knowles-Carter. She is both accepted and rejected as a feminist; her behavior is both applauded and criticized; she is viewed as both empowering and disempowering; and she is both credited with bringing women's issues to the attention of a larger audience and accused of being a "terrorist" to the feminist movement of the day.

Beyoncé occupies a space earlier generations may have never imagined–a singing, dancing, acting, Black woman who is an entertainment mogul (Griffin 2011). Nonetheless, she is a part of a long lineage of Black women who use their voices to describe their feelings about being Black women and, through this process, give other Black women power from their messages (Whittington & Jordan 2014).

Today, her messages are said to be feminist. However, she gives "feminism" a "makeover" (Zimmerman 2014). She does not fit the usual physical form or behave in the ways of the "Feminazi" (Bennett 2014). As an entertainer, Beyoncé is "universally loved, virtually unquestioned, and flawless," and as a wife, she is not a "man-hater" (Bennett 2014).

During a media interview with Jane Gordon in 2010, Beyoncé initially said, "I think I am a feminist in a way." Three years later in a *Rolling Stone* interview, she embraced her identity and called herself a "modern-day feminist" (Cubarrubia 2013). In addition to her declaration, there are other connections to feminism. She was on the cover of the Spring 2013 issue of *Ms.*

magazine. In late 2013, *Time* magazine's Eliana Dockterman, wrote "Beyoncé has become the embodiment of modern feminism for a generation that has been reluctant to claim the word." In 2014, she posted a picture of herself on Instagram as the iconic "Rosie the Riveter." She wrote an open feminist essay entitled "Gender Equality Is a Myth!" for *The Shriver Report* (Knowles-Carter 2014). At the 2014 MTV Video Music Awards, she performed with the word "FEMINIST" in large capital letters. This performance was seen as the "holy grail" of "feminist endorsement" by the "most powerful celebrity in the world" (Bennett 2014). Suddenly, the word was "Beyoncé-fied," rendered empowering and beautiful, trendy and hyper-relevant" (Zimmerman 2014).

The Crunk Feminist Movement Collective (2013), a blog that facilitates discussions among Hip-Hop generation feminists of color, outlined five reasons to support Beyoncé as a feminist. They were: (1) "She's a work in progress," which recognizes her feminist declarations have changed, modified and progressed. (2) "Sometimes bitches do need to bow down," which supports moments when women should not accept less from anyone. (3) "Academic feminism ain't the only kid on the block," which acknowledges feminist voices can come from various people of all occupations and educational levels. (4) "I'm here for anybody that is checking for the f-word, since so many folk aren't," which notes the limited support of feminism requires a requisite support of those willing to embrace it. (5) "King Bey always brings her A-game and manages to have fun while doing it," which identifies the contradictory voices and hatred for those within and outside the movement that Beyoncé seems to rise above and succeed despite of their existence.

The dichotomy present in the discourse surrounding Beyoncé's connection to feminism is multifaceted, contradictory and by no means easy to decipher. Her "fierce feminism" raises attention and debates. She even provoked the ire of famed scholar, bell hooks, who during a discussion at The New School in New York City in 2014, said, "I see a part of Beyoncé that is in fact anti-feminist—that is a terrorist, especially in terms of the impact on young girls." Brittney Cooper (2014) of the Crunk Feminist Collective classified hooks' labeling of Beyoncé as "an act of discursive violence" and plain "bullshit" (18, 20). Cooper does acknowledge Beyoncé should show more empathy for the "cultural Black girl struggle," but pushed back on those who reduce her to a commodity and as being anything more than just a "bigger cog" in the wheel of the capitalist society (2014, 17).

Best known for her dancing and her lyrics, Beyoncé is an important part of popular culture, and, historically, mass media, including popular lyrics, furnish stereotypes for youth, women, and Blacks (Riesman 1957). Popular lyrics have undergone scrutiny by social scientists, because there is an assumption that useful knowledge can be obtained through the study of lyrics for they provide insights into societal values, including soul music that is an expression of Black culture and descriptive of listeners' experiences (Freudiger & Almquist 1975). Lyrics are also important to investigate, as there is little interference related to their analysis. Researchers can focus on just words and meaning, and not distractions, such as music, tonal emphasis of the singer, dancing, nonverbal cues and costumes.

Conducting a textual analysis of her five albums, the purpose of this study is to: (1) investigate if Beyoncé's work aligns with black and Hip-Hop feminist theory tenets, (2) identify what themes are present within her lyrics and pinpoint any shifts in lyrical themes after motherhood and marriage as well as the overall maturation of her career, (3) provide an understanding of the alignment of her lyrics with historic Black female stereotypes, sexual scripts and sexual roles, and (4) determine if her work overall supports notions of empowerment.

Beyoncé, Role Models and Black Girls

Young girl dances while wearing a Beyoncé-inspired shirt (courtesy Tia C.M. Tyree).

Girl Power is a concept that teaches girls can do, be, and have anything they want (Pomerantz, Raby & Stefanick 2013). It is a term that goes well with the concept of Black Girls Rock, which is the mantra that is coupled with a movement of a nonprofit designed to help promote female youth empowerment and mentoring among women of color as well as spawn dialog about representations in the media. Within today's current empowerment discourse, there are some who are called role models and further push the conversations of female empowerment. Beyoncé is one of them.

However, Levande (2008) asserts "feminism has been hijacked and its hijackers use female pop stars to sell behaviors and attitudes about sexuality itself. The most popular myth is the equation of stripping, prostitution, and pornographic imagery with power" (301). Over time, women move from talent to tramp, and they are "getting naked to get heard," which is a failed attempted to challenge the status quo (Levande 2008, 305). It could be said Beyoncé exhibits some of these behaviors.

She, too, is said to be a "diva," which presents a powerful image of femininity that embodies the inherent contradiction of its performativity being consciously constructed (Loth 2013). Beyoncé's cloak of perfection, beauty and power is a problematic one. In a study of primary school girls' role models and constructions of the "popular" girl, Barbara Read (2011) labeled Beyoncé the face of the popular Black girl (as quoted by Short 2015), and Read also asserted Beyoncé's performance of femininity is anti-feminist and possibly harmful to young girls. Seeing her pretty, hypersexualized behavior and overexposed image can lead to damaging, unhealthy and disempowering behaviors and competition among girls and women (Read 2011).

However, it is deeper than simply Beyoncé, as she is a reflection of Black culture. Society is filled with conflicting messages about Black women's sexuality, femininity and statuses in both the Black community and U.S. society, but Black girls still must learn to navigate their construction and develop their identity as Black women (Emerson 2002). Cultural productions of Black female artists can reflect those contradictions, including hypersexual imagery and those that denigrate and deny the beauty of the Black female body. Yet, a strategy of self-representation of Black female artists allows them to reappropriate explicit images to achieve control over their own sexuality (Emerson 2002).

Studies have shown the importance of pop culture and Hip-Hop to African American youth and how they use them to make sense of the world in which they live (Ferguson 2000; Patillo-McCoy 1999). Therefore, there is much to expect of Black female role models in the music business. They are supposed to reject the sexualized vices of the Jezebel stereotype and exhibit the virtues of the asexual, nurturing Mammy (Austin 1997). Further, professional Black role models have usually acquired stature and power in the white world, because they project a safe, assimilated posture unthreatening to white people, which then erases their "clout to wield on behalf of other Blacks ... being what they are" (Austin 1997, 295). Beyoncé's acceptance as a role model is easier in U.S. society, because she is an entertainer, a long-accepted role for Black women, and a sex symbol, an unthreatening position in society (Griffin 2011).

Representations of Black Women, Feminism and Connections to Hip-Hop Culture

As a critical social theory, Black feminist thought conceptualizes Black female identities as organic, fluid, interdependent, multiple and dynamic socially constructed locations within specific historical contexts (Peoples 2008). It also describes Black women as a unique group that exists in a place within U.S. social relations where intersectional processes of race, ethnicity, gender, class and sexual orientation shape Black women's individual and collective consciousness, self-definition and actions (Collins 1990). Patricia Hill Collins (1990) located four major themes in the construction of Black feminist thought that are generated from a Black woman's standpoint. First, Black women empower themselves by creating self-definitions and self-valuations that establish positive, multiple images and repel negative, controlling representations of Black womanhood. Second, Black women oppose and disassemble the overarching and interlocking structure of domination in terms of race, class and gender oppression. Third, Black women interconnect intellectual thought and political activism. Finally, Black women recognize a distinct cultural heritage that provides them with the skills needed to resist and transform daily discrimination.

Black feminist thought takes elements and themes of Black women's culture and infuses them with new meaning, articulating a consciousness that gives African American women an essential tool of resistance against all forms of subordination (Scott 1985). However, like the mainstream feminist movement, Black feminism has been critiqued by Black female writers for failing to address the current realities and needs of a young generation of Black women largely impacted by popular music and Hip-Hop culture (Peoples 2008). Coining themselves as Hip-Hop feminists, scholars initiated a dialog between two unlikely partners: Hip-Hop and feminism. Similar to the approaches advanced by earlier Black feminists, Hip-Hop feminism remains deeply invested in intersectional analyses of Black women's experiences (Durham, Cooper, & Morris 2013).

Peoples (2008) noted three major themes present in Hip-Hop feminist writing that also resonate in the theorizing of older generations of Black feminists. The themes were: (1) empowerment, (2) the importance of images and representation, and (3) Black women's involvement in coalitional politics (Peoples 2008). Through these themes, Hip-Hop feminists work to expand the focus of the Black feminist agenda toward Hip-Hop and push forward a model of feminism "brave enough" to challenge older feminists' perspectives (Morgan 1999, 59). Hip-Hop feminists contend that Hip-Hop is a site of expression for Black girls and women that can be used to develop a critique of "gender politics within communities of color" (Durham, Cooper, & Morris 2013, 723). Acknowledging the misogyny in Hip-Hop culture, they push forward a "sociopolitical agenda of uplift aimed at self-empowerment for women and girls through political education based on feminist modes of analysis" and explore ways in which Hip-Hop enables Black women to assert agency and control of their sexuality (Peoples 2008, 28; Emerson 2002).

Elizabeth Whittington and Mackenzie Jordan (2014) heap additional criticisms onto Black feminists. With respect to Beyoncé, they assert Black feminism is seemingly not reaching the precise women it is designed to empower, but "Bey Feminism" reaches them and gives them voice in a society that often silences them. They coined her unique grassroots style of feminism, "Bey Feminism." They assert "every day Black women" embrace Bey Feminism to help them with "negotiating, co-creating, reinforcing and challenging" their identities in society, and Black feminist should not separate from Bey Feminism, but understand its appeal and ways it can be replicated to overcome oppressive patriarchy (Whittington & Jordan 2014).

Methodology

This is not the first attempt to study Beyoncé's lyrics. In fact, there are two studies worthy of mentioning in this essay. Brooks (2008) analyzed one album, which was *B'Day*; Short (2015) analyzed lyrics from two albums, *Beyoncé* and *4*. However, this study is important for it analyzes all of Beyoncé's albums, which are *Dangerously in Love* in 2003, *B'Day* in 2006, *I Am … Sasha Fierce* in 2008, *4* in 2011 and *Beyoncé* in 2013, under the same framework. It is important to note "deluxe," "platinum" or final released albums were included in the sample. This approach provided the best opportunity to increase the range and scope of songs in the study. This sample did not include "Bow Down," as it did not appear on a final album and was said to be folded into the concepts within "Flawless" on the *Beyoncé* album (Newman 2013; Kornhaber 2014). In this study, a textual analysis of the lyrics was conducted, which is an interpretative tool researchers employ to understand the world, and it is a systematic way to uncover how text create meaning (McKee 2003; Hallahan 1997). Analyzing lyrics should take into consideration the era in which the song is made popular, the contexts of the performance, dimensions of class, race and ethnicity, gender and sexual preferences and how the consumption of the song might impact how audiences read and interpret media culture (Kellner 1995; Denisoff & Peterson 1972). Yet, the authors of this essay were keenly aware other work in this book would study responses to Beyoncé's songs by listeners. Therefore, no emphasis was placed on predicting the types of emotional reactions or behaviors that listeners may experience after hearing a song. Instead, the important and much-needed contribution of this study was analyzing her lyrical catalog as a cultural artifact.

This study utilized several aspects from past studies that analyzed Beyoncé's lyrics, soul music and other Hip-Hop texts. First, only lyrics sung by Beyoncé are under analysis. Each song was a unit of analysis, and themes were established for each song. Second, lyrics were analyzed to determine if they reflect components of Black and Hip-Hop feminism identified earlier in this essay. Third, gender traits, historic Black female stereotypes and sexual scripts were identified. Sexual scripts commonly found in Hip-Hop music, including the freak, earth mother, gangsta bitch and gold digger, were analyzed. The historic Black stereotypes were those commonly found in mass media, including the angry Black woman, Black lady and mammy. Gender traits for females were supportive, inconsistent, submissive, dependent, hesitant and beautiful; male traits were demanding, consistent, aggressive, independent, confident, and active (Freudiger & Almquist 1975, 55). Fourth, a song was identified as empowering, if the overall message rejected the dimensions of knowledge that perpetuate objectification and dehumanization of Black women; highlighted Black women's efforts of racial uplift; supported racial solidarity and self-definition; suggested the choice and power to act, regardless of the bleakness of a situation; showcased the desire for Black women to achieve greater equal opportunity and status, including in areas of reproductive rights, politics and poverty; or emphasized concerns of legal status and rights, discrimination and sexual victimization (King 1988; Collins 2000).

Findings and Discussion

In total, 77 songs were analyzed for this study from five albums. Each album had its own distinct narrative, signaling the evolution of a woman who transitioned from being single to a businesswoman, feminist, mother, and wife. (Overall album narratives are provided in Table 1.) However, despite these life transitions, the overall song themes remained relatively consistent. Love, relationships and sex were the most dominant themes, with love being the most prominent.

Of the 77 songs under investigation, 46 were related to the topic of love. Throughout the five albums, Beyoncé discussed love in a variety of ways, creating a multilayered discourse about her romantic pursuits as they related to successes and failures in relationships. However, just as Beyoncé used the theme of love to profess her adoration for the men in her life, she also spoke of love from the stances of betrayal, disdain and heartbreak, creating messages with polarizing extremes about Black womanhood and sexuality.

The theme of sex was present throughout all five albums, as Beyoncé embraced her sexuality on multiple songs in an attempt to seduce men, explore her sexuality and celebrate her body. By her fifth album, she asserted her sexual agency in relation to a sex-positive feminist lexicon. On this album, Beyoncé celebrated her sexual exploits and presented a narrative that related to Carol Queen's (2001) views on sex-positive feminism that pushed women to embrace their sexuality and not "denigrate, medicalize, or demonize any form of sexual expression except that which is not consensual" (94).

Table 1—Album Narrative Summaries

Album Name	Overall Album Narratives
Dangerously in Love	Love and relationships are dominant themes. She is over sexualized with 13 of the 15 songs fitting into a sexual scripts or historic Black stereotypes. Early tracks move from mostly the freak stereotype with a celebration of connections and sex with men to a metaphysical connection to love. She describes herself as crazy, but in most cases, it is a direct result of breaking traditional gender roles in relationships.
B'Day	This album is mostly about a woman who is betrayed, scorned or ignored by her lover, but she is finding her voice and able to express it. She is financially stable, successful and buying her own items as well as those of her lover. She is not willing to accept mistreatment and is threatening to move on to the next relationship at any moment.
I am … Sasha Fierce	Songs take on polarizing extremes. She is often a needy, dreamy, crazed lover or a strong, financially independent woman securing her position in a relationship. She is exploring and claiming what she wants as well as what makes her feel good. She now is speaking more to and for other women.
4	Traditional soul music themes and ideals dominate the album with her wanting to be loved and being betrayed. She is a faithful lover who is pledging her allegiance to her man. A few songs take a more aggressive independent stance ("Best"/"Start Over"/"End of Time"). She is asserting herself more and demanding what she wants. The last two songs create a notable coupling. "I Was Here" stresses her desire

Album Name	Overall Album Narratives
	to make a positive impression on the world, and by "Run the World" following it, the message of her wanting female empowerment is then connected.
Beyoncé	Beyoncé has embraced her sexuality, again, and multiple songs celebrate sexual exploits. The biological "daddy" she sung of in her first album is replaced with her sexual "daddy" in five songs. She has increased her direct call and response lyrics to women, and she is sharing more thoughts of what it means to be a mother, daughter and wife. She is more active, beautiful and aggressive than in any other album.

Conversely, Beyoncé also pushed forward a slightly conservative message that suggested a strong reverence for the traditional family structure and its value system. For example, in "Daddy," "Dangerously in Love," "1+1," "Blue," and "Ring Off," Beyoncé celebrated her family members and their varying roles for the greater purpose of issuing a message of communal uplift. While Beyoncé's views on her family were initially sporadic references in the first four albums, in *Beyoncé*, the singer discussed being a daughter, wife and mother. This finding was particularly important given Beyoncé's standpoint as a Black woman and its impact on the themes of her music. As noted by Bart Landry (2000), the preservation of the collective family has been pivotal in the pursuit of racial uplift for the Black community. Black women intellectuals and activists have held a range of political ideas, intellectual perspectives, and ideological commitments that demonstrated a devotion to improving their communities by working alongside Black men (Watkins 2006), including a threefold commitment to their family, career and social movement with multiple roles as activists, career women, mothers, wives among others (Landry 2000).

Representations of Empowerment in Beyoncé's Lyrics

Of the songs under investigation, 29 were labeled as overall having empowering messages to women, which represented 38 percent (37.66) of her musical catalog. Empowerment for Beyoncé meant being treated properly in a relationship, preferably as an equal partner. It also came through messages of financial freedom, including buying her items and those of her lover. Further, empowerment involved Beyoncé speaking her mind; expressing distinct control of her career and life; being sexually free and comfortable with her flaws; and voicing her concerns when being mistreated. In some cases, empowerment meant empathizing with and speaking for women who were being mistreated as well as acting as a teacher by telling "ladies" and "girls" what to do in certain situations.

What is most interesting is that while critics lauded her last album as her most empowering, it was not the one to carry the most empowering messages. It was *B'Day* that carried the most empowering messages with a total of 11 songs, representing 69 percent (68.75) of the album's tracks. Between the release of her first album and second album, she established Beyond Productions LLC in 2004, the company that produced her lucrative fashion lines, and she had not married yet. She was a self-proclaimed "worldwide woman." It was at this time she likely began to earn significant money, experienced an increase in her fame and felt empowered as a young, rich and powerful woman in her twenties.

Beyoncé's lyrics often couched her empowering messages using what is labeled in this work as the "but" factor. The word "but" is a coordinating conjunction that joins words, sentences, clauses and phrases. In language, conjunctions help with coherence, as they link concepts and discourse functions, and without using one or using the wrong one, listeners may not be able to discern relationships between statements (Bliss, McCabe, & Miranda 1998). In songs when Beyoncé would begin to raise concerns about who she is, what she wanted or what she believed, they were structured in ways that had her voicing concerns after the word "but." The educated common-sense view of language is one that respects the understanding it is guided by a distinct set of rules associated with word usage (Bolinger 2014). Therefore, the usage of the word "but" to connect empowering ideas and statements for her listeners is not to be ignored.

Some songs including the "but" factor were "Me, Myself and I," "Listen," "Ring the Alarm" and "Broken-Hearted Girl." For example, in "Broken-Hearted Girl," she was finding the strength to tell her lover, who she admitted hurt her and she hated, about her feelings. Beyoncé confessed to being afraid to tell him, a confirmation of the power struggles often present in male-female relationships. Yet, she did voice her issue. Another example was found in "No Angel," when she admitted to driving her lover crazy and not being perfect, but then questions if he preferred she be a "machine" who did not notice when he was lying or late. This was perhaps a nod to the book and movie "*The Stepford Wives*" (1975/2004), in which ultra-submissive wives in a Connecticut neighborhood were robots.

Black Feminism and Hip-Hop Feminism Tenets within Beyoncé's Lyrics

Whether intentionally or unintentionally, Beyoncé's lyrical catalog consistently incorporated elements of Black and Hip-Hop feminism. Each album represented multiple tenets of both areas of feminist thought, and the

complexity of her messages grew with each album. The most common concepts in her albums were of the collaborative nature and power of sisterhood;
resistance to the oppressive gender roles in love relationships; contestation
of the power dynamics present between women and men; concerns of images
and representations; need for financial independence and individual freedom;
demand for the respect of the intellectual capacity of Black women; and creation of agency for Black women's experiences. More specifically, in "Ring
the Alarm," she flexed her intellectual muscles by voicing concerns that if she
left her lover his future companion would profit from what she taught him,
and in "Upgrade U," she discussed social power dynamics when she noted
the world was run by men, but women were responsible for keeping its tempo.
In "Listen," she contested status quo by demanding her dreams be fulfilled
and refused to allow them to be sidelined and turned into her lover's dreams.
(See Chart 1 for details.)

Chart 1—Breakdown by Album of Black Feminist and Hip-Hop Feminist Tenets

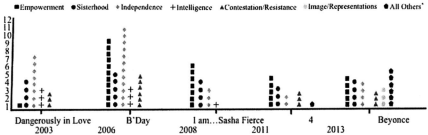

Black Feminist and Hip-Hop Feminist Tenents in Lyrics

■Empowerment ●Sisterhood ♦Independence +Intelligence ▲Contestation/Resistance ◎Image/Representations ●All Others*

Dangerously in Love	B'Day	I am...Sasha Fierce	4	Beyonce
2003	2006	2008	2011	2013

*The other tenents included change, oppressive standards, tensions, partnerships and Black women as unique.

An important lyrical connection to Black feminist thought was Beyoncé's
connection to sisterhood. She called out her girls, crew, friends, ladies and
women in multiple songs. Whether highlighting her thoughts and experiences
or theirs, she acted as supporter, teacher and proverbial voice for women.
The most popular example was "Single Ladies," but others included "Flawless,"
and "Run the World (Girls)." Evoking her proverbial sisterhood was often
signaled by a call-and-response tradition, which has deep ties in the Black
community.

Her last album offered the most dynamic representations and included
multiple lyrics covering a variety of different concepts, including "Pretty
Hurts," which dealt with image and representations and her questioning
Vogue magazine's definition of beauty; "Ring Off," in which she empathized

with her divorced mother and encouraged her to put herself first in her life, "Mine," in which Beyoncé acknowledged the common postpartum issue of not feeling yourself after having a baby; "Blue," in which she celebrated motherhood, "Flawless," in which she called upon her sisterhood to accept their flawlessness and tell others about it, and finally, "Partition," in which she embraced her sexuality and left the listeners with a solid understanding of the connections of sex to feminism.

Her connections to Hip-Hop culture were very evident in her lyrics. From her descriptions of her clothing and behaviors to her experiences and materialism, lyrics were ripe with Hip-Hop references. It is perhaps in this context one might begin to understand the contradictions within her lyrics, such as when she objectified herself, called other women T.H.O.T.S. (i.e., that hoe over there), tricks and bitches, or when she even called herself a bitch. These are common ways women are represented in Hip-Hop. This is problematic, as historically rappers objectify, denigrate, and oppress young Black females through negative language, and this behavior is destructive to Black females emotions and self-esteem as well as sustains the negative stereotypes present within White patriarchal America (Tyree 2009). However, like many other women in Hip-Hop, Beyoncé did lyrically fight for her voice to be heard and contested ways women are represented.

From a Hip-Hop standpoint, her most notable song was "Hip-Hop Star." She took on an aggressive tone and reversed the normal Hip-Hop discourse of the man objectifying the woman. In the song, she dared her a man to undress her, asked him if he wanted to get nasty with her and whether he wanted to ride with her. These were all messages with clear sexual overtones, but she was in control. She even sung of wearing her pants down low, a style usually associated with men.

This was not the only time Beyoncé presented herself in this feminist space through gender role reversals. Other examples were in songs, such as "If I Were a Boy," "Suga Mama," "Get Me Bodied" and "Disappear." Through the role reversals, she acknowledged male privileges and male statues often found in relationships. In "If I Were a Boy," Beyoncé noted she would drink beer, hang with guys, and be with anyone she wanted to be with and never be confronted, because her friends would stick up for her. She also suggested ways in which she would treat women better. In "Suga Mama," she took on the role of the "sugar daddy," a longstanding stereotype in which a male exchanges money for sexual favors or companionship with a younger woman. In "Get Me Bodied," Beyoncé was the aggressor in the club who was making her "rounds" and trying to find a man.

Beyoncé's Balance of Lyrical Conformity and Nonconformity with Gender Traits

Beyoncé's lyrical catalog provided an incredibly balanced portrayal of male and female traits. Beyoncé songs were categorized as having female traits 47 times and male traits 48 times. There were 28 songs in which she was only in the female category, 29 only in the male category and 19 songs with her simultaneously exhibiting male and female traits. (See Table 2 for full details.)

Table 2—Male and Female Traits in Beyoncé's Songs

ALBUM	Overall Songs With Male Traits	Overall Songs With Female Traits	Female Trait with No Male Trait in a Song	Male with No Female Trait in a Song	Male + Female Traits in Same Song
Dangerously in Love	10	11	5	3	6
B'Day	11	6	5	10	1
I am…Sasha Fierce	8	12	9	5	3
4	6	6	6	6	0
Beyonce	13	12	3	5	9
TOTAL	48	47	28	29	19

When Beyoncé's lyrics were solely exhibiting female traits, she was overwhelmingly portrayed as dependent followed by dependent-submissive and inconsistent. When solely exhibiting male traits, she was virtually evenly portrayed as independent, active and independent-active. When songs had both male and female traits, she was mainly beautiful-aggressive, supportive-confident and submissive-aggressive-active. The last category is an admittedly hard one to be constructed, but one that supported the complex balance of lyrical content within her catalog. Examples of songs fitting this category were "Blow" and "Rocket" from the *Beyoncé* album. More specifically, in "Blow," she stated the man can be the boss, a submissive trait, but the majority of the song had her in an aggressively, active sexual posture boasting about how she would show her lover her stroke, give her love until she is empty and make love nonstop until morning arrives.

The pattern in which her male and female traits were distributed throughout her catalog is worthy of highlighting. Lyrics in her first album were nearly even in songs with female and male traits, 11–10, respectively. About half of the album—6 of 15—had songs with both traits. Her second album had the most empowering songs in it, and this album presented Beyoncé singing 11 songs with male traits, ten of which only included male traits. Again, she was not a mother or wife at this time, but was a budding businesswoman. The third album was released a few months after she was married. The traits shifted more heavily to female ones, the most songs in any album with female only traits, but tied the percentage of her last album. There was a 100 percent decrease in the number of lyrics categorized with male only traits. The fourth album *4* was stark in its presentation of traits. Six were in the male category; six were in the female category. None overlapped. It was either completely serendipitous, or a perfectly conscious effort to present an album neither too feminine nor too masculine. Beyoncé's fifth album, heralded by many as her most feminist, returned back to having more songs categorized with male traits than female traits at 13–12, respectively. Yet, the album had the most couplings of male-female traits at nine songs, perhaps neutralizing the impression.

Female Stereotypes, Sexual Scripts and Sexual Roles

Beyoncé's labeling as both historic Black stereotypes and as sexual scripts is very interesting. In total, 36 songs were noted, with four situating her simultaneously as having characteristics of two stereotypes. Lyrically, she fit into the following categories: freak, earth mother, gangsta bitch, Black lady, diva, hood rat, and angry Black woman. She is labeled the most in her first album with 12 of the 15 (80 percent) songs situating her as a sexual script, namely the freak and earth mother for her sexual exploits and discussions of metaphysical concepts, respectively. Her next three albums had her labeled a total of 14 times, which is only slightly more than the total in her first album. Her predominate category was the freak.

Her last album had the second highest appearance of stereotypes at 10 of 17 (58 percent) of the tracks. This album's content was extremely sexual in nature, and it had her labeled the most as a freak with eight of the ten songs. The question then is if she is a self-proclaimed "modern day feminist" at the time of her last album, what becomes of her sexualized content? Beyoncé best answers this question herself in the outro of the "Partition" remix. A woman is speaking in French, and it is purportedly sampled from the French version of *The Big Lebowski* movie (Haglund & Wickman 2013). The woman is asking if a man likes sex. More specifically, she asks if he likes coitus. She then corrects a misconception about feminists by stated men think feminists hate sex. However, she asserts women love this natural and stimulating activity (Haglund & Wickman 2013).

Her connection to the angry Black woman stereotype was also notable. An unfortunate trend in her music was the idea of Beyoncé being an uncontrollable lover who was frequently crazed or driving her lover crazy, which is a representation that does not run contrary to the stereotypical imagery of the angry and out of control Black woman in mass media. Further, in support of Short's (2015) findings, Beyoncé's entire catalog of music positioned her multiple times in the earth mother sexual script. Beyoncé's lyrics contained spiritual and environmental metaphors as well as questions regarding metaphysics. Beyoncé often spoke of her soul, praying, angels, sin, heaven and being blessed. She even had a song entitled "Ave Maria"—which is the Latin translation of Hail Mary.

It is important to note the metaphorical space is one usually privileged for White males, conferring it with the ability to contemplate values, abstract objects, facts, necessities and physical things (Mohanram 1999; Merleau-Ponty 2002). In contrast, Franz Fanon (2008) noted the Black body is usually one with no agency; instead, it is one with only a discursive construct. The Black body is usually only able to exist in reality (Mohanram 1999). Therefore, Beyoncé's ability to be in this metaphorical space within pop culture is a powerful expression to the world.

Conclusion

Each of Beyoncé's five albums had its own distinct narrative, signaling the evolution of a woman who transitioned from being a single young artist, to a businesswoman and later to a powerful, feminist, mother, wife and business mogul. When situated within the history and themes of Black and Hip-Hop feminisms, it is apparent Beyoncé could represent both the problem and proposed solution for these feminist movements. From one standpoint, she sang some misogynistic lyrics and others that evoked historic Black stereotypes and sexual scripts counterproductive for Black female representation in mass media. From another standpoint, in the midst of her presumed self-objectification, she presented lyrics that opened up metaphorical spaces for Black women that have been previously privileged for White men. She, too, had multiple elements of Black and Hip-Hop feminisms that promoted the collaboration and power of sisterhood; expressed resistance to the oppressive gender roles in love relationships; contested gendered power dynamics; raised concerns about the images and representation of Black women; and articulated an increased need for Black women to have independence and individual freedom.

As noted by Mackay (2015), "Not everyone is feminist, not everything is feminist, not every comment or decision that a woman makes or takes is a feminist comment or a feminist choice." In the case of Beyoncé, she self-identifies as a feminist. For some, it is enough to accept this as truth. For others, the complexity of who she is as an individual and artist offers too many contradictions to accept her personal labeling. For others, they may just need proof. This study can serve the very purpose of drawing the proverbial line in the sand to determine exactly which side Beyoncé should be situated—feminist or antifeminist.

Yet, there are two final issues to consider. First, musical performance is complex. It is more than lyrics. It is more than Beyoncé donning a wig, cooing into a microphone and shaking on stage with her all-female band playing in the background. Simon Frith (1999) identifies three strata in popular musicians' performances, which can be simultaneously present. First is the "personally expressive" component, an individual singing from her own experience, but the other two layers are "involved in a process of double enactment: they enact both a star personality (their image) and a song personality, the role that each lyric requires, and the pop star's art is to keep both acts in play at once" (186, 212). Auslander (2004) working from Frith's (1996) definitions acknowledges three layers of performance: the real person, the performance persona and the character. Beyoncé plays the part. She is a performer who owns her performance—complex, flawed and contradictory as it may be.

Second, this is about choice. While recognizing patriarchal and capitalistic forces are at play in the media and music industries, no one is technically forcing Beyoncé to do what she does or sing what she sings. Could she present a different, less eroticized Beyoncé with every song being empowering? Sure. Could she be a sell-out focusing not a single song on topics that speak to, for and about experiences relevant to Black women and girls? Sure. Yet, she does not. She is a voice for Black women. Perfect she might not be, but she is needed, applauded, wildly popular and bringing attention to the issues of Black women and girls to the world. All may not universally agree upon her approach, but it is Bey Feminism, a new way to change the world. And, it may just be time for Beyoncé's critics to respectfully, well, bow down.

REFERENCES

Auslander, Philip. 2004. "Performance analysis and popular music: A manifesto." *Contemporary Theatre Review* 14:1–13.
Austin, Regina. 1997. "Sapphire Bound!" In *Critical Race Feminism: A Reader*, edited by Adrien Katherine Wing, 289–296. New York: New York University Press.
Bennett, Jessica. 2014. "How to Reclaim the F-Word? Just Call Beyoncé." Last modified August 26, 2014. http://time.com/3181644/beyonce-reclaim-feminism-pop-star/.
Bliss, Lynn S., Alyssa McCabe, and Elisabeth A. Miranda. 1998. "Narrative Assessment

Profile: Discourse Analysis for School-Age Children." *Journal of Communication Disorders* 31: 347–363.

Bolinger, Dwight. 2014. *Language, the Loaded Weapon: The Use and Abuse of Language Today*. New York: Routledge.

Brooks, Daphne A. 2008. "'All That You Can't Leave Behind': Black Female Soul Singing and the Politics of Surrogation in the Age of Catastrophe." *Meridians: Feminism, Race, Transnationalism* 8: 180–204.

Collins, Patricia Hill. 1990. *Black Feminist Thought*. New York: Routledge.

_____. 2000. *Black Feminist Thought: Knowledge, Consciousness, and the Politics of Empowerment* (2nd ed.). New York: Routledge.

_____. 2015. "Black Feminist Thought in the Matrix of Domination." Last modified July 22, 2015. http://www.turningthetide.org/files/feminist percent20thoughtper cent20andpercent20matrixpercent20ofpercent20domination.pdf.

Conley, Mikaela. 2011. "Beyoncé Joins Michelle Obama's Initiative to Fight Childhood Obesity." Last modified April 29, 2011. http://abcnews.go.com/Health/beyonce-drops-music-video-fight-childhood-obesity/story?id=13482133.

Cooper, Brittney. 2014. "On Bell, Beyoncé, and Bullshit." Last modified May 20, 2014. http://www.crunkfeministcollective.com/2014/05/20/on-bell-beyonce-and-bull shit/.

Crunk Feminist Collective. 2015. "5 Reasons I'm Here for Beyoncé, the Feminist." Last modified June 3, 2015. http://www.crunkfeministcollective.com/2013/12/13/5-reasons-im-here-for-beyonce-the-feminist/.

Cubarrubia, RJ. 2013. "Beyoncé Calls Herself a 'Modern-Day Feminist.'" *Rolling Stone*.

Denisoff, R. Serge, and Richard A. Peterson. 1972. *The Sounds of Social Change*. Chicago: Rand McNally and Co.

Dockterman, Eliana. 2013. "Flawless: 5 Lessons in Modern Feminism from Beyoncé." Retrieved December 17, 2013. http://time.com/author/eliana-dockterman/.

Durham, Aisha, Brittney Cooper, and Susana Morris. 2013. "The Stage Hip-Hop Feminism Built: A New Directions Essay." *Signs: Journal of Women in Culture and Society* 38: 721–737.

Ellison, Jo. 2013. "Beyoncé Makes *British Vogue* Cover Debut." Last modified April 3, 2013. http://www.vogue.co.uk/news/2013/04/beyonce-makes-british-vogue-cover-debut-may-issue-vogue.

Emerson, Rana. 2002. "'Where My Girls At?' Negotiating Black Womanhood in Music Videos." *Gender & Society* 16: 115–35

Fanon, Frantz. 2008. *Black Skin, White Masks*. New York: Gross Press.

Ferguson, Arnett Ann. 2000. *Bad Boys: Public Schools in the Making of Masculinity*. Ann Arbor: University of Michigan Press.

Freudiger, Patricia, and Elizabeth M. Almquist. 1978. "Male and Female Roles in the Lyrics of Three Genres of Contemporary Music." *Sex Roles* 4: 51–65.

Frith, Simon. 1996. *Performing Rites: On the Value of Popular Music*. Cambridge: Harvard University Press.

Gordon, Jane. 2010. "Beyoncé: The Multi-Talented Star Reveals What She Is Planning Next." Last modified August 15, 2010. http://www.dailymail.co.uk/home/you/article-1301838/Beyoncé-the-multi-talented-star-reveals-planning-next.html.

Green, Tyere. 2014. "Grammy Greats: 12 Artists Who've Broken Grammy Award Records." Last modified January 22, 2014. http://www.ibtimes.com/grammy-greats-12-artists-whove-broken-grammy-award-records-1546281.

Griffin, Farah Jasmine. 2011. "At Last…? Michelle Obama, Beyoncé, Race & History." *Daedalus* (Winter): 131–141.

Grillo, Tina, and Stephanie M. Wildman. 1997. "Obscuring the Importance of Race: The Implication of Making Comparisons between Racism and Sexism (or Other Isms)." In *Critical Race Feminism: A Reader*, edited by Adrien Katherine Wing, 44–50. New York: New York University Press.

Haglund, David, and Forrest Wickman. 2013. "Beyoncé Sampled the French Version of The Big Lebowski." Last modified December 13, 2013. http://www.slate.com/blogs/browbeat/2013/12/13/beyonc_french_lyrics_on_partition_did_beyonc_sample_the_big_lebowski.html.

Hallahan, Kirk. 1997. *The Consequences of Mass Communication: Cultural and Critical Perspectives on Mass Communication*. New York: McGraw-Hill.

Hobson, Janell. 2013. "Beyoncé's Fierce Feminism." *Ms.* Spring.

hooks, bell. 1992. *Black Looks: Race and Representation*. Boston: South End Press.

Jamila, Shani. 2002. "Can I Get a Witness? Testimony from a Hip-Hop Feminist." In *Colonize This! Young Women of Color on Today's Feminism*, edited by Daisy Hernandez and Bushra Rehman, 382–94. New York: Seal Press.

Kellner, D. 1995. "Cultural Studies, Multiculturalism and Media Culture." In *Race, Gender and Class in Media: A Text Reader*, edited by Gail Dines and Jean M. Humez, 5–17. Thousand Oaks, CA: Sage.

King, Deborah K. 1988. "Multiple Jeopardy, Multiple Consciousness: The Context of a Black Feminist Ideology." *Signs*: 42–72.

Knowles-Carter, Beyoncé. 2014. "Gender Equality Is a Myth." Last modified January 12, 2014. http://shriverreport.org/gender-equality-is-a-myth-beyonce/.

Kornhaber, Spencer. 2015. "Beyoncé's 'Flawless': The Full Story." Last modified June 22, 2015. http://www.theatlantic.com/entertainment/archive/2014/06/the-full-story-of-beyonces-flawless/373480/.

Landry, Bart. 2000. "Black Women and a New Definition of Womanhood." *Black Working Wives: Pioneers of the American Family Revolution*, edited by Bart Landry, 56–81. Los Angeles: University of California Press.

Levande, Meredith. 2008. "Woman, Pop Music, and Pornography." *Meridians: Feminism, Race, Transnationalism* 8: 293–321.

Lopez, Korina. 2014. "Beyoncé Takes Philanthropic Initiative #BeyGOOD Global." *USA Today*. Last modified March 5, 2014. http://www.usatoday.com/story/life/music/2014/03/05/queen-bey-takes-philanthropic-initiative-beygood-global/6079073/.

Loth, Jo Marie. 2013. "The Diva Re-Vamped: Destabilising Notions of the Diva in the Cabaret of Paul Capsis and Meow Meow." *Popular Entertainment Studies* 4:57–73.

Mackay, Finn. 2015. "Feminism at the Crossroads." *Institute of Arts & Ideas IAI News* 22.

McIntyre, Hugh. 2014. "Beyoncé Is Now the Most Nominated Woman in Grammy History." *Forbes*. Last modifed December 6, 2014. http://www.forbes.com/sites/hughmcintyre/2014/12/06/beyonce-is-now-the-most-nominated-woman-in-grammy-history/.

McKee, Alan. 2003. *Textual Analysis: A Beginner's Guide*. London: Sage.

Merleau-Ponty, Maurice. 2002. "The Spatiality of One's Own Body and Motility." *Phenomenology of Perception*. London: Routledge.

Mohanram, Radhika. 1999. *Black Body: Women, Colonialism, and Space*. Minneapolis: University of Minnesota Press.

Morgan, Joan. 1999. *When Chickenheads Come Home to Roost: My Life as a Hip-Hop Feminist*. New York: Simon & Schuster.

Newman, Jason. 2015. "Beyoncé Goes Gangsta Rap on New Track 'Bow Down/I Been On.'" Last modified July 1, 2015. http://www.fuse.tv/2013/03/beyonce-bow-down-i-been-on.

Patillo-McCoy, Mary. 1999. *Black Picket Fences: Privilege and Peril among the Black Middle Class*. Chicago: University of Chicago Press.

Peoples, Whitney. 2008. "'Under Construction': Identifying Foundations of Hip-Hop Feminism and Exploring Bridges between Black Second-Wave and Hip-Hop Feminisms." *Meridans* 8: 19–52.

Pomerantz, Shauna, Rebecca Rab, and Andrea Stefanik. 2013. "Girls Run the World? Caught Between Sexism and Postfeminism in School." *Gender and Society* 27: 185–207.

Pough, Gwendolyn D. 2004. *Check It While I Wreck It: Black Womanhood, Hip-Hop Culture and the Public Sphere*. Boston: Northeastern University Press.

Queen, Carol. 2001. "Sex-Radical Politics, Sex-Positive Feminist Thought, and Whore Stigma." *Identity Politics in the Women's Movement*, edited by Barbara Ryan, 92–102. New York: New York University Press.

Read, Barbara. 2011. "Britney, Beyoncé, and Me—Primary School Girls' Role Models and Constructions of the 'Popular' Girl." *Gender & Education* 23: 1–13.

Riesman, David. 1957. "Listening to Popular Music." In *Mass Culture: The Popular Arts in America*, edited by B. Rosenberg and D.M. White, 111. Glencoe, IL: The Free Press.

Scott, James. 1985. *Weapons of the Weak: Everyday Forms of Peasant Resistance*. New Haven: Yale University Press.

Short, Lucy R. 2015. "Still Haunted: Tending to the Ghosts of Marriage and Mother-hood in White Feminist Critiques of Beyoncé Knowles-Carter and Michelle Obama." *Tapestries: Interwoven Voices of Local and Global Identities* 4(1): 22.

The Stepford Wives, dir. Bryan Forbes. 1975. Fads in Cinema Associates and Palomar Pictures.

The Stepford Wives, dir. Frank Oz. 2004. Paramount Pictures.

Stephens, Dionne, and Layli Phillips. 2003. "Freaks, Gold Diggers, Divas and Dykes: The Socio-Historical Development of African American Female Adolescent Scripts." *Sexuality and Culture* 7: 3–47.

Thompson, Krissah. 2014. "Michelle Obama and Beyoncé: Friends and Feminists?" *Washington Post*. Last modified January 7, 2014. http://www.washingtonpost.com/lifestyle/style/michelle-obama-and-beyonce-friends-and-feminists/2014/01/07/3d31b9aa-77ad-11e3-af7f13bf0e9965f6_story.html.

Tyree, Tia. 2009. "Lovin' Momma and Hatin' on Baby Mama: A Comparison of Misog-ynistic and Stereotypical Representations in Songs about Rappers' Mothers and Baby Mamas." *Women and Language* 32: 50–58.

Watkins, Valethia. 2006. "New Directions in Black Women's Studies." In *The African American Studies Reader*, edited by Nathaniel Norment, 229–240. Durham: Car-olina Academic Press.

Whittington, Elizabeth, and Mackenzie Jordan. 2014. "'Bey Feminism' vs. Black Fem-inism." In *Black Women and Popular Culture: The Conversation Continues*, edited by Adria Y. Goldman et al., 155–172. Lanham, MD: Lexington Books, 155.

Zimmerman, Amy. 2014. "The Perils of Glitzy Celebrity Feminism Having a Moment." Last modified October 15, 2014. http://www.thedailybeast.com/articles/2014/10/15/the-perils-of-glitzy-celebrity-feminism-having-a-moment.html.

Birthing Baby Blue
Beyoncé and the Changing Face of Celebrity Birth Culture

NATALIE JOLLY

When Beyoncé reported to *Vogue* (Gay 2013) that she "really [under-stood] the power of my body" and that she felt "no shame" and "a lot more confident" after her daughter's vaginal unmedicated delivery, she challenged the birth narrative that has marked celebrity culture since Madonna opted for a cesarean delivery over two decades ago. With elective cesarean section long being the celebrity delivery method of choice and with nearly one in three babies being delivered via cesarean nationally, Beyoncé's affirmation of unmedicated vaginal birth after her January 7, 2012, delivery of Blue Ivy Carter marks a watershed moment in celebrity culture and in mainstream birth culture more generally. In this essay, I look at three aspects of birth discourse that Beyoncé's childbirth experience has challenged: pain avoidance as standard labor protocol, women's general lack of body confidence and its manifestation in childbirth, and bodily shame in connection with birth. To do so, I analyze Beyoncé's public commentary about her experience delivering Blue Ivy (in settings such as her March 2013 *Vogue* interview [Gay 2013] and her *Life Is but a Dream* [Knowles 2013] documentary) in light of both celebrity birth trends and current birth practices in the U.S. Beyoncé's commentary can be read as a rejoinder to current trends in the medicalization of birth and to the increasingly common practice of celebrity cesarean. I argue that Beyoncé also draws on her birth experience to inform a new body politics, one based on bodily competency rather than body distrust/disgust. I use this analysis to suggest that Beyoncé's departure from the celebrity pattern of cesarean delivery promises to open a space for a more diverse understanding of what contemporary birth culture might engender and how such a refiguring may challenge notions of conventional femininity.

Madonna's confession, during her labor in 1996, that she "just want[s] this to be over" and that she "can't bear this" (Taraborrelli 2001, 281) led not only to her decision to deliver via cesarean, but portended the changing nature of celebrity birth culture. "Let's just have a C-section," said Kate Hudson of her 2004 delivery (Calanni 2011). "I have a feeling I'm going to have an operation," said Britney Spears just before her 2005 cesarean delivery of her first son (Millea 2005). "It ended up being the greatest thing," reported Angelina Jolie of her first cesarean delivery of her daughter in 2006 (Tracy 2009, 98). "I don't want any surprises," said Christina Aguilera when discussing her motivation for scheduling her son's 2008 cesarean delivery (Wihlborg 2008). "It all turned out perfectly," declared Pink of her daughter's 2011 cesarean birth (Staff 2011). And after her fourth cesarean in 2011, Spice Girl Victoria Beckham's surgical deliveries have prompted pundits to ponder, are celebrities too posh to push? (Song 2004).

Celebrity practices are often an augury of coming social trends, and this has certainly held true for birth, where delivery via cesarean section has grown tremendously during the last fifty years. In 1965, the cesarean rate was 4.5 percent, growing to 22.5 percent by 1985 (Taffel, Placek, and Liss 1987). Today, nearly one in three babies are delivered via cesarean section, making it the most common surgery in America (Quinlan 2015). Developments in fetal monitoring technology and a more widespread surveillance of the fetus during labor has corresponded with a higher rate of cesarean section, as has policies that mandate subsequent cesareans after an initial cesarean (Taffel, Placek, and Liss 1987, Anderson 2004). In addition, fear of litigation, a decrease in the practice of forceps delivery, and medical insurance mandates are also thought to be behind the steady rise in cesarean delivery. Still others have suggested that maternal request, or patient-choice cesarean, is driving c-section numbers upwards (Weaver, Statham, and Richards 2007). Each of these factors has, to some degree, fostered a climate favorable to surgical delivery and led to an increase in the medicalization of childbirth.

The rising rate of cesarean delivery is of concern for a variety of reasons, not the least because of the dangers it poses to mother and baby (Morris 2013). With a longer recovery time, higher rates of infection, risk of blood clots and increased complications during future pregnancies, cesarean section poses serious maternal risk. Infants delivered via cesarean section face both short-term risks associated with lung and breathing complications and long-term risks of hospitalization from conditions ranging from asthma and juvenile rheumatoid arthritis, to inflammatory bowel disorder, immune system defects, leukemia and other tissue disorders during their lives (Sevelsted 2015). Since 1985, the international healthcare community has considered a national cesarean rate of 10 percent to be ideal, and the rising rate of surgical delivery continues to be of concern (WHO 2015). Because of the increased health risks that cesarean section poses to both mother and child, it is of interest that the procedure continues to enjoy such prominence. Why do women increasingly see surgical delivery as a viable, even desirable, method of delivery despite the pernicious risks associated with it? Does the practice of "celebrity cesarean" (Jolly 2007) normalize or possibly even incentivize surgical delivery for women? Certainly an examination of "the context and the milieu in which women give birth" is necessary, particularly because "the very concept of informed choice and consent can seduce us into believing that choice exists as an independent, value-neutral entity that is not influenced or constructed by the surrounding context and culture" (McAra-Couper, Jones, and Smythe 2012, 94). Below, I analyze the cultural environment within which women find themselves to understand why medicalized birth and surgical delivery may have such wide appeal. I consider whether Beyoncé's testimony can be read as a response to and critique of these normative birth practices. Certainly the cultural currency commanded by a celebrity such as Queen Bey suggests that her actions are more than just simple deeds. I consider "the Beyoncé effect," and wonder what her disavowal of the celebrity cesarean means for birth norms.

Beyoncé: "Everything that scared me just was not present in that room"

When Britney Spears famously declared in a 2005 *Elle* magazine interview that she "[did not] want to go through the pain" (Millea 2005) of vaginal childbirth, her words gave voice to a growing sentiment: the pain associated with labor and vaginal delivery was frightening, hence her decision to electively schedule a cesarean delivery for her son. Four out of five pregnant women experience fear of childbirth, with 20 percent experiencing a "clinical fear of childbirth" severe enough to pose complications to their pregnancy and/or their delivery (Saisto and Halmesmäki 2003, 202). And while not all cesarean deliveries are scheduled, there is growing evidence that "fear of giving birth vaginally [has] emerged as the primary reason to request a cesarean section" (Fenwick et al. 2009, 395). Why has vaginal birth become so frightening, and how might we "interrogate and problematise the milieu in which birthing decisions are made so to avoid slipping into a sensibility that birth is socially decontextualized and that all caesareans are freely chosen?" (Bryant et al. 2007, 1200). In this section I explore the fear of pain associated with childbirth and consider the consequences of pathologizing birth anxiety. Beyoncé's experience can be read as a puissant retort, and I suggest that she creates space for an alternative to a celebrity birth culture built on fear and anxiety.

Jessica Simpson told Jay Leno that "labor is really going to hurt" just before deciding to forego vaginal delivery and instead schedule an elective cesarean for her daughter in 2012 (and later, her son in 2013). Fear of the pain associated with labor and delivery is not new, but this widespread anxiety seems to render conventional pre-birth jitters quaint by comparison. And because birth is seen as a biomedical event to be managed, it is increasingly common "to treat women's fear of childbirth by offering a greater range of medical controls and technology" (Nilsson and Lundgren 2009, e8). Thus, birth anxiety has become a personal malady, an artifact of individual psychological distress that can be addressed at the scale of the individual rather than the social. Psychotherapies and cognitive therapies designed to treat women suffering from clinical fear of childbirth (also called *tokophobia*) have been gaining popularity because of their ability to "focus on one target problem with the active role of the therapist and [reformulate] the problem in a limited time" (Saisto and Halmesmäki 2003, 205). What has been missing is an examination of the social and cultural features that may foster and exacerbate women's fear of pain and more general anxiety about childbirth. Failure to situate tokophobia within a wider social context risks dismissing birth anxiety as an individual particularism and risks pathologizing women's bodily experiences. "That women may see the pain, work, and the indignities of vaginal birth as distasteful and unfeminine should be of little surprise in a culture of femininity that inoculates women against a sense of body—and self-confidence" (Jolly 2015). Thus the allure of the celebrity cesarean stems in some part from a desire to "give birth like a girl" (Martin 2003). Tokophobia and the pain-avoidance practices it motivates are likely emblematic of a femininity which reinforces women's fragility.

So when Beyoncé spoke publicly (and positively) about her unmedicated vaginal birth, she challenged existing celebrity birth conventions and replied more generally to the cultural anxiety that increasingly characterizes vaginal birth as fearsome. In 2012, she released the statement: "Hello Hello Baby Blue! We are happy to announce the arrival of our beautiful daughter, Blue Ivy Carter, born on Saturday, January 7, 2012. Her birth was emotional and extremely peaceful, we are in heaven. She was delivered naturally at a healthy 7 lbs and it was the best experience of both of our lives" (Finn 2012). Her statement showcased Blue Ivy's natural delivery without couching the experience in terms of pain or anxiety. In not choosing a celebrity cesarean, Beyoncé opened a space for considering the positive potential of unmedicated vaginal delivery, one centered on peace and emotion rather than fear.

In a 2013 *Vogue* magazine interview, Beyoncé expanded on this sentiment and truly reveled in the physicality of her unmedicated vaginal delivery. She stated,

I felt very maternal around eight months, and I thought I couldn't become any more [maternal] until I saw the baby. But it happened during my labor because I had a very strong connection with my child. I felt like when I was having contractions, I envisioned my child pushing through a very heavy door [Gay 2013].

In her discussion of Blue Ivy's birth, Beyoncé focused on her maternal connection to her daughter and prioritized that over her own nervousness and/or anxiety about the delivery. For her, the pain associated with labor did not warrant discussion; instead Beyoncé focused on her ability to imagine labor from her daughter's perspective, and empathized with her baby. The strong and no doubt painful experience of unmedicated vaginal birth, then, became—for Beyoncé—a way to deepen her connection to her daughter and widen the experience beyond her own perspective. In doing so, she challenged the conventional celebrity practice of equating vaginal delivery with fear. Instead she asserted that, rather than something to avoid, an unmedicated vaginal delivery has positive potential.

Beyoncé drove this point home, stating, "I imagined this tiny infant doing all the work, so I couldn't think about my own pain[....] We were talking. I know it sounds crazy, but I felt a communication" (Gay 2013). Here Beyoncé more explicitly demanded that the conversation not center on her individual experience of pain. For her, the physicality of her delivery fostered the context within which she could communicate with her baby. The pain of labor was not something to avoid through medication or through surgery; instead, the pain allowed Beyoncé a moment of bonding that she clearly relished. In discussing Blue Ivy's birth in this way, Beyoncé has mapped out new terrain, refusing to frame the discussion in terms of pain and her own birth anxiety. Beyoncé acknowledged that pain and anxiety play a role in childbirth, but rejected the fear-based narrative that has characterized celebrity birth, stating, "My family and my closest people were there when I gave birth. Everything that scared me just was not present in that room" (Gay 2013). In doing so, she reframed the conversation to center the positive potential of the pain, what it allowed for rather than what it cost. Beyoncé acknowledges that fear may be present in the birthing room, but fear was not a sentiment that she would allow to characterize her birthing experience.

Beyoncé responds to the tokophobia that increasingly characterizes celebrity birth culture by saying, "So for me to really let go and really appreciate every contraction. It was the best day of my life" (Gay 2013). Beyoncé's birth story asks that we consider the unrealized potential of unmedicated delivery. In doing so, we must reckon with conventions that have normalized (and even celebrated) cesarean delivery and have made pain avoidance during labor de rigueur. The deep connection Beyoncé was able to establish with her daughter, her ability to expand her perspective beyond her own experience, and her willingness to find value in the pain and even "appreciate every con-traction" (Gay 2013) created space for an alternative to a celebrity birth culture built on fear and anxiety. In framing her birth story in this way, Beyoncé veered away from the tokophobic assumptions that have normalized pain avoidance as a customary part of birth culture. She not only challenged the precedent of celebrity cesarean, she also asked that we consider the positive potential of non-medicated delivery. What can we learn about female embod-iment from Beyoncé's experience of vaginal birth?

Beyoncé: "Right now, after giving birth, I really understand the power of my body"

Body dissatisfaction is a hallmark of celebrity culture. No body part is spared examination in the parade of bodily scrutiny. "My breasts are saggy, I've got cellulite, my hips are bigger [...] every actress out there is more beau-tiful than me" (OK! Staff 2010). So opined Jessica Alba about her celebrated body, and she is not alone in focusing a critical eye on herself. "I have so much saggy skin on my stomach and I have no bum at all," complained Vic-toria "Posh Spice" Beckham (Morton 2007, 260). Britney Spears lamented, "I wish my hair was thicker, and I wish my feet were prettier. My toes are really ugly. I wish my ears were smaller. And my nose could be smaller, too" (Heatley 2008). Angelina Jolie was certain that her legendary lips "take over my whole face" (US Weekly 2011). "I have a love/hate relationship with my body," said Madonna of her feted figure (ET Online 2014). Such sentiments are prosaic, and body aversion animates women's lives both on the red carpet and off. An undermining of body confidence is a cornerstone of normative femininity, as is a romanticization of weakness, passivity and docility. Uber alles, women are not buoyed by their relationship to their body, and femi-ninity does not telegraph strength. In this section, I chart the goals and ambi-tions that animate normative femininity and explore how these norms lie in perfect sympathy with surgical delivery. I offer Beyoncé's thoughts on Blue Ivy's delivery as a rejoinder to a culture of femininity that privileges body critique over body confidence.

How does the physical experience of childbirth align with the tenets of normative femininity? Certainly the carapace of femininity imposes a par-ticular architecture, a tyranny of nice and kind (Gilligan 1982) that celebrates women's docility and weakness, even during seemingly biological experiences such as birth. It would seem that gender norms permeate women's experiences of childbirth, causing them to "give birth like a girl" (Martin 2003) and to manifest the all the punctilio of femininity within the experience. Coupled with the pseudo-romantic notion of women being rescued from difficulty, this politics of passivity poses a paradox to birthing women. How do women confront the physicality of labor and vaginal delivery within the context of a femininity that undermines their ability to do so? "That normative femininity devalues a woman's ability to endure pain, to work hard, and to prevail in the face of adversity and instead celebrates a woman's rescue from difficult situations has material consequences for her bodily experience of birth" (Jolly 2015). The gestalt of femininity, then, is more than merely a lack of body confidence or a celebration of fragility. It is a pervasive social context within which women are left with little to help them navigate the physically demanding terrain of unmedicated childbirth and without a language to speak of the possible benefits that might result from such an encounter.

The fingerprints of femininity are easy to spot when celebrities such as Christina Aguilera reported an elective cesarean delivery motivated by not "want[ing] any [vaginal] tearing." "I didn't want any surprises" (Wihlborg 2008), said Aguilera of her decision to schedule her son's cesarean delivery. Femininity is the counterpoint to strength, perseverance and capacity, and the sense that the female body does not work—cannot work—pervades even a woman's expectations about birth. And yet, Beyoncé does not seem to brook such sentiments, building an empire on her legendary Stakhanovitian work ethic while still managing to personify all that is emblematic of normative femininity. "I just feel my body means something completely different" (Gay 2013), said Beyoncé after her daughter's delivery, in response to a culture that continues to praise her body for its decorative properties. "Right now, after giving birth, I really understand the power of my body" (Gay 2013). In couching the discussion in terms of power and a new bodily knowledge, Beyoncé found that her unmedicated vaginal delivery of Blue Ivy offered her something novel: a conception of femininity based on bodily achievement rather than on the body as adornment. For Beyoncé, birth enabled the creation of a new way to know her body, one where the female body was measured by its ability to be powerful rather than as an object for consumption. She dismissed the conventional metric of femininity, stating, "Even being heavier, thinner, whatever. I feel a lot more like a woman" (Gay 2013). Rejecting an orthodox definition of womanhood centered on body size and appearance, Beyoncé drew on her birth experience to refigure what it means to be a woman based on physical prowess.

Beyoncé's new definition of femininity incorporates physical endurance, bodily capacity, perseverance, and success, attributes not conventionally associated with womanhood. "It comes from knowing my purpose and really meeting myself once I saw my child," Beyoncé explained. "I was like, 'OK, this is what you were born to do.' The purpose of my body became completely different" (Ellison 2013). What well and truly is the purpose of a woman's body? If the dictates of femininity normalize the female body as ornament, then asking a woman to use her body as an instrument poses an inconsistency. This disconnect was made more stark when Beyoncé gave birth, as she was forced to juxtapose the decorative body with the laboring body. That she rejected the body as object is telling, as is the value she finds in recuperating the laboring body. "I feel a lot more confident about it," said Beyoncé of her body after her daughter's birth (Gay 2013), begging the question: what might be possible if femininity was conceived of as competency, of prevailing over adversity, of being physically dexterous and intrepid? And if gender norms allowed for a femininity steeped in body confidence, might women be able to carry that outlook to other aspects of their lives?

Beyoncé: "More feminine, more sensual. And no shame"

"I felt like a complete failure." So admitted Kate Winslet after her daughter's cesarean delivery. "My whole life, I'd been told I had great child-bearing hips," said the British actress, who reported feeling "traumatized" by not being able to "handle childbirth" (Reynolds 2013). Unable to reconcile the aesthetic body with the laboring body, Winslet lied about her cesarean delivery and confessed, "I've gone to great pains to cover it up." Only after vaginally delivering her son four years later does Winslet come clean about the ruse, calling her second labor and delivery "amazing." "It was an incredible birth. It was really triumphant" (Reynolds 2013). Winslet's embarrassment at not joining what she termed "the powerful women's club" nods at the larger culture of femininity, in which shame plays a leading role. "Shame, as what we might call a primary structure of a woman's lived experience […] becomes integral to a generalized sense of inferiority of the feminine body-subject" (Kruks 2001, 64–65). From menses to menopause, femininity seems architected upon bodily shame writ large (Schooler et al. 2005, Bessenoff and Snow 2006).

In navigating a culture where menstruation is suppressed and menopause is medicated, women are left with "the perception of female physiology—and thus womanhood—as inherently flawed" (Moloney 2010, 156). A sense of bodily shame has become an insignia of femininity, and suggests women not trust the biological functioning of their bodies. Within this cultural milieu, women become fluent in the knowledge of bodily distrust, and birth becomes yet another moment where that bodily shame metastasizes to the point of undermining a woman's confidence in her body's ability. Beyoncé offered a retort in stating that her unmedicated vaginal birth left her feeling "more feminine, more sensual. And no shame" (Gay 2013). In refusing to countenance the parameters of conventional femininity, Beyoncé is impenitent about her female body. Rather than adhere to an anorexic version of femininity prefaced on bodily shame, Beyoncé deftly plucks body distrust out from the tenets of womanhood. Much like Kate Winslet's "triumphant" birth discussed above, Beyoncé's response to her birth experience suggested that unmedicated birth might allow for one possible conception of femininity built on bodily capacity rather than bodily distrust.

In bringing the laboring body, the capable body, the strong and successful female body into her definition of femininity, Beyoncé was able to recast the feminine as aptitude rather than liability. Such a refiguring liberated Beyoncé from the tenets of conventional femininity: "I don't feel like I have to please anyone. I feel free" (Gay 2013), she said, in reflecting on her birth experience. In particular, Beyoncé seemed to see her birth experience as a rejoinder to the infantilizing nature of femininity, claiming, "I feel like I'm an adult. I'm grown" (Gay 2013). In drawing on the embodied experience of delivering her daughter, Beyoncé articulated a femininity laden with power. Her birth experience allowed her to appropriate aspects of conventional masculinity into her revised conception of femininity, saying, "I can do what I want. I can say what I want" (Gay 2013). What was it about her unmedicated vaginal birth that allowed for such a transformation, particularly one that had such resonance even after Beyoncé had left the delivery room? Rather than becoming another moment of manifested bodily shame, birth for Beyoncé was instead an opportunity to stare down the barrel of conventional gender norms. In doing so, she put normative femininity in her crosshairs and pulled the trigger. Indeed the ramifications of this revisioned femininity left no part of her perspective unmarred, and she pushes further, saying, "I can retire if I want. That's why I've worked hard" (Gay 2013). The physicality of birth reminded Beyoncé of what she was capable: hard work. Her sense of accomplishment translated beyond Blue Ivy's delivery. It served as a cauterizing truth and one that demanded a more capacious understanding of what it means to be a woman today.

Beyoncé voiced her dissatisfaction with a femininity that had not lived up to its billing. It was in the bodily experience of pregnancy and birth that she found relief from the confines of conventional femininity, stating, "There is something so relieving about life taking over you like that" (Knowles 2013). Which poses an interesting question: Who (or what) was this "you" that was taken over? It would appear that Beyoncé is nodding to the normative "you" that is lost in the briar patch of gender conventions, the "you" of a desiccated femininity. "Bodies have all the explanatory power of minds" (Grosz 1994, vii), Elizabeth Grosz reminds us, and Beyoncé is relentless in her admonition that we take seriously the potential of birth to refigure what it means to be a woman in this world. "You're playing a part in a much bigger show," said Beyoncé of her experience birthing Blue Ivy. "And that's what life is. It's the greatest show on earth" (Knowles 2013). What might be possible if the birthing body became primary (Sullivan 2001, 2), not in a reductionist way that equates all women with the reproductive capacity of their bodies, but instead in a way that attends to the corporeality of female existence within a culture of femininity fraught with shame?

Beyoncé: "I felt more powerful than I've ever felt in my life"

In reflecting on Blue Ivy's birth, Beyoncé said, "It's just magical. It makes me so proud to be a woman because it's just unexplainable what happens to your body—it's incredible" (Chiu 2012). In a culture where women's bodies are valued as ornament, and where the physiology of the female body is seen as shameful and grotesque, is it an act of magic for a woman to have a positive experience of female embodiment? Her unmedicated vaginal delivery allowed Beyoncé to feel "connected to my body" (Chiu 2012) in a way she hadn't previously. Beyoncé sums up her birth experience by stating, "I felt like I knew my purpose in the world" (Chiu 2012). Birth, for Beyoncé, offered new possibilities for femininity. In particular, her unmedicated vaginal delivery allowed Beyoncé to construct a femininity girded by body confidence and self-assuredness. Rather than cast labor as something to fear or to avoid, Beyoncé asks women to consider the liberatory potential of an unmedicated vaginal birth. She concluded that after Blue Ivy's birth she "felt more powerful than I've ever felt in my life" (Chiu 2012). Such lauding of unmedicated vaginal delivery is a stark reply to the practice of celebrity cesarean and the culture of surgical delivery that has increasingly come to characterize birth today. Beyoncé offers us a way to heed the World Health Organization's (WHO 2015) charge to lower cesarean rates, and in doing so asks that we refigure femininity in the process.

Beyoncé's birth of Blue Ivy allowed her an opportunity to define femininity in terms of physicality rather than desirability, passivity, shame or any of the other tenets of conventional femininity. Her experience laboring and delivering her daughter permitted her a glimpse into what might be possible if femininity endorsed a conception of self predicated on strength and tenacity. "The purpose of my body became completely different," said Beyoncé after her daughter's birth. "The way I view it and everything. There's a sensuality and an audacity that I'm OK with sharing. And I'm not uncomfortable about it. I'm not shy about it" (Ellison 2013). For Beyoncé, then, birth stripped away the veneer of conventional femininity, and returned the possibilities of her body to her. In a society that champions the aesthetic value of the female body over all else, it is indeed an audacious claim to redefine femininity in terms of physicality, strength, fearlessness and confidence. In her refusal to apologize for embracing this newfound confidence, Beyoncé adroitly sculpts a feminine defiance that errors on the side of audacity and makes legible the constraints of conventional femininity.

REFERENCES

Anderson, GM. 2004. "Making Sense of Rising Caesarean Section Rates." *BMJ: British Medical Journal* 329.7468: 696–97.
Bessenoff, Gayle R., and Daniel Snow. 2006. "Absorbing Society's Influence: Body Image Self-Discrepancy and Internalized Shame." *Sex Roles* 54: 727–31.
Bryant, Joanne, Maree Porter, Sally K. Tracy, and Elizabeth A. Sullivan. 2007. "Caesarean Birth: Consumption, Safety, Order, and Good Mothering." *Social Science & Medicine* 65: 1192–201.
Calanni, Antonio. 2011. "Kate Hudson." *Orlando Sentinel.*
Ellison, Jo. 2013. "Mrs Carter Uncut." *Vogue.*
Fenwick, Jennifer, Jenny Gamble, Elizabeth A. Nathan, Sara Bayes, and Yvonne Hauck. 2009. "Pre- and Postpartum Levels of Childbirth Fear and the Relationship to Birth Outcomes in a Cohort of Australian Women." *Journal of Clinical Nursing* 18: 667–77.
Finn, Natalie. 2012. "Beyonce and Jay-Z Finally Make Baby News Official: 'We Are in Heaven.'" *E Online.*
Gay, Jason. 2013. "Beyonce Knowles: The Queen B." *Vogue.*
Gilligan, Carol. 1982. *In a Different Voice.* Cambridge: Harvard University Press.
Grosz, Elizabeth. 1994. *Volatile Bodies: Theories of Representation and Difference.* Bloomington: Indiana University Press.
Heatley, Michael. 2008. *The Book of Rock Quotes.* New York: Omnibus Press.
Jolly, Natalie. 2007. "Cesarean, Celebrity and Childbirth: Students Encoutner Modern Birth and the Question of Female Embodiment." In *Curriculum and the Cultural Body* edited by Stephanie Springgay and Debra Freedman, 175–87. New York: Peter Lang.
_____. forthcoming. "Does Labor Mean Work? Querries into the Role of Femininity in Childbirth." In *Birth and Its Meanings* edited by Nadya Burton. Toronto: Demeter Press.
Kruks, Sonia. 2001. *Retrieving Experience: Subjectivity and Recognition in Feminist Politics.* Ithaca: Cornell University Press, 2001.
Leon, Anya, and Alexis Chiu. 2012. "Beyonce: How I Prepared for Blue's Birth." *People Magazine.*
Martin, Karin. 2003. "Giving Birth Like a Girl." *Gender & Society* 17: 54–72.
McAra-Couper, Judith, Marion Jones, and Liz Smythe. 2012. "Caesarean-Section, My Body, My Choice: The Construction of 'Informed Choice' in Relation to Intervention in Childbirth." *Feminism & Psychology* 22: 81–97.
Moloney, Sharon. 2010. "How Menstrual Shame Affects Birth." *Women and Birth* 23: 153–59.
Morris, Theresa. 2013. *Cut It Out: The C-Section Epidemic in America.* New York: New York University Press.
Morton, Andrew. 2007. *Posh & Becks.* New York: Simon & Schuster.
Nilsson, Christina, and Ingela Lundgren. 2009. "Women's Lived Experience of Fear of Childbirth." *Midwifery* 25: e1–e9.
Quinlan, J., and N. Murphy. 2015. "Cesarean Delivery: Counseling Issues and Complicaiton Management." *American Family Physician* 91: 6–20.

Reynolds, Mark. 2013. "Why Kate Lied About Mia's Birth." *The Daily Mail.*

Saisto, Terhi, and Erja Halmesmäki. 2003. "Fear of Childbirth: A Neglected Dilemma." *Acta Obstetricia et Gynecologica Scandinavica* 82: 201–08.

Schooler, Deborah, L. Monique Ward, Ann Merriwether and Allison Caruthers. 2005. "Cycles of Shame: Menstrual Shame, Body Shame, and Sexual Decision-Making." *Journal of Sex Research* 42: 324–34.

Sevelsted, A., J. Stokholm, K. Bonnelykke, H. Bisgaard. 2015. "Cesarean Section and Chronic Immune Disorders." *Pediatrics* 135:6–15.

Sullivan, Shannon. 2001. *Living across and through Skins: Transactional Bodies, Pragmatism, and Feminism.* Bloomington: Indiana University Press.

Taffel, S.M., P.J. Placek, and T. Liss. 1987. "Trends in the United States Cesarean Section Rate and Reasons for the 1980–85 Rise." *American Journal of Public Health* 77: 955–59.

Taraborrelli, Randy. 2001. *Madonna: An Intimate Biography.* New York: Simon & Schuster.

Tracy, Kathleen. 2011. *Angelina Jolie: A Biography.* Westport, CT: Greenwood Publishing Group.

Weaver, Jane J., Helen Statham, and Martin Richards. 2007. "Are There 'Unnecessary' Cesarean Sections? Perceptions of Women and Obstetricians About Cesarean Sections for Nonclinical Indications." *Birth* 34: 32–41.

WHO (World Health Organization). 2015. "Caesarean Sections Should Only Be Performed When Medically Necessary."

Wihlborg, Ulrica. 2008. "I'm Head Over Heels." *People* Magazine.

Beyoncé and Blue
Black Motherhood and the Binds of Racialized Sexism

SONITA R. MOSS

In July 2014, a woman named Jasmine Toliver created a Change.org petition called "Petitioning Blue Ivy—Comb Her Hair," addressed to Beyoncé and Jay-Z. The petition obtained more than 5,000 signatures before closing. Toliver stated her concerns as the following:

> As a woman who understands the importance of hair care. It's disturbing to watch a child suffering from the lack of hair moisture. The parents of Blue Ivy. Sean Carter A.K.A Jay-Z and Beyoncé has failed at numerous attempts of doing Blue Ivy Hair. This matter has escalated to the child developing matted dreads and lint balls. Please let's get the word out to properly care for Blue Ivy hair [Toliver 2015].

After drawing the ire of many, Toliver denounced the petition as a joke on her Facebook page:

> My petition has put the damn world at a stand still. Yes the baby needs her hair done I'll stick by that! Tuh! But the petition is obviously a joke and thanks to everyone who had common sense to realize it. Doesn't mean anything but a laugh among friends and family member when I pointed out that it was a mess. But again I'm done with society it's so easy to get blood sucked into it and brainwashed. I'm going to CONTINUE TO BE ME! NOTHING WILL CHANGE. My thick skin got me through this hilarious experience! I was raised in a no nonsense household and tell it how it is. That's exactly what I did! Thank god for all-lll of my friends and family members on FB on and off to agree with me and seen the humor in it. I made it baby!!! Google me b*tches! Lmao!" [Rogers 2014].

Several days later, after a paparazzi picture surfaced of Blue Ivy's hair in a neatly braided style, Toliver posted, "I saved her life. She gone thank me when she gets older. As we can see it petitions work! Power to the people!" (Rogers 2014).

Toliver's words reveal that within a racist and sexist social system, Black women often propagate and instantiate extant hatred of Black womanhood. Within this framework, Black females are expected to meet a standard of beauty, regardless of their age. Blue Ivy was two years old when this petition circulated, revealing the unscrupulousness of racialized sexism. Black children are often not regarded as precious or needing to be protected as white children (Roberts 1997). Although she was a toddler, the plea to her parents was actually a profound attack on the worthiness of Blue Ivy. In addition, this petition joins a historical legacy of demonizing Black motherhood (Roberts 1997; hooks 1981; Collins 2000; Abdullah 2012; Geronimus 2003; Sewell 2013). Blue Ivy is unacceptable for her appearance and Beyoncé is unacceptable for not controlling her appearance.

Blue Ivy Knowles-Carter inherited a beautiful and terrible legacy. Beautiful because by virtue of her birth, Blue embodies the link of two living legends, Jay-Z and Beyoncé, who are arguably two of the most celebrated artists and entrepreneurs of this century. Terrible because Blue Ivy is a Black girl, and to be a Black female in America is to inherit an undeserved hatred, revulsion, marginalization, and hyper-scrutiny. As Harris-Perry deemed it, Black womanhood in America means "standing upright in a crooked room" (Harris-Perry 2011, 29). Blue Ivy's existence has been, and will continue to be challenged as much as it is celebrated. As her mother, Beyoncé has experienced racism and sexism, although she occupies a space that is unique to Black women in America due to her iconic status as an artist, mogul, tastemaker, and activist. However, this unique position did not protect her from being pathologized as a bad Black mother. I argue that while Beyoncé and Blue occupy different spaces within this spectrum of racism and sexism, both mother and daughter endure the oppression of a denigrated social position. Furthermore, the extreme policing of Blue's personage reflects a modern form of racialized sexism that is designed to control Black femininity under the guise of respectability politics. These politics have materialized into contemporary policies enforced in institutions that seek to tame Black hair. Yet, these politics also enabled Beyoncé's status as an icon. Racialized sexist beauty politics promote Beyoncé's body and simultaneously tear down her daughter. In this way, racialized sexism hurts all Black women—there is no "winner." However, Black feminist activists and Black mothers resist these binds to protect and uplift Black girls and women.

In this essay, I will use the "Comb her hair" petition to assert an argument about the contemporary issues of racialized sexism that Black women face: Black womanhood, Black girlhood, and Black motherhood and Black female bodies are in a constant state of redress in the socio-cultural consciousness. I borrow Crenshaw's theory of intersectionality to articulate racialized sexism as a space in which Black women face both racism and sexism from power structures that create unique oppressions (Crenshaw 1991; Cho, Crenshaw, and McCall 2013). Simply explaining situations facing white women as racism *or* sexism is inadequate because of the propensity for activists to see racism as an issue facing Black men and sexism as an issue facing Black women (Hull, Scott, and Smith 1982). I also use the concept of "misogynoir" to underscore how racialized sexism is increasingly propagated through the media, in this case, digital space. Moya Bailey coined the term misogynoir to "describe the particular brand of hatred directed at Black women in American visual & popular culture" (Bailey 2010). Trudy, creator of the Black feminist blog *Gradient Lair* expands upon the term as specific to the Black experience because of "anti–Black projections from non–Black people onto Black people and thereby internalized and proliferated by Black people" (2015). Thus, a Black woman as the arbiter of racialized sexism against a young Black girl is an example of misogynoir. Racialized sexism is not a new phenomenon, but part of a long tradition of subjugating Black female bodies. The implications of this inequity are reflected in extant attempts to control Black female bodies structurally and institutionally. Beyoncé is a global star, one who exists in an almost untouchable space from daily issues facing most people, let alone Black women, yet her Black womanhood takes the fore in the case of Blue Ivy's body. Beyoncé's stardom cannot save her from being pathologized as a Bad Black mother, and nepotism cannot protect Blue Ivy from denigration. However, Black women have resisted oppression and continue to do so, countering these narratives with activism and innovative images that capture the fullness of Black personhood.

Controlling Black Female Bodies

To understand the tradition of America's relationship to Black female bodies is to understand the genesis of the "Comb her hair" petition against Blue Ivy. This stems from slavery: "the devaluation of Black womanhood occurred as the result of the sexual exploitation of Black women during slavery" (hooks, 1981, 53). While Toliver claims that concern for the good of Blue's hair was the catalyst for the petition, Black bodies in the United States have been subject to control and subjugation since their arrival as chattel slaves (Roberts 1997). Black women's role in slavery was inextricable from sovereignty over their bodies—slave owners needed their physical labor and sexual reproductive abilities for financial gain (Roberts 1993, 7; Roberts 1997). African women produced property, living breathing capital, and therefore the Black woman's body became a site of ownership, not agency: "They were robbed of their womanness as persons, and robbed of their personhood as women, dismembered by sexuality turned against motherhood, and motherhood turned against sexuality" (Martinot 2007, 90). Because the race of a child's mother dictated its status as free or enslaved, even the bi-racial products of slaveholders' sexual assaults on Black women produced slaves (Martinot 2007). There was no escape for a Black woman or her offspring from the institution that punished, surveilled, and controlled as a birth rite. And while Black women endured this abuse, their sexuality was turned against them:

> The designation of all Black women as sexually depraved, immoral, and loose had its roots in the slave system. White women and men justified the sexual exploitation of enslaved Black women by arguing that they were the initiators of sexual relationships with men [hooks 1981, 52].

The vestiges of this social and cultural institution produced tightly enforced controlling images that Toliver's petition reflects today, the indelible mark that permeates the subconscious of Americans today.

Patricia Hill Collins argues that "controlling images" of Black women are designed to make racism, sexism, poverty, and other forms of social injustice appear to be natural, normal, and inevitable parts of everyday life (Collins 2000, 70). These mythic images began in slavery, where the Black female body was manipulated physically and degraded socially. "Marked not only physically but also emotionally, intellectually, socially, and sexually, the Black female slave acts as a beginning point to which we can examine what the sin which the Black female body becomes a sight for presentation in popular mediums" (Sewell 2012, 324). These images, far from being relegated to obsolescence or irrelevance, continue to shape perceptions of Black women and reify their degradation as full citizens. The petition against Blue Ivy degraded her parents and her personhood, and reflects modern day controlling images. While all of these images impact Black women today, this petition specifically evokes images of the Mammy, the Jezebel, and the Sapphire.

The Mammy was constructed as the faithful and maternal slave, tirelessly working to care for her white charges (Collins 2000; Roberts 1997; Sewell 2012; Simmons 2008; West 2012). She was often portrayed as overweight, older, and inevitably asexual—thus, she was not a threat to the white mother of the children she tended. The Jezebel was the binary opposite to the Mammy, named after a character in the bible whose "sexual prowess led men to wanton passion" (Roberts 1997). While the Mammy was harmless, servile, and needless, the Jezebel was the representation of the animalistic, hypersexual, African savage who sought to use her body for immoral lust and pleasure—typically to bed her white slave master (Collins 2004; Simmons 2008). Martinot argues that constructing the African woman as culturally hypersexualized was a means to reify white women as sites of sexual purity, a mythic womanhood that legitimized motherhood (Martinot 2007, 91). Jezebel served the purpose of reifying "real" womanhood and excusing assault on Black women's bodies because of a supposed intrinsic promiscuity: "Constructing the lascivious, wanton, and hypersexual Black woman was a way to reconcile the treatment of Black women as not fully women, idealized as modest and fragile. It also rationalized the brutality of Southern whites" (Hobson 2012, 55). The Sapphire, perhaps the most trenchant controlling image of Black women, birthed popular culture's venerated image of the neck-rolling, finger snapping, sharp tongued Angry Black Woman. Sometimes referred to as the Black Bitch, Sapphire was loud, bossy, hateful, and evil (West 2012; Harris-Perry 2011). The Sapphire image was popularized by the *Amos 'n' Andy* show, creating sympathy for Black males and antipathy for Black females. It reinforced the notion that Black women were unlovable and that Black males were unable to stand them because of their bad attitudes (Simmons 2008, 43).

Critical race scholars assert that these images have transformed into contemporary images that still paint Black womanhood with a broad stroke of depravity, hypersexuality, laziness, and unworthiness (Sewell 2012; Collins 2004; Davis 1993). The cunning recasting of Black women in similar roles with different names is partially effective because of a broadly disseminated notion of equality of opportunity and treatment in the U.S, regardless of race and gender. Though the U.S. media, particularly since the election of Barack Obama, proclaims to have entered into a post-racial era, empirical studies disprove this notion (Bonilla-Silva 2014; Omi and Winant 2015; Feagin 2010). Rather, the U.S. embraces a colorblind ideology that imposes subtle forms of racism and leverages cultural pathology arguments to rationalize the vast material realities between Black Americans and whites. Bonilla-Silva argues that this is "designer racism": "Instead of relying on name calling (niggers, spics, chinks), color-blind racism otherizes softly ('these people are human, too'); instead of proclaiming that God placed minorities in the world in a servile position, it suggests they are behind because they do not work hard enough; instead of viewing interracial marriage as wrong on a straight racial basis, it regards it as 'problematic' because of concerns over the children, location, or the extra burden it places on couples. Yet this new ideology has become a formidable political tool for the maintenance of the racial order" (Bonilla-Silva 2014, 30).

For Black women, colorblind racism almost makes a mockery of itself through its enduring negative images of Black women in popular culture. Indeed, the media is a powerful medium through which to reinforce these messages of Black female inferiority: "Because her body and performance have signified a specific vision of what it means to be Black, producers and writers built roles around common stereotypes associated with her in hopes to not only fulfill the fantasy of whites but also maintain the status quo in America at large" (Sewell 2012, 324). The Black female body embodies new and old images of an unworthy being, something that needs to be surveilled and controlled at all times. Hobson argues that Black female bodies are rendered as unsettling within this framework of racism and sexism: There's a "national distress" over Black female bodies, in part due to the cultural legacy of racism and sexism in relationship to the Black female body (Hobson 2012, 66). As an object of distress, the Black female body is not innocent, is it constantly read as "deviant, illicit sexuality, and criminality" (Hobson 2012, 66). Thus, this unsettling notion of Black femininity is reproduced through the media and meaningful in shaping the experiences of Black women and girls.

Understanding the historical subjugation of Black female bodies is also a way to make sense of the stereotypical media portrayals that exist today. The criminalization of Blackness, Black bodies, and Black women began as a legal institution. The legacy of these images has transformed into a "cultural logic, a means of valorizing its actions and truth claims as natural" (Martinot 2007, 81). The twenty-first century Jezebels, Mammys, and Sapphires are packaged differently in the post-racial, digital era: the Black Bitches, the Gold Diggers, the Video Hos, the Welfare Queens, and the innumerable images of Black women on reality television shows encapsulate the dangerous Black woman who is out of control, wayward, and immoral. The Black Bitch is a central trope of Black womanhood because of its timeless assessment of Black women as unattractive, unwanted, and ineffable. The predominance of misogynistic and "misogynoir-istic" images of Black women often attributed to hip-hop was a hand-me-down from references to Black Bitches in slavery (Simmons 2008). Collins argues that working class Black women have taken the brunt of this trope in part because they are identified as not being "ready" for integration into mainstream middle-class white society: "Poor and working-class Black culture was routinely depicted as being 'authentically' Black whereas middle- and upper-middle class Black culture was seen as less so. Poor and working-class Black characters were portrayed as the ones who walked, talked, and acted 'Black,' and their lack of assimilation of American values justified their incarceration in urban ghettos. Representations of poor and working-class authenticity and middle-class respectability increasingly came in gender-specific form" (Collins 2004, 122–123). Being uniquely positioned to be economically exploited, Black women are more likely than their white counterparts to be poor, uneducated, single mothers. Hence, racism and sexism articulated the perfect object of scorn; Black women.

Imagine being Beyoncé the morning after the explosion about Blue Ivy's hair, or perhaps even Blue Ivy herself when she is old enough to understand. The dominant representations of Black women have a psychological impact

(West 2012; Seccombe, James, and Walters 1998; Harris-Perry 2011). Melissa Harris-Perry argues that these tropes demand that Black women play the Strong Black Woman: "The social construction of Black women's citizenship and identity around the theme of self-sacrificial strength is a recurrent motif in Black women's lives and politics" (Harris-Perry 2011, 21). This myth mis-recognizes Black women, and thus Black women are forced to "tilt and bend themselves to fit the distortion" (Harris-Perry 2011, 29). Thus, many Black women also adhere to the unforgiving racist and sexist expectations that demonize Black women; in a focus group, some Black women agreed that stereotypical images that portray Black women as angry, promiscuous, or lazy are grounded in reality (Harris-Perry 2011, 34). As a method to resist the psychological harm of being shamed for their existence, some Black women are just as likely to support inflexible and harmful double standards that pun-ish Black women (Harris-Perry 2011, 62–63). The "Comb her hair" petition is an example of such punishment. Toliver is a Black woman, and she was moved to take a public stance against Blue Ivy, but moreso against Blue Ivy's body. Within the Black community, certain Black bodies are policed more than others—particularly those that stray from prescribed norms of Black acceptability. Blue Ivy's hair was not considered acceptable, which is also a legacy of racism and sexism from slavery.

Black or Beautiful

I suspect that Toliver's petition evoked such a response from the Black community—both support and revulsion—due to the deeply rooted and painful politics of hair and beauty within the Black community. Under patri-archy, women's value is attached to beauty. Beauty in this instance is concep-tualized as skin color, facial features, and hair texture (Collins 2000). Black women have long been considered unattractive, ugly, and not having signifi-cant access to beauty by virtue of features that run counter to Eurocentric beauty standards (Hobson 2005). Though beauty standards have shifted, its depictions remain irrevocably white—fair skin, silky, shiny hair, light eyes, narrow features. Blackness is not a monolith, but it is represented simplisti-cally in mainstream media and specifically designated as ugly in relation to a whitened personification of beauty: "Within the binary thinking that under-pins intersecting oppressions, blue-eyed, blond, thin White women could not be considered beautiful without the Other—Black women with African features of dark skin, broad noses, full lips, and kinky hair" (Collins 2000, 89). Hobson incisively outlines the connection between historical treatment and exhibition of Black women to the fraught depictions of Black women's bodies today (Hobson 2005). Many of these depictions support the subjugation of

Black women (Hobson 2005, 143), and while this ultimately subjugates all Black people, Black women bear the brunt of these ideologies. U.S. institutions have supported ideological conceptualizations of the ugly or inappropriate Black body, and such practices carry on today. Hobson discusses the connection between the dethroning of Vanessa Williams, the first African American Miss America, and the institutionalization of white femininity. In 1937, contestants were required to be "the white race," which "shaped an irreproachable ideal of the national body that linked beauty and femininity with racial and virginal purity" (Hobson 2005, 121). After Williams won the crown in 1983, although she was a light-skinned African American with blue eyes, she received death threats for threatening systemic racialized sexism (Hobson 2005, 121). When Penthouse published nude photos Williams' had taken two years prior, Williams was denounced by Miss America and her title revoked. As the first and only winner to be dethroned, although Miss America recently issued an apology (Wagner 2015), Williams' repudiation symbolizes the tenuousness of beauty and femininity for Black women. In this sense, Black women constantly face a challenge or threat to self-ascribed or externalized notions of beauty.

Since the exploitation and posthumous dissection of the "Hottentot Venus," the Black female body has been subject to intense scrutiny from dominant cultural gaze. Hobson argues that the treatment of Hottentot Venus, born Sara Bartmann, is allegorical to contemporary treatment of the Black female body as "deviant" (Hobson 2005, 2–3). Contemporary media analyses of Black female bodies as deviant or improper continue this legacy by characterizing these bodies as "suffering" or lacking, and thus this Black woman of the past is linked to Black women's "collective present" (Hobson 2005, 7). While all women are hyperscrutinized and judged by their appearance in a patriarchal society (Collins 2004), Black women must overcome popular notions that beauty is less available to them due to their skin tone, facial features, hair, or body shape. Indeed, Black women face the twin extremes of being judged as hypermasculine or hyperfeminine. In the case of Baartman, her large buttocks, breasts, and labia became the intense site of scrutiny of the European historians and further proof of the Black body as oversexed (Hobson 2005, 24). Hobson argues that the propagation of Black women's bodies as both savage and sexual, ugly and impetuous served to reify notions that Africans and Europeans are essentially racially inferior (Hobson 2005, 36–40, 50, 94). Under such ideology, "Black" becomes a stand in for sullied and impure, while whiteness, and white femininity stands in sharp relief as innocent and pure. It is critical to remember Sara Baartman, not because of her ascribed "freakishness," but because the power of the dominant gaze to define and re-instantiate notions of essentialized Blackness remain powerful in contemporary culture—the stereotyping of Black women's body and sexuality takes the familiar form of Baartman as ultimately problematic. This ideology places Black female bodies as unladylike and wanting compared to their white counterparts (Hobson 2012). Thus, Black women are constantly poised as proving themselves in opposition to the dominant ideology: "Black women need to be considered respectable in order to counter the guilt associated with the Black body" (Hobson 2012, 73).

The history of African enslavement in the U.S. and subsequent colorism is a partial reflection of racism and sexism that Black women experience. During slavery, Black women's bodies were exploited as sexual conquests by white males. The resulting enslaved children reflected a range of lighter brown skin tones and hair textures, eye colors, and facial features inherited from both African and European phenotypes. Slaveholders used these physical differences to create a hierarchy of beauty and social status that privileged the lighter skin and more European facial features: "African" physical features were considered less attractive and intelligent, and therefore designated to manual labor outside (Collins 2000, 291). Biracial children brought higher prices on the slave market, and white males favored fairer-skinned female slaves for sexual unions (Keith and Herring 1991). Preferential treatment brought material advantages: house servant positions afforded slaves better food, clothing, shelter and ability to adopt qualities venerated in the larger white society such as mannerisms and ways of speaking (Keith and Herring 1991, 762–763). Biracial enslaved peoples were enabled to secure employment post–Emancipation and emerged as an elite Black caste with professional positions and a privileged social status (Keith and Herring 1991). This effectively created an intra-racial hierarchy of Blackness which privileges physical features closer to whiteness.

Perhaps one of the most painful legacies of colorism is the rift it creates within the Black community. Lighter-skinned people are conditioned to believe they are more beautiful, yet often experience their identity or loyalty to Blackness challenged or questioned (West 2012, 291). Darker-skinned Black women experience of the pain of being locked out of romantic relationships and are taught to believe they are less attractive than lighter skinned women (West 2012, 291). Global beauty industries profit from Black women's racist and sexist inheritance—beauty industries promulgate an aesthetic that supports white supremacy through constructing darkness as inferior (Phoenix 2014, 102). Lighter skin is so exalted that people of color worldwide bleach their skin and obtain surgical enhancements to leverage white privilege and reap the material benefits: "Lighter skinned people earn more money, complete more years of schooling, live in better neighborhoods, and marry higher-status people than darker skinned people of the same race or ethnicity" (Phoenix 2014). Men of color, who can disrupt or reinforce dominant Beauty standards in digital space, often proliferate racism and sexism that denigrates darker skinned Black women as unattractive in comparison to lighter skinned Black women on Twitter and Instagram (Phoenix 2014, 98). Smith theorizes that discussing the prominence of colorism in the Black community is taboo because it is a reminder of how we have been taught to despise our "Afrocentric characteristics": "...nappy or kinky hair, wide noses, thick lips, and dark skin" (Smith 2015, 1). Since the first study of African American skin shade in 1946, Black Americans have attributed characteristics to specific skin colors that are widely internalized and externalized today, with light-skinned Black possessing superior attitudes and looks, and darker skinned Blacks as inferior. The study was repeated in 2010—the categories had changed, but broadly the consensus was the same (Smith 2015, 3).

The broad discourse of the petition reflects Black insecurity about Black female bodies, but the specificity of hair is irrevocable to Black women's painful denial to white supremacist beauty standards. The hair politics of Black women are informed by a tradition of escaping the hair texture that Toliver stated needed to be "combed"—unkempt, tangled, kinky, coily, and nappy hair. Black people are made aware of the painful standard in childhood; wooly, thick locks that require time, patience, and effort to "subdue" is "bad" hair, while the long, silky, curly, loose locks deemed as "effortless" hair is "good" hair (Collins 2000). Ingrid Banks delineates the difference between having a "bad hair" day and having "bad hair" in the black community: "Bad" hair speaks to the texture of tightly coiled black hair that is juxtaposed with straighter hair, otherwise known as "good" hair" (Banks 2000, 13). However, it is far easier to have a good hair day with "good" hair within the ideology of white supremacy. If Blue had loosely curled locks, would Toliver have created such a petition? Hair texture is so powerful that some African Americans consider it a trump card to skin color and facial features: lighter skinned girls with "whiter" features and "good" hair are largely considered more attractive, but darker-skinned women with "good" hair can escape social ostracism (Banks 2000, 30–31). Today, Black women have access to dominant beauty standards through wearing a multitude of hairstyles that use hair extensions to lighten, lengthen, and alter the texture of the hair (Collins 2004). It cannot be understated that Black women venerate and express a range of physical appearances, often unsung arbiters of fashions, dance moves, and lexicon adapted by the white mainstream. However, Black female bodies are policed, particularly those bodies that stray from respectability politics (Durham 2012). "Hair texture, a female feature that is far more malleable, also matters greatly in re-creating femininity in the context of the new color-blind racism"(Collins 2004, 195). This speaks to the punishment that Black girls and women who dare to wear their hair as it grows naturally receive—since there are many options for Black hair, choosing "bad" hair threatens standards of colorism and beauty within the Black community.

Beyoncé is one of the most prominent examples of transcending racial beauty politics and achieving "mainstream" appeal through her physical appearance. Beyoncé's beauty falls squarely within the realm of respectable Black beauty; fair skinned, light eyes, and silky blond hair. The many images circulating of Beyoncé as a baby showcase light brown, curly, "good" hair. Beyoncé's fair skin, ethnically ambiguous features, and yes, her "good" hair are all central to her lionization as a sex symbol, a specter, a beauty icon within the black community. Part of Beyoncé's crossover appeal is due to her successful negotiation of raced, gendered, and classed beauty standards. Durham (2012) argues that Beyoncé often underscores a higher classed Black femininity through the physical, particularly her hairstyles. Through careful deployment of a down-to-earth ghetto girl and an upper-crust, feminine agent, Beyoncé carefully negotiates the constraints of Black female sexuality and bodies (Durham 2012). Yet, for the duration of her career, Beyoncé's indivisibility from a myriad of wigs, weaves, braids, and extensions reify the importance and cost of the obsession with reformulating our roots in our own image. Fans and critics have become so enamored with the image of Beyoncé—the untouchable modern Black idol—that the reality of physical and phenotypic inheritance is unbearable. Through Collins' lens of controlling images, Blue's Black beauty contradicts Beyoncé's supremacy as a transcendent Black Queen—an unstoppable force, acquiring an estimated one billion dollar net worth alongside her Black husband, all wearing blonde weaves and carefully crafted sexuality. Black mothers do not have access to the symbolic space that Beyoncé inhabits, and thus her child should reflect her status. Blue Ivy looks like Beyoncé and Jay-Z, but the distinct allegiance she bears to her father in skin tone, facial features, and hair texture is disruptive and distressing. And thus it is Beyoncé's duty to " comb her hair," to make her acceptable, to hide the shame of one iteration of Black features.

"Black children are born guilty"

In *Killing the Black Body*, Dorothy Roberts argues, "Black children are born guilty" (21). The innocence typically granted to all children simply for being born has been routinely denied to African American children since slavery. Part of this is due to the physical and figurative bondage Black women faced during the period. Enslaved women's bodies were used as tools to bear fruit for slaveholders. "Black women bore children who belonged to the slave owner from the moment of their conception" (23). Considered property instead of free human beings, such infants were relegated to an "in-waiting" status: waiting to be sold, whipped, shackled, and forced—to labor, to breed, to exist for the monetary gain of another human being. Conventional wisdom about the dehumanization of Black Americans often forgets that Black children are not an exception to this unspoken rule.

Black life in general is usually covered in the media as problematic: absent fathers, single mothers, prison, obesity, ghetto life and violence. Rarely is family life discussed without mention of the prevalence of broken homes and young mothers. A Bill Moyers 1986 special report, entitled "The Vanishing Family: Crisis in Black America," is emblematic of a pathological perspective of Black family life, blaming irresponsible parenting for an endless cycle of poverty and despair. While discussing the poor choices of the impoverished, single mothers and cavalier fathers, the camera cuts to the faces of the children, which I interpret as a way to elicit pity or judgment of the parents. The judgment cast upon the parents is also indirectly targeting the children. Objects of scorn, neglect, or ignorance, the children are cast as "mistakes" or victims, rather than precious and deserving of care. These children are born unlucky, marred by their circumstances, and therefore less prized than middle-class or white children. "What's happening goes far beyond race. Why, then, do so many teenage girls get pregnant and have children? Why do so many fathers abandon their children? The answer starts here," Moyers states at the opening of the now infamous special report ("The Vanishing Family: Crisis in Black America" 1986). He argues plainly that race is not a major factor in such outcomes, but his calculus is as old as American racism. These images and words only serve to reify existing conceptualization of hypersexual and criminal Black children. In a searing critique of the film *Beasts of the Southern Wild* bell hooks elucidates how the Black girl cast in the role of Hushpuppy is simultaneously eroticized and abused, cast as a miniature "strong Black woman" (hooks 2015). Racialized sexism confiscates innocence from Black girls. The intersection between racism and sexism is a nexus that swallows the complexity of Black girlhood and Black womanhood. Through this framework, Black women are attributed the pathologies of biological and cultural inferiority while also saddled with a hypersexual, unwieldy, and inappropriate sexuality. The anxiety around the Black female body does not begin in puberty, but rather starts in childhood. The bodies and beings of Black girls are flattened and reduced to mere images and punished for not operating under the tight strictures of respectability politics. These judgments are magnified in the digital age, when a short video, tweet, or in this case paparazzi photos are disseminated, and a petition is created against a two-year-old.

Through this lens, age is irrelevant. The beauty ideology that punishes Black women's natural hair, features, and bodies is far from dead, even in a so-called post racial context. Blue's story underscores how Black girlhood is under constant scrutiny and attack. When the petition was released, Blue Ivy was two years old. Blue Ivy was the recipient of public shaming that many other young Black girls endure. The spectators reflect the internalized racialized sexism in their commentary about hair matters. Tolliver herself voiced a common thread in the African American community about punishing "truths"—that she's just telling it "like it is." Other famous Black girls have been degraded in similar ways by the media. Gabrielle Douglas, Olympic Gold Medalist and World Champion gymnast was sixteen when her historic first place performance at the 2012 Olympic Games was overshadowed by increasingly degrading jokes about her hair on social media (Wells 2015). There is also the Onion.com tweet about 8-year-old Quvenzhané Wallis in which she was jokingly called "kind of a c*nt" while at the Academy Awards as a nominee for Best Actress for her performance in *Beasts of the Southern Wild* (Hailey 2015). The Onion issued an apology for the joke, but the casual tone of the tweet suggests that the author was rubbed the wrong way by the confident and self-possessed Wallis.

The public and private realms are connected through official and de facto codes of conduct. Thus, the public shaming of famous Black girls is connected to the everyday lives of "regular" Black girls. The individual, structural, and institutional ways that Black girls bodies are controlled is connected by racist and sexist ideology. For instance, several Black girls in recent years have been punished in schools for the natural state of their hair, deemed distracting or inappropriate (Douglas 2013; Hobdy 2015; Clutch 2015). The U.S. Army issued policies curtailing hairstyles Black women frequently wear while serving, such as cornrows and two-strand twists (Byrd and Tharps 2014). The troubling issue with these regulations is that these hairstyles require considerable time and effort to produce. Thus, having Black hair that cannot be worn naturally and be considered neat is punishable, and remedies to both protect and tame the hair are still unacceptable. After an outcry from the Black community, arguments from Black congresswomen, and a popular sketch by comedian Jessica Williams on the *Daily Show*, the regulations were modified (Rhodan 2015). While protests against these discriminatory standards were successful, the Army attempted to exact confusing and unfair standards against Black bodies. This is the result of racialized sexism; this is trying to stand upright in a crooked room.

Black girls understand the rules of the game; the difficulties of adhering to beauty standards that privilege specific aesthetics of skin color, hair texture, and body shape while also avoiding hypersexualization. In one study, a focus group with Black teen girls revealed that they believe that white girls are less likely to be punished for showing skin because of their body shape, and more likely to be considered attractive even with "messy" hair (Lamb and Plocha 2015, 95–96). Black girls also echoed classic depictions of lightness as more beautiful than darker skin. Racialized sexism saddles Black girls with the undeserved weight of shame and unattainable beauty standards. This punishment is also preparation for degradation as Black women, and potentially, Black mothers.

Bad Black Mothers

The first comment on the "Comb her hair" petition states: "I hate when a mother looks like a million dollars with their hair all done and the child looks like they haven't seen a comb since they were born" (Toliver 2015).

Beyoncé is an idol, but she is also a mother to a Black child. Her living legend status did not protect her from racialized sexism; perhaps it even magnifies it. The media has diligently promoted confounding images of Black motherhood as capable of Mammyhood—caring for and even nursing white children, diligently, thanklessly—yet lacking the ability or desire to parent biological Black children without pathology. The media's obsession with promoting the pathology of Black mothers has treaded beyond ink and keystrokes, but is materially consequential to Black women: involuntary sterilization is a historical and contemporary truth for Black women (Roberts 1997), which some see as a strategy to prevent bad Black babies from maturing into criminals, baby machines, or government dole cheaters.

The petition reflects similar ideology of the failing and selfish Black mother. The language that the author uses points to Beyoncé as a failure because her daughter's hair, does not meet constructed standards of "good" Black hair. There are many ways that Black women are punished for parenting in ways that subjugate hegemonic ideals of beauty. Yet, white mothers are often praised for allowing their children to subvert expected norms, particularly around appearance. White mothers of Black children do not fear the same reprisal of tightly controlling their children's appearance (Cushing 2008, 96–97). The critical piece here is not that children should not be offered options, but that Black women are punished when they provide sovereignty to their children. White motherhood and Black motherhood are intertwined in this way; in order to maintain the privileged status as normal and "good," Black mothers must suffer and "be the primary targets of moral condemnation" (Geronimus 2003, 889). In the case of Blue Ivy's hair, we do not know if her hairstyle the day of the photographs was her choice or her mother's, but this petition punishes Beyoncé for an apparent dereliction of her duty.

Motherhood is a state of intense contention and contestation across race, class, and gender lines. However, there are contours of Black motherhood that are particular to the intersection of racialized sexism. In the case of Blue Ivy's body, Beyoncé has dominion and is expected to bestow presumably intrinsic gifts of beauty and grace onto her daughter. The lifestyle of royalty is central to Beyoncé and Jay-Z's image as transcendental Black Americans, crossing racial and gender lines. In this case, having any luxury that money can buy is also translated to the constantly glamorous and lavish appearance of Beyoncé's body: particularly her hair, make-up and clothing. Blue Ivy is then expected to reflect the glory of Black financial and social success.

The petition that insinuated Beyoncé was inexcusable to present her child in this way was calling attention to the force of money that can transcend— since Blue Ivy's hair was uncoiffed she was like any other Black child, who does not meet the standard of Beyoncé's image. Beyoncé's seed should only complement her presumed perfect brand and image. Blue Ivy's body is a threat to the belief that Beyoncé is a surreal superhuman Black woman—discernible connection to her Creole ethnicity complete with a French name, light-skin, mainstream beauty, wealth, and a "Beyhive" of followers ready to digitally desecrate anyone daring enough to speak out against her. Thus, from this lens Blue Ivy's body is a dangerous reminder of the fallibility of Black womanhood. From this perspective, the Black female body needs to be controlled, controlled, contained, nipped, tucked, starved, and constantly wrested into submission.

Black motherhood is constantly under attack, even when done in the name of scientific reason and the production of knowledge. For instance, one study proclaims that the achievement gap between Black men and white men is actually a byproduct of Black and white mothering differences. The solution is white women; the authors claim that white women raise Black boys who are better equipped to cultivate the necessary skills and habits that lead to success in education, employment, and wealth (Arcidiacono et al. 2015). The authors assert that parenting practices and speech, not racial discrimination, ultimately explains these differences (Arcidiacono et al. 2015). Such studies are so troubling because they perpetuate the notion that internal and external racial differences are so marked that the essence of "good" motherhood is out of reach for Black women.

From the *Moynihan Report*'s culture of poverty theory that attributed the failure of the Black family to single Black mothers, to the 1990s "crack babies" media frenzy, Black mothers loom large in the public consciousness as the source of imbalance and the downfall of Black families (Roberts 1997; Roberts 1993). Oppositional narratives have emerged in defense of Black mothers who so often take care of fictive kin and their own children while facing severe obstacles (Stack 1974). Hill Collins (2000) theorizes that even narratives of empowerment that valorize the "strong Black woman" limit recognition of Black women's oppression: "praising Black mothers for strength while not contextualizing the issues they face, the labor they routinely perform thanklessly is a different type of controlling image" (174). This image lends itself to the notion that Black women need to be self-sacrificing, and it explains why they are so ruthlessly punished by the Black community when they come up short.

Jada Pinkett-Smith, actress and wife of actor Will Smith, has been the target of online punishment for her permissive parenting style, particularly around the body of her daughter Willow, 15. Willow shaved her head at 12 and Pinkett-Smith responded to her critics, stating:

> The question why I would LET Willow cut her hair. First the LET must be challenged. This is a world where women, girls are constantly reminded that they don't belong to themselves; that their bodies are not their own, nor their power or self determination. I made a promise to endow my little girl with the power to always know that her body, spirit and her mind are HER domain. Willow cut her hair because her beauty, her value, her worth is not measured by the length of her hair. It's also a statement that claims that even little girls have the RIGHT to own themselves and should not be a slave to even their mother's deepest insecurities, hopes and desires. Even little girls should not be a slave to the preconceived ideas of what a culture believes a little girl should be. More to come. Another day [Sieczkowski 2012].

Pinkett-Smith defies both the constraints of Black motherhood and patriarchy in one fell swoop.

Black motherhood is a revolutionary act. The wholesale destruction, rape, and exploitation of Black women and the ability to parent unmolested means that to be a U.S. Black mother is to defy the dominant narrative; that Black women should not have children, nor can they properly raise Black children. Black women are held to different standards than white mothers because of racism and sexism. Therefore, this racialized sexism creates unique challenges for U.S. Black mothers, regardless of advantages such as wealth, education or ethnicity. Even Beyoncé Knowles. While many see Beyoncé as superhuman, she is also a Black mother who faces very mortal, and sometimes highly specific challenges. Critics have sought to remove Beyoncé from her experience as a mother—many media outlets frenzied to claim Beyoncé was faking her pregnancy (Cabrera 2015). Yet Beyoncé is finding ways to promote her feminist political project, not simply as a woman, but as a Black woman and mother.

On the fourteenth track of her eponymous "visual album," Beyoncé simply titles the song "Blue," and in a haunting, soothing, and loving croon across a blithe, melodious harp, Beyoncé implores her daughter to hold on to her mother, that together they can make it last forever. Her husband too has a song entitled "Blue," but Beyoncé's version feels visceral, embalmed in the sanctity between mother and child. In the music video, Beyoncé looks upon her child with the most loving gaze, lifting her high into the air. She carries her daughter on her hip, hugging her close, and closing her eyes, savoring the moment of blending her love for art and family into song. At the very end, we hear Blue's voice, a tiny voice, garbled yet filled with glee, calling out for her mommy. This song and video are divine, ensconced with love and protection.

Black mothers have a history of subverting oppression through relationships to their children (Abdullah 2012). Beyoncé is joining this long tradition, in part through activism. Since 2013, Beyoncé is a self-proclaimed feminist and using her platform to advance equality for women in society. While even her own proclamation of the label "feminist" has roused suspicion amongst white feminists and black spectators, Beyoncé's political statements are powerful as a Black mother of a Black child. Her social media campaigns, #WhatisPretty and #BanBossy challenge her fans and critics to reinterpret articulations of beauty and femininity. Beyoncé penned an open letter in the Shriver Report, arguing for women's pay equality, joining a long line of Black women who have protested unfair working conditions (Knowles-Carter 2015). As an entertainer and business mogul, Beyoncé has suffered greatly in the public eye as much as she has financially profited from it—accusations that she is a not a "real feminist" is one of the latest attacks (Johnson 2015; Fears 2014; Vagianos 2015). However, she is undeniably a feminist because she is championing justice for women covertly and overtly; when Beyoncé unapologetically posts pictures of her Black child on Instagram, she is resisting controlling images of Blue. When Beyoncé sings that "pretty hurts," she is resisting controlling images of Black women and beauty. When Beyoncé fired her father as manager and began to command her own career, including the release of her self-titled visual album without warning, Beyoncé is innovating and transgressing the racism, sexism, and capitalism that subdues Black female artists. As far as Blue, Beyoncé is a role model to her child and shamelessly in love with her child.

Conclusion

For witnesses who were hurt, confused, and angry by the petition, there are some who will minimize this as an individual act of ignorance instead of a clear example of Black women's social reality—a complex nexus of racism and sexism. To write this off as an individual act of meanness is an underestimation of Black women's barriers in society materially, emotionally, economically, and physically. A study examining interracial dating practices among college students found that Black women were the least desired racial group because of stereotypical images of the Black Bitch with "bad attitudes" (Bany, Robnett, and Feliciano 2014). Black women get paid the least of all racial and gendered groups, with the exception of non-white Hispanic women (Leber 2015). Black trans and gender-nonconforming women face alarming rates of violence, homelessness, and criminalization (Grant, Mottet, and Tanis 2011). Black women have high rates of depression and untreated mental illness, some of which is attributed to the controlling image of the "strong Black women" (Harris-Perry 2011; West 2012). Black women are more than twice as likely than white women to die at the hands of a former or current partner (Sugarmann 2013; "When Men Murder Women: An Analysis of 2011 Homicide Data" 2013). Initiatives often center the experiences of Black men and boys, and when critics respond to highlight the plight of Black girls, some Black figures stave off criticism as illegitimate (Wogan 2015; Martin 2014). Black women are expected to wait their turn, be patient, stop complaining. This happened Post-Emancipation, during Civil Rights, and especially now in a "post-racial" U.S. However, Black women continue to organize for justice, and are beginning to receive long-deserved recognition. Sandra Bland's suspicious death in a federal holding facility launched the SayHerName hashtag into transnational virality (Desmond-Harris 2015; "#SayHerName—AAPF" 2015). Largely because of the labor of Black feminists who demand that Black communities and outsiders acknowledge the harrowing barriers Black women are expected to endure silently (Croom 2015; Lemieux 2014). The extrajudicial killings of Black bodies that launched the Black Lives Matter movement is not a phenomenon only facing Black men—Black women are similarly criminalized and killed (Hamsher 2014; Blanco 2014; Cooper 2015). The unwarranted killings of innumerable Black bodies, many of them young, galvanized a new generation of Civil Rights leaders, demanding accountability for physical and mental lashings to the Black body. The founders of the Black Lives Matter movement are all queer, Black women (Garza, Tometi, and Cullors 2015). Thus, there is suppression, but there is also resistance.

In this essay, I attempted to deconstruct the "Comb her hair" petition against Blue Ivy's hair as a contemporary example of endless attempts to control and degrade the Black female body. While this act may appear singularly extreme or humorous, it is the legacy of historic treatment against the Black female body. Black women began as a vessel for capital, which transmuted into mythic, controlling images of Black femininity that smother, shame, and punish Black women. As a result, Black motherhood is pathologized and Black girlhood is arrested. Blue Ivy Knowles-Carter was targeted because Black girls' physical appearances are stringently surveilled and constricted. However, Beyoncé publicly empowers her child with unapologetic love and celebration of her Blackness. Blue Ivy inherited a beautiful and terrible legacy; a unique link to performance, art, creativity and the innovative brilliance of Blackness, but also the wounds and continued harm of racialized sexism. Nevertheless, Blue Ivy is a precious child, and a reminder of what is taken when Black girls inhabit racist and sexist social systems. Beyoncé and a legion of Black feminists continue to resist and challenge the tangled roots of racialized sexism—and that has nothing to do with the texture of Blue Ivy's hair.

REFERENCES

Abdullah, Melina. 2012. "Womanist Mothering: Loving and Raising the Revolution." *Western Journal of Black Studies* 36 (1).

Arcidiacono, Peter, Andrew Beauchamp, Marie Hull, and Seth Sanders. 2015. "Exploring the Racial Divide in Education and the Labor Market through Evidence from Interracial Families." *Journal of Human Capital* 9 (2): 198–238.

Bailey, Moya. 2010. "They Aren't Talking About Me." Crunk Feminist Collective. March 14. http://www.crunkfeministcollective.com/2010/03/14/they-arent-talking-about-me/.

Banks, Ingrid. 2000. *Hair Matters: Beauty, Power, and Black Women's Consciousness.* New York: New York University Press.

Bany, James, Belinda Robnett, and Cynthia Feliciano. 2014. "Gendered Black Exclusion: The Persistence of Racial Stereotypes Among Daters." *Race and Social Problems* 6 (3): 201–13.

Blanco, Marcie. 2014. "America Is Punishing Black Girls for Doing the Things White Girls Do All the Time." www.mic.com. December 12. http://mic.com/articles/106264/america-is-punishing-black-girls-for-things-white-girls-do-all-the-time#.Aw55ZV04l.

Bonilla-Silva, Eduardo. 2014. *Racism without Racists: Colorblind Racism and the Persistence of Racial Inequality in America.* Fourth. Lanham, MD: Rowman & Littlefield.

Byrd, Ayana, and Lori L. Tharps. 2014. "When Black Hair Is Against the Rules." *New York Times*, April 30. http://www.nytimes.com/2014/05/01/opinion/when-black-hair-is-against-the-rules.html.

Cabrera, Daniela. 2015. "Beyonce Has Been Pregnant Since September & More Absurd Rumors About Queen B." *Bustle.* Accessed December 5. http://www.bustle.com/articles/58682-beyonce-has-been-pregnant-since-september-more-absurd-rumors-about-queen-b.

Cho, Sumi, Kimberlé Williams Crenshaw, and Leslie McCall. 2013. "Toward a Field of Intersectionality Studies: Theory, Applications, and Praxis." *Signs* 38 (4): 785–810. doi:10.1086/669608.

Clutch. 2015. "Principal Pulled Eighth Grader Out of Class Because of Her 'Poofy' Natural Hair." *Clutch* Magazine. Accessed December 5. http://www.clutchmagonline.com/2015/11/principal-pulled-eighth-grader-out-of-class-because-of-her-poofy-natural-hair/.

Collins, Patricia Hill. 2000. *Black Feminist Thought: Knowledge, Consciousness, and the Politics of Empowerment.* Second. New York: Routledge.

_____. 2004. *Black Sexual Politics: African Americans, Gender, and the New Racism.* New York: Routledge.

Cooper, Brittney. 2015. "She Was Guilty of Being a Black Girl: The Mundane Terror of Police Violence in American Schools–Salon.com." *Salon.* October 28. http://www.salon.com/2015/10/28/she_was_guilty_of_being_a_black_girl_the_mundane_terror_of_police_violence_in_american_schools/.

Crenshaw, Kimberlé. 1991. "Mapping the Margins: Intersectionality, Identity Politics, and Violence against Women of Color." *Stanford Law Review* 43 (6): 1241–99. doi:10.2307/1229039.

Croom, Phyllis. 2015. "Say Her Name: Billie Holiday and the Erasure of Black Women's Experience." *The American Prospect.* July 1. http://prospect.org/article/say-her-name-billie-holiday-and-erasure-of-black-womens-experience.

Davis, Angela. 1993. "Outcast Mothers and Surrogates: Racism and Reproductive Politics in the Nineties." In *American Feminist Thought: At Century's End: A Reader*, edited by Linda S. Kauffman. Cambridge, MA: Blackwell.

Desmond-Harris, Jenee. 2015. "#SayHerName Project Explained | PopularResistance.Org." *Popular Resistance*. May 29. https://www.popularresistance.org/sayhername-project-explained/.

Douglas, Deborah. 2013. "Why Are Black Women Punished for Having Natural Hair?" *AlterNet*. December 3. http://www.alternet.org/civil-liberties/stop-policing-my-hair-when-black-girls-shine-we-shine.

Durham, Aisha. 2012. "Check on It: Beyoncé, Southern Booty, and Black Femininities in Music Video." *Feminist Media Studies* 12 (1): 35–49.

Feagin, Joe R. 2010. *The White Racial Frame: Centuries of Racial Framing and Counter Framing*. New York: Routledge.

Fears, Niki. 2014. "Annie Lennox Slams Beyonce for Fake Feminism." *Inquisitr*. October 22. http://www.inquisitr.com/1555590/annie-lennox-slams-beyonce-for-fake-feminism/.

Garza, Alicia, Opal Tometi, and Patrisse Cullors. 2015. "Herstory | Black Lives Matter." *Black Lives Matter*. Accessed December 6. http://blacklivesmatter.com/herstory/.

Grant, Janet, Lisa Mottet, and Justin Tanis. 2011. "Injustice at Every Turn: A Report of the National Transgender Discrimination Survey." Washington, D.C.: National Center for TransgenderEquality and National Gay and Lesbian Taskforce. http://endtransdiscrimination.org/PDFs/BlackTransFactsheetFINAL_090811.pdf.

Hailey, Jonathan. 2015. "The Onion Calls Quvenzhane Wallis a 'C*nt.'" *The Urban Daily*. Accessed December 5. http://theurbandaily.com/2013/02/25/the-onion-quvenzhane-wallis-cunt/.

Hamsher, Jane. 2014. "The Real 'Orange Is the New Black': Women Are the Fastest Growing Prison Population—Shadowproof." *Shadow Proof*. June 9. https://shadowproof.com/2014/06/09/the-real-orange-is-the-new-black-women-are-the-fastest-growing-prison-population/.

Harris-Perry, Melissa. 2011. *Sister Citizen: Shame, Stereotypes, and Black Women in America*. New Haven: Yale University Press.

Hobdy, Dominique. 2015. "Florida School Threatens to Expel African-American Girl for Wearing Natural Hair." www.essence.com. Accessed December 5. http://www.essence.com/2013/11/26/florida-school-threatens-expel-african-american-girl-wearing-natural-hair.

Hobson, Janell. 2005. *Venus in the Dark: Blackness and Beauty in Popular Culture*. New York: Routledge.

_____. 2012. *Body as Evidence: Mediating Race, Globalizing Gender*. Albany: State University of New York Press.

hooks, bell. 1981. *Ain't I a Woman: Black Women and Feminism*. Winchester, MA: Pluto Press.

_____. 2015. "No Love in the Wild." *NewBlackMan (in Exile)*. Accessed November 25. http://www.newblackmaninexile.net/2012/09/bell-hooks-no-love-in-wild.html.

Hull, Gloria T., Patricia Bell Scott, and Barbara Smith. 1982. *But Some of Us Are Brave: Black Women's Studies*. Old Westbury, NY: Feminist Press.

Johnson, Maisha. 2015. "Men Like How I Dance, and Other Racist Reasons to Question My Feminism." *BGD*. Accessed December 5. http://www.blackgirldangerous.org/2015/01/men-like-dance-racist-reasons-question-feminism/.

Keith, Verna M., and Cedric Herring. 1991. "Skin Tone and Stratification in the Black Community." *American Journal of Sociology* 97 (3): 760–78.

Knowles-Carter, Beyonce. 2015. "The Shriver Report—Gender Equality Is a Myth!" Accessed December 5. http://shriverreport.org/gender-equality-is-a-myth-bey once/.

Lamb, Sharon, and Aleksandra Plocha. 2015. "Pride and Sexiness: Girls of Color Discuss Race, Body Image, and Sexualization." *Girlhood Studies* 8 (2).

Leber, Rebecca. 2015. "The Gender Pay Gap Is Bad. The Gender Pay Gap for Women of Color Is Even Worse." *New Republic*. April 14. https://newrepublic.com/article/ 121530/women-color-make-far-less-78-cents-mans-dollar.

Lemieux, Jamilah. 2014. "Black Feminism Goes Viral." *Ebony*. March 3. http://www. ebony.com/news-views/black-feminism-goes-viral-045#axzz2zkm0pTID.

Martinot, Steven. 2007. "Motherhood and the Invention of Race." *Hypatia, the Reproduction of Whiteness: Race and the Regulation of the Gendered Body* 22 (2): 79–97.

Martin, Roland. 2014. "Black Elites Look Silly Over 'My Brother's Keeper' Criticism on Creators.com." www.creators.com. August 8. http://www.creators.com/ opinion/roland-martin/black-elites-look-silly-over-my-brothers-keeper-criti cism.html.

Omi, Michael, and Howard Winant. 2015. *Racial Formation in the United States: From the 1960s to the 1990s*. Third. New York: Routledge.

Phoenix, Aisha. 2014. "Colourism and the Politics of Beauty." *Feminist Review*, 97–105.

Rhodan, Maya. 2015. "U.S. Military Rolls Back Restrictions on Black Hairstyles." www.time.com. Accessed December 5. http://time.com/3107647/military-black-hairstyles/.

Roberts, Dorothy. 1993. "Racism and Patriarchy in the Meaning of Motherhood." *Journal of Gender and Law* 1 (1): 1–38.

_____. 1997. *Killing the Black Body: Race, Reproduction, and the Meaning of Liberty*. New York: Knopf Doubleday Publishing Group.

Rogers, Jazmine Denise. 2014. "Petition Creator Who Urged Beyoncé to Comb Blue Ivy's Hair Claims She Was 'Joking' | MadameNoire." *MadameNoire*. June 17. http://madamenoire.com/439626/petition-creator-urged-beyonce-comb-blue-ivys-hair-claims-joking/.

"#SayHerName—AAPF." 2015. http://www.aapf.org/sayhername/.

Seccombe, Karen, Delores James, and Kimberly Battle Walters. 1998. "'They Think You Ain't Much of Nothing': The Social Construction of the Welfare Mother." *Journal of Marriage and Family* 60 (4): 849–65. doi:10.2307/353629.

Sewell, Christopher J.P. 2012. "Mammies and Matriarchs: Tracing Images of the Black Female in Popular Culture 1950s to Present." *Journal of African American Studies* 17 (3): 308–26. doi:10.1007/s12111-012-9238-x.

Sieczkowski, Cavan. 2012. "Jada Pinkett Smith Blasts Critics of Daughter Willow's Hair." *The Huffington Post*. November 29. http://www.huffingtonpost.com/2012/ 11/27/jada-pinkett-smith-willow-smith-hair-critics-girls-should-not-be-a-slave-facebook_n_2198183.html.

Simmons, Anita. 2008. "Black Womanhood, Misogyny, and Hip-Hop Culture: A Feminist Intervention." *Cultural Studies Association* 1 (2): 27–48.

Smith, Monesca. 2015. "The Blacker the Berry?" *Journal of Colorism Studies* 1 (1): 1–4.

Stack, Carol B. 1974. *All Our Kin: Strategies for Survival in a Black Community*. New York: Basic Books.

Sugarmann, Josh. 2013. "Black Women Face a Greater Risk of Domestic Violence."

The Huffington Post. October 14. http://www.huffingtonpost.com/josh-sugar mann/black-women-face-a-greate_b_4157659.html.

"The Vanishing Family—Crisis in Black America." 1986. *Bill Moyers 1986 Special Report.* CBS.

Toliver, Jasmine. 2015. "Blue Ivy: Comb Her Hair." *Change.org.* Accessed December 5. https://www.change.org/p/blue-ivy-comb-her-hair.

Trudy. 2015. "Explanation of Misogynoir." *Gradient Lair.* Accessed November 6. http://www.gradientlair.com/post/84107309247/define-misogynoir-anti-black-misog yny-moya-bailey-coined.

Vagianos, Alanna. 2015. "Why Beyoncé's Latest 'Feminist' Move Was So Problematic." *The Huffington Post.* September 10. http://www.huffingtonpost.com/entry/why-beyonces-latest-feminist-move-was-so-problematic_55eee575e4b093be51bc05aa.

Wagner, Laura. 2015. "Miss America Pageant Apologizes to 1983 Winner Vanessa Williams." Accessed November 6. about:reader?url=http percent3A percent2F percent2Fwww.npr.org percent2Fsections percent2Fthetwo-way percent2F2015 percent2F09 percent2F14 percent2F440274068 percent2Fmiss-america-pageant-apologizes-to-1983-winner-vanessa-williams.

Wells, Veronica. 2015. "Cut It Out! The Ridiculous Discussion Surrounding Gabby Douglas' Hair." *MadameNoire.* Accessed December 5. http://madamenoire.com/202014/cut-it-out-the-ridiculous-discussion-surrounding-gabby-douglas-hair/.

West, Carolyn. 2012. "Mammy, Jezebel, Sapphire and Their Homegirls: Developing an 'Oppositional Gaze' Toward the Images of Black Women." In *Lectures on the Psychology of Women.* Fourth. 286–99. New York: McGraw Hill.

"When Men Murder Women: An Analysis of 2011 Homicide Data." 2013. Washington, D.C.: Violence Policy Center. http://www.vpc.org/studies/wmmw2013.pdf.

Wogan, JB. 2015. "My Brother's Keeper Is Great, but What About the Girls?" *Governing.* May 15. http://www.governing.com/topics/urban/gov-brothers-keeper-black-girls-obama.html.

BDSM, Gazes and Wedding Rings
The Centering of Black Female Pleasure and Agency in Beyoncé

EVETTE DIONNE BROWN

Beyoncé is a popular culture phenomenon. With more than 115 million albums sold (Menza 2014), international tours that sell out in mere moments (Sosa 2013), and a Super Bowl halftime performance that was watched by 104 million viewers (Gallo 2014), Beyoncé is one of the most influential, successful and recognizable entertainers in the world. On December 13, 2013, Beyoncé released her eponymous fifth album with no promotion, fanfare, or warning while she was traveling for the Mrs. Carter Show World Tour (Menza 2014). The unexpected release of 14 new songs and 17 associated videos ushered in a new era of promoting and releasing albums (Menza 2014).

The release of *Beyoncé* also situated her in the musical tradition of Black feminist pop stars. *Beyoncé* is Beyoncé's Black feminist opus. Through visuals for multiple songs, including "Blow," "Partition," and "Yoncé," Beyoncé articulates a black feminist commitment to liberation via the politics of pleasure. The politics of pleasure is an emerging framework within the Black feminist thought tradition, which centers pleasure as an ingress to a Black feminist identity. Through a textual analysis of "Blow," "Haunted," "Drunk in Love," "Partition," and "Yoncé," I aim to use a hip-hop Black feminist lens to explore how Beyoncé's fifth album is a subversive musical triumph that resists trauma as an entrance point to Black feminist identity.

In an effort to examine Beyoncé's fifth album as a hip-hop Black feminist text, I will first position Beyoncé as a hip-hop Black feminist pop star thorough a chronological explanation of her tenuous relationship with the term "feminist" and her continuous process to strengthen her Black feminist commitments. Then, I will utilize a literature review to place Beyoncé in the context of other hip-hop Black feminist pop stars, including Janet Jackson, Nicki Minaj, and Rihanna, who have illuminated issues at the intersections of race and gender through the lens of pleasure. Black feminist thought, and hip-hop Black feminism as its offspring, will then be positioned and justified as the theoretical lens through which Beyoncé's fifth album will be explored. A thematic dissection of five videos from *Beyoncé* will be used to analyze how the overall album is a Black feminist text. Ultimately, this research explores how Beyoncé uses music to situate herself as a hip-hop Black feminist with a concentrated commitment to fore fronting pleasure. An analysis of *Beyoncé* will further popular culture as a contested, but rich, site of Black feminist inquiry while also exploring how the politics of pleasure are critical to imagining liberation for Black women.

Beyoncé's Feminist Evolution

From the start of her career, Beyoncé has written and performed music that emboldens women to assert their control. As the lead singer in female R&B group, Destiny's Child, Beyoncé explored themes ranging from financial independence (Bills, Bills, Bills) to surviving emotional abuse in intimate relationships (Girl). Once she launched a career as a soloist in 2003, Beyoncé continued to explore empowerment through music, releasing hits like "Single Ladies," which focused on a woman rebounding after a breakup, and "Kitty Kat," an ode to withholding intimacy when a relationship begins to sour. In particular, Beyoncé's second album, *B'Day*, was her first to explore the "ever-sophisticated range of emotions tied to Black women's personal and spiritual discontent, satiation, self-worth, and agency" (Brooks 2008, 183).

Despite her commitment to uplifting women through her work, and employing an all-female band, Beyoncé was hesitant to publicly identify as a feminist, and even more reluctant to emerge as a Black feminist pop star. In an interview with *British Vogue* in 2013, Beyoncé's response to a question about labeling herself as a feminist was telling.

> That word can be very extreme. But I guess I am a modern-day feminist. I do believe in equality. Why do you have to choose what type of woman you are? Why do you have to label yourself anything? I'm just a woman and I love being a woman. I do believe in equality and that we have a way to go and it's something that's pushed aside and something that we have been conditioned to accept. But I'm happily married. I love my husband [Ellison 2013].

Her response exposed the ahistorical dichotomy between feminist identification and sustaining significant relationships with the opposite sex. Despite her initial hesitance, Beyoncé's stance on feminism evolved. In an interview with *The Daily Mail* in 2010, Beyoncé revealed that she considers herself somewhat feminist.

> I think I am a feminist, in a way. It's not something I consciously decided I was going to be; perhaps it's because I grew up in a singing group with other women, and that was so helpful to me," she told the magazine. "It kept me out of so much trouble and out of bad relationships. My friendships with my girls are just so much a part of me that there are things I am never going to do that would upset that bond. I never want to betray that friendship, because I love being a woman and I love being a friend to other women [Gordon 2010].

In *Yours and Mine*, a short autobiographical film, Beyoncé explained her tenuous relationship with the term "feminist" and what it represents.

> I've always considered myself a feminist, although I was always afraid of that word because people put so much on it. When honestly, it's very simple. It's just a person that believes in equality for men and women. Men and women balance each other out, and we have to get to a point where we are comfortable with appreciating each other.

Beyoncé's public claiming of the term feminism reached its apex in 2014 at MTV's Video Music Awards (Traister 2014). In the middle of an unprecedented 15-minute performance of her fifth album, Beyoncé stood before an emblazoned pink image of the word "feminist" as Nigerian author, Chimamanda Ngozi Adichie, spewed the textbook definition of the word (Bennett 2014; Traister 2014). In that moment, Beyoncé claimed feminism as an integral aspect of her identity and relinquished her previous hesitance to embrace the term (Traister 2014). The response from self-identified feminist writers, critics, and theorists was immediate. Writer Rebecca Traister declared it the most feminist moment of her lifetime, writing that her performance "showed a woman of color as a sexually confident, high-octane talent and as a powerful business woman, as an adoring mother and an equal partner" (Traister 2014). In an evolution of her public persona as a feminist, Beyoncé also appeared on the cover of *Ms.* magazine, which is considered a flagship feminist publication, where she was described as a feminist with immense power "to delight in one's beauty and sexuality" (Hobson 2015). She also appeared in the Ban Bossy campaign where she proclaimed that she's not bossy, but is instead, the boss. Beyoncé's also emerged as a Black feminist concerned with gun violence as well as the gender wage gap (Wallace 2013). For the Shriver Report, Beyoncé wrote about the widening pay gap between men and women in the workforce. "Women are more than 50 percent of the population and more than 50 percent of voters. We must demand that we all receive 100 percent of the opportunities" (Knowles-Carter 2014). Beyoncé also expressed similar sentiments in GQ when she said, "Let's face it, money gives men the power to run the show. It gives men the power to define value" (Wallace 2013).

Given Beyoncé's embodiment of feminism as both an interpersonal and political commitment, academic discourse has emerged in multiple disciplines, including women's studies, communication studies, and performance studies. "Politicizing Beyoncé: Black Feminism, U.S. politics, and Queen Bey" is a course offered at Rutgers University (Winsor 2014). The course utilizes black feminist thought to examine how Beyoncé resists and reifies stereotypes with her lyrics and music videos (Winsor 2014). However, Beyoncé's emergence as a political figure also opens her to feminist criticism, which has been leveraged against her for not challenging power structures, specifically capitalism.

Black feminist theorist, bell hooks, said Beyoncé's image, which includes trademark blonde-weaved tresses, is "in service of imperialist, white supremacist capitalist patriarchy" because it doesn't challenge dominant ideals of whiteness as a beauty standard (hooks, Mock, Lynch, and Blackman 2014). When referencing Beyoncé's portrait on the cover of *Time*, hooks referred to her as both anti-feminist and a terrorist who is "colluding in the construction of herself as a slave" (hooks, Mock, Lynch, and Blackman 2014). Other feminist writers have also criticized Beyoncé for not challenging the racial hierarchy that values whiteness at the expense of Black women as well as her decision to reveal outfits in an attempt to appeal to the male gaze (Ball 2013; Freeman 2013; Winfrey-Harris 2013). In an essay for *Madame Noire*, Ball writes that *Beyoncé* is "a pageantry of opulence and extravagance" that upholds the power of the wealthy instead of challenging it (Ball 2013).

Black feminism makes space for accountability, which is the reason why Beyoncé deserves critique. As a wealthy, heterosexual, and cisgender Black woman, Beyoncé occupies a contentious space where she simultaneously marginalized and privileged (Winfrey-Harris 2013). However, Beyoncé's fifth album offers pleasure as an alternative entrance into Black feminist Thought, which is worthy of exploration. In contextualizing her significance among Black feminist musicians, it is possible to explore the grayness of Black feminism that Beyoncé exists in.

Beyoncé in the Lineage of Black Feminist Pop Stars

Beyoncé's fifth album places her in a growing legion of U.S. Black American singers, including her contemporaries like Rihanna and Nicki Minaj, who are read as Black feminists (Beaudoin 2015; Blay 2015; Carroll 2015; Givhan 2014). Hip-hop black feminist scholars, including Durham (2012) and Hobson (2015), see Beyoncé as a disruptor tasked with wrecking essentialist Black feminist concepts in order to forge her own interpretation of liberation. Beyoncé's a member of a tradition of pop stars who recognize pleasure as a critical piece of liberation and assert that within their music through audacious discussions of sexual pleasure; the empowerment of other women through the rejection of the male gaze; and the illumination of social issues that have a disproportionate impact on Black women. In particular, multiple scholars trace the origins of pleasure as a Black feminist commitment within popular culture to Janet Jackson.

When Jackson released her third album, *Control,* in 1986, it was a declaration of her independence. In opposition to the safer and more acceptable music from her first two musical efforts, Jackson's *Control* positioned her as a woman in complete control of her sexual autonomy, leading Smith (2014) to dub it "the album that launched a thousand feminist music careers" (Smith 2014, 1). Her first single, "What Have You Done for Me Lately," was an ode to separating from a partner whose complacent in the relationship. The subsequent single, "Nasty" narrated a particular incident when Jackson was harassed outside of a hotel she was residing in while recording her album. When asked about what motivated her to record and release "Nasty," Jackson said the song was "born out of a sense of self-defense" after she felt sexually threatened and emotionally abused (Ritz 1993). In addition to exploring relationship issues, *Control* is the album that "helped redefine what it meant to be a Black female superstar, and arguably, a Black superstar period" (Smith 2014).

One vital aspect of the reimaging of the Black female superstar as Black feminist is a keen focus on sex that is consensual and fulfilling (Hobson 2003; Lindsey 2013). In choosing to embrace sexual desire as critical to their performance as entertainers and Black women, Black feminist pop stars signal "a subversion, and arguably, an outright rejection of gendered racial and sexual stereotypes about Black women" (Lindsey 2013, 56). In her exploration of singers Ciara and Kelly Rowland's sexual expressivity in their discographies, Lindsey (2013) finds that Black feminist pop stars transgress the boundaries that have surrounded Black female sexuality since slavery. In doing so, these Black feminist pop stars create space to theorize Black female pleasure (Lindsey 2013). For Jackson, bold sexuality is integral to her performance as a Black feminist pop star (Vogel 2014). In a 1993 cover story of *Rolling Stone,* Jackson described her album, *janet,* as one about "a woman who finally feels good enough about her sexuality to demand a man's respect" (Ritz 1993). "If," one of the signature songs on *janet,* is a about a woman fantasizing about what she'd like to do sexually to a man in a committed relationship if she were given an opportunity (Ritz 1993). In *janet,* Jackson "announced herself as a sexual agent" (Cliff 2015). In a 1993 *Rolling Stone* cover story, Jackson said:

> On a psychological level, though, good sex, satisfying sex, is also linked with losing yourself, releasing, using your body to get out of your body. Well, for the first time, I'm feeling free. I love feeling deeply sexual—and don't mind letting

the world know. For me, sex has become a celebration, a joyful part of the creative process [Ritz 1993].

Janet Jackson's unflinching sexual expression translated to subsequent musical acts, like R&B trio TLC, who "offered a unique demonstration of feminist-minded principles within the mainstream music industry's confines" (Mastrangelo 2013). Their first single, "Ain't Too Proud to Beg," was specifically about not being ashamed of wanting sex. In "Red Light Special," a song about an intimate night with a beau, TLC demanded sexual satisfaction from their partners. On "Girl Talk," the lead single from their fourth album, TLC lambasts egotistical men who brag about their sexual skills, but aren't fulfilling their partners in the bedroom. Not only does "Girl Talk" signal that women can be unapologetically sexual, it also flips the script so women are positioned in control of sexual encounters (Mastrangelo 2013). Sex-positivism "accounts for women making decisions about their sexual selves and self-identifications based upon their desires to engage or not engage in sexual activity," which has been integral to the politics of black feminist pop stars (Lindsey 2013, 58).

Demanding sexual gratification has been essential to rapper Nicki Minaj's entertainment career (Frank 2015; Rio 2015; Willoughby 2015). Minaj's bravado, within her lyrics, videos and performances, commands the reduction of the male gaze and re-centers her desires as paramount to her relationships (Rio 2015). In an interview with *Cosmopolitan*, Minaj said, "I demand that I climax. I think women should demand that" (Sandell 2015). Her comments echo Jackson's, who said in her 1993 *Rolling Stone* profile, "Women want satisfaction. And so do men. But to get it, you must ask for it. Know what you need. Say what you want. Sexual communication is the name of the game" (Ritz 1993).

The release of Minaj's "Anaconda," a song celebrating derrieres, prompted a frenzy of feminist dialog around acceptable and respectable expressions of sexuality (Rio 2014; Smith 2014). "Anaconda" was brash and defiant by rejecting the male gaze and focusing on Black female sexuality (Rio 2014). Yet, the response to "Anaconda" was a power struggle over who gets to control Black female bodies (Smith 2014). In the video, Minaj is in complete control of her sexuality, a feat that guides multiple Black feminist pop stars, including Ciara.

In her analysis of Ciara's "Ride" video, which was banned from Black Entertainment Television for being too provocative, Lindsey (2013) finds that the video received backlash because it positioned Ciara as a protagonist in control of her desires. Despite these responses, Black feminist pop stars continue rejecting the hetero-male gaze. When asked in a 2014 *Rolling Stone* profile about the response to "Anaconda," Minaj said, "I'm a grown-ass fucking woman! I stand for girls wanting to be sexy and dance, but also having a strong sense of themselves" (Rolling Stone 2014). Essentially, the work of Ciara, TLC, Janet Jackson, and Nicki Minaj shifts the role of black female musicians from reproducing controlling images to establishing of "sex-positive, African-American female-authored sites of sensual, erotic, and sexual expressivity" (Lindsey 2013, 60).

Social Justice as a Musical Responsibility

On her classic 1989 release *Rhythm Nation 1814*, Jackson explored multiple intersectional feminist themes, including racial discrimination, homophobia, and socioeconomic classism. Janet Jackson uses music to transform "communal suffering into communal power" (Vogel 2014). In his research on Jackson's transcendent musical influence, Vogel (2014) compares *Rhythm Nation 1814* to Marvin Gaye's iconic album *What's Going On* because both records "fused the personal and the political." *The Velvet Rope*, Jackson's 1997 album, also discussed depression and domestic violence, which continued her history of producing socially-conscious music (Smith 2014).

Merging the personal and political is standard within the discographies of black feminist pop stars. From the onset of their careers, TLC developed a reputation for being socially conscious (Mastrangelo 2013). Often, the three group members donned condoms as eye-patches to raise awareness about HIV. Their music also addressed political topics, including HIV, street harassment, and unrealistic beauty ideals (Mastrangelo 2013). R&B singer Rihanna, who also exists in contentious black feminist space, addressed rape in the lyrics and video for her song "Man Down." In the video, Rihanna stars at the protagonist who is raped after she dances with her rapist in a club. Rihanna chooses to shoot her attacker, which "reinforces a very basic point: the choice to be sexual and sensual on the dance floor should not be read in any way as consent for future sexual activity" (Crunk Feminist Collective 2011).

Rihanna also evokes her agency in the controversial "BBHMM" video, which posits her as a woman who opts to kidnap another woman whose husband owes her money. The video is graphic and violent, which led some white feminists to deem it repulsive and anti-feminist (Lewis 2015; McVeigh and Helmore 2015; Vine 2015). Despite the woman-on-woman violence depicted in the video, Carroll (2015) declares the video feminist because it illuminates a Black woman placing her needs over a white woman and also explores the way state-sanctioned violence impacts black women. Positioning Black feminist thought, and subsequently, hip-hop black feminism, as a theoretical lens to explore Beyoncé's role as a Black feminist figure further expands upon the complexity of Black feminist pop stars.

Black Feminist Thought as Theory

Black feminist thought (BFT) is a theoretical and sociopolitical lens created to resist the erasure of U.S. Black American women at the intersections of race and gender (Hill Collins 1986). Arising from mainstream feminism's second wave, BFT is rooted in the "outsider within" (Hill Collins 1986, 15) epistemologies of U.S. Black American women. To acknowledge oppressions as multiplicative rather than additive, BFT locates and centers multiple Black American female voices.

To resist dominant constructions of Black female personhood, BFT is concerned with several core tenets, including centering Black women's lives, voices and experiences; encouraging self-definition; recognizing the interlocking nature of oppressions; building stable and interdependent coalitions among marginalized groups; and challenging systemic power wherever and however it appears (Hill Collins 1990). Rooted in the encouragement of self-definition and recognition of oppression on the micro and macro levels, BFT challenges controlling images. Patricia Hill-Collins contends that controlling images or "portraying African-American women as stereotypical mammies, matriarch, welfare recipients and hot mommas" (1990, 76) justifies the oppression of Black women across the intersections of gender, race and class. Controlling images were created in slavery, and are still circulated to present social issues like poverty and racism as "natural, normal and inevitable parts of everyday life" (77).

The jezebel pinpoints black women as hyper and deviant (Hill Collins 2009). The creation of the jezebel was used to justify the sexual terrorism committed against Black women during slavery (hooks 1981; Hill Collins 1990). Black women were accused of seducing their owners, while simultaneously repulsing them. This allowed white men to escape legal prosecution. The historical caricature of U.S. Black American women as hypersexualized is still circulated and reinforced through multiple vehicles. Black feminist thought is a plausible framework for theorizing Black female sexuality given its commitment to self-definition and intersectionality. However, BFT's rooting in the second-wave limits its ability to locate pleasure in the Black female body without first necessitating pain and oppression. Hip-hop feminism offers a bridge between complex Black sexual politics and feminism that can be used to analyze Beyoncé.

Bridging the Gap between BFT and Hip-Hop Feminism

Hip-hop feminism is a branch on the genealogical tree of Black American feminisms that includes BFT (Morgan 1999; Durham, Cooper & Morris

2013). The centering of Black female epistemologies creates a dialogical relationship between BFT and hip-hop feminism; however, their respective rooting in the second-wave and third-wave alters the usage of the two frames (Durham, Cooper & Morris 2013). Aisha Durham, Brittney Cooper and Susana Morris (2013) refer to the disruption of hip-hop in feminism as percussive, or the "striking of one body with or against another with some degree of force, so as to give a shock; impact; a stroke, blow, knock" (724).

Percussive feminist models, like hip-hop feminism, entertain contradiction as a legitimate space for sociopolitical inquiry. Hip-hop feminism disrupts second-wave conceptualizations of good or bad feminist identities. Instead of conforming to a feminist essentialism, hip-hop generation feminists embrace "feminism brave enough to fuck with the grays" (Morgan 1999, 59). Hip-hop feminism recognizes the racialized patriarchy that pathologizes Black womanhood, but challenges feminists to exact their agency. So, hip-hop feminism negates victimhood as an origin of feminist thought (Durham, Cooper & Morris 2013; Morgan 1999). Hip-hop feminism is concerned with strengthening female agency; using hip-hop as one of several complex avenues for Black American women to locate their voice; and offering space for women to "talk back" (hooks 1992, 9) to multiplicative oppressions. Given the commitment of hip-hop feminism to advocating for paradoxical, hip-hop feminism can be situated to theorize pleasure as a political act of reclamation. Subsequently, I will utilize hip-hop Black feminism to analyze how Beyoncé's fifth album forefronts pleasure through the queering of desire; a keen focus on butts; and the embrace of marriage.

Beyoncé *as a Hip-hop Black Feminist Pleasure Text*

Queering, or "a position opposed to normative heterosexual regimes," is essential to developing a politics of pleasure within Black feminist thought (Harris 1996, 4). In calling for an interrogation of how Black female eroticism has been policed across the intersections of race, gender, and heterosexuality, queering offers a framework for Black feminists to define their sexuality outside of standard markers of femininity, Blackness, and heteronormativity (Harris 1996). Queering acknowledges and resists the limitations imposed on Black female eroticism (Harris 1996). In an effort to unlink trauma and violence from the historical and contemporary sexual lives of Black women, agency is at the forefront of the pleasure politic (Morgan 2015). Agency affords Black women space to define their sexuality instead of having it defined for them (Smith 1977; Harris 1996; Morgan 2015).

I experience Beyoncé's fifth album as an audacious and brash queering of desire and pleasure. *Beyoncé* is an acknowledgement of the impact of racialized sexism on Black female sexual expression and a brazen unwillingness to conform to respectability. Through the themes of her music, and the accompanying visuals, Beyoncé situates herself, her marriage, and her desires as a critical aspect of her Black feminist politic. Sex, in particular, "is the most obvious terrain on which Beyoncé challenges boundaries between self and other" (Lordi 2013). Instead of subscribing to a chaste ideology that values modesty above pleasure, Beyoncé's fifth album is as Brittney Cooper explains, "asking us to think about what it means for Black women to be sexual on our own terms" (Qureshi 2013). "Drunk in Love," "Blow," "Partition," "Rocket," and "Yoncé" are all unflinching explorations into sexual pleasure. "Drunk in Love" is an ode to drunken sex while "Rocket" is about utilizing sex as an act of appreciation within a functional relationship. "Blow," "Partition," and "Yoncé" are brazen explorations of sexual acts, most implicitly, oral sex.

The queering of desire dominates the visuals for the song, "Haunted," which is about the ghosts that tend to hover over the memories of previous relationships. In the "Haunted" video, Beyoncé pulls up to a mansion in a green vintage automobile stuffed with luggage, as if she plans to remain in the mansion for an extended period. She's adorned in a white fur coat and black pumps and her hair is styled in fingerwaves. She approaches the door with her baggage and drops it as soon as she crosses the threshold. A butler lights a cigarette for her as she eyes him and then she tosses the cigarettes on the ground and crushes it. The opening scene reinforces the notion that Beyoncé has complete ownership over herself, her actions, and the actions of those in her orbit.

It is soon revealed that Beyoncé is in a whorehouse and she assumes the role of a madam who finds pleasure in her role as the orchestrator of the mansion. Evidenced by the crown that she adorns throughout the video, Beyoncé is ruler of this sexual domain. There's a different scene in each room Beyoncé walks past. Three women are performing a lap dance in one room while another woman, wearing pasties, is painting herself with black latex. Though Beyoncé is in control of the mansion, she's not an active participant in the sexual acts. Yet, the sexual scenes are interspersed with dance scenes that Beyoncé participates in. In one of the rooms, Beyoncé and several dancers are thrusting in rhythm to the music. Beyoncé is also solo in another room where she's sticking her butt out and gyrating on a couch. Though she isn't involved in the explicit sexual acts in other rooms, where money is exchanged between sex workers and patrons, Beyoncé is of this element. She's the maestro, so incorporating BDSM as well as sex work into the visuals for "Haunted" is an explicit act of agency.

Queering desire also includes the rejection of heterosexuality as default sexual orientation. In the video for "Yoncé," a song about asserting authority in the music business as well as sexual relationships, Beyoncé enlists the assistance of three supermodels, Chanel Iman, Joan Smalls, and Jourdan Dunn, to subvert heterosexuality as natural order. The "Yoncé" video has no particular plot, but instead, focuses on the four women finding pleasure in each other. The camera cuts between specific body parts, like the lips, teeth, and breasts, as the models gaze lustfully at Beyoncé. One model licks Beyoncé's breast as she stares at the camera. The video is very homoerotic. It bends patriarchal heteronormativity and centers the desires of the women. Even as they walk down the street together and Beyoncé squeezes on her breasts, it's about the women. Men are an afterthought in *Beyoncé*, though there is a simultaneously intense focus on marriage as an integral component to Beyoncé's Black feminism. The video for "Blow," a song about receiving satisfying oral sex, is set in a skating rink. When Beyoncé walks in, an afro-clad man attempts to grab her arm in an effort to gain her attention. She's uninterested and quickly pulls her arm out of his grasp. Refusing to be harassed, she proceeds to skate and dance with other women, implying that the solidarity she shares with them matters more than the appeal of male attention.

The Booty

Pleasure is articulated through a multitude of visual means, including a keen focus on the movement of booties. Aisha Durham coins American culture's fascination with booties as a "backward gaze" that demonizes racially-marked signs of "exotic beauty and primitive sexuality in the Western imagination" (Durham 2012, 38). The backward gaze is designed to reduce Black American women to the sum of their body parts, but when Beyoncé finds pleasure in gazing at and moving her butt it's a rejection of the racialized sexism that functions to shame her into respectable submission. It also functions as a rejection of the hetero-male gaze.

Throughout the "Haunted" video, Beyoncé is surveilled through video cameras. The entire time, it appears as if Beyoncé is being surveilled. We see her through a bird's eye views, both through an overhead camera as well as on a television. In these moments, Beyoncé is viewing herself through the glare of the television and the surveillance camera. She signifies that her gaze is most important, which rejects the heteronormative male gaze that often dominates the construction of Black female pop stars (Durham 2012). Throughout *Beyoncé*, "Beyoncé works to redefine the engagement with her body" (Durham 2012, 43), and that often appears through keen focus on the significance of Beyoncé's gaze as most important. In "Partition," the entire video is shot from Beyoncé's perspective. There's a striking scene in "Partition" where Beyoncé is sitting backward on the edge of a black stage, so the camera is situated on her buttocks. As the camera pans her ass, she rubs over her back and waist. Though this scene could be read as an act of objectification, since the camera is focusing on a singular part of Beyoncé's body instead of her entire being, she subverts that idea by donning a smile and continuously throwing her head back in ecstasy.

Aisha Durham (2012) sees Beyoncé's engagement with her butt as a revolutionary act. She writes "her signature dance is in part a reclamation of the Black booty that is prevalent in vernacular culture throughout the African diaspora," since "looking at one's self challenges the male gaze where the booty—or the batty—is reserved for male erotic pleasure only" (Durham 2012, 43). In "Partition," there's an emphasis on specific body parts—like the ass, the lips, and the breasts, which are all considered sexualized sections of women's bodies. The fragmenting of Black female bodies has historically been used to disenfranchise Black women (Balaji 2010).

We become defined and labeled by our body parts, reinforcing the racialized patriarchy that led to the enslavement of Sarah Baartman. However, Black American women can and should reclaim our bodies as sexual and cultural commodities that we are the sole proprietors of. Reimagining these coded areas as sites of pleasure disrupts the pathology of Black female expression. Beyoncé's consistent gaze on her butt in "Partition" is an act of resistance that inverts objectification and commodification (Balaji 2010). Celebrating the butt challenges "assumptions that the Black body, its skin color and shape, is a mark of shame" (hooks 1992, 63).

In "Partition," Beyoncé performs a risqué burlesque show for her husband. She swings her hair and her butt as she dances behind a leopard curtain before performing a complicated acrobatic routine on a chair. The entire performance is about everybody's gaze being on her. Unconsciously, Beyoncé's "Partition" video inspired other Black women to claim ownership over their bodies. In her New School conversation with bell hooks, Shola Lynch, and Marci Blackman, transgender activist Janet Mock (2014) said:

> Having "Partition" come out a couple months before my book came out—when I am writing about sex work and sexual abuse and issues with my body, my sexuality—it was freeing to have Beyoncé owning her body and claiming that space.

While she's performing for her husband, Beyoncé also exacts implicit agency by finding pleasure in being sexually desired by her partner.

Marriage as Liberation

Most of Beyoncé's fifth studio album is an ode to the extreme highs and lows of love and marriage. From "Drunk in Love" to "XO," Beyoncé's music exposes the effort and sacrifices required to sustain a marriage while ballads like "Jealous" and "Mine" explore how adultery can spark marital strife (Lordi 2013). Marriage is an integral part of Beyoncé's Black feminist commitments, but as professor Kevin Allred explains, her fifth album stresses the importance of "equality and partnership over traditional gender roles" in an effort to break away from oppressive gender roles (Winsor 2014). For Black women, who were once forbidden from getting hitched in America, a union can be an act of agency. In her "Yours and Mine" film, Beyoncé pushes back against critics who see marriage as stifling when she says, "People feel like they lose something when they get married, but it doesn't have to be that way. There's nothing more exciting than having a witness to your life."

Thematically, this idea percolates on Beyoncé, as her husband, rapper Jay-Z, costars in several of the videos. Beyoncé finds pleasure in her husband finding her attractive. In "Partition," Beyoncé is walking in a trench coat and lingerie while a car's headlights follow her. She is in complete control of what she shows and to whom she shows it. Her body belongs to herself alone. We then see her in the back of a limousine with her husband. They're intimately touching each other as she kisses on his neck. She guides his hand where she wants it to go. Again, Beyoncé's in control, even as her husband becomes her audience during the burlesque dance in "Partition." As she rises from the floor in a sequined ensemble, she is performing for him. Instead of marriage serving as a source of shackling, it is instead a partnership that encourages her to be sexier and more in control of her body.

"Drunk in Love" continues Beyoncé's exploration of marriage as a facet of liberation. Emily Lordi interprets the "Drunk in Love" song and video as "being about a long-term married couple working to keep the spark alive" (Lordi 2014). Spark requires effort, which Beyoncé offers in the "Drunk in Love" video. Beyoncé's walking on the beach in a black bikini top and bottoms as well as a sarong. As she approaches the camera, we see her carrying a trophy—almost as if she's not the trophy in the video or the marriage—but her husband is. From there onward, the video is a celebration of carefree love. Beyoncé's dancing isn't choreographed and pristine. Instead, she appears carefree as she kicks her legs in an on-beat twerk. She also gyrates her hips while kneeling in the sand and walks toward the camera. In that moment, nobody matters more than the superstar. She is the focus. There's a moment where she touches her own breasts and makes the sign of the cross, essentially telling her partner, or husband, that he'll need Jesus to handle her sexually.

It isn't until 3 minutes and 19 seconds into the video that Jay-Z makes his initial appearance. Even then, Beyoncé is the focal point of the camera's lens. We see her face as she leans into her husband's neck and stares into the camera. There are genuine moments of goofiness and laughter. Talking about sex brings the giddiness out of Beyoncé. Even Jay-Z's small portion in the video is about his admiration of his wife, especially sexually. It's a celebration of sex, of all-night sex, and everything that entails. At some point, she tells Jay-Z to "stop it" as she smiles, as if there's a secret between them that's not made for the world's consumption. Beyoncé's marriage isn't just a marriage—it is a crucial cultural symbol of what's possible for Black feminist women who desire partnership.

Pleasure as an Integral Part of Black Feminism

Beyoncé's fifth album revolutionized the distribution of music and also situated her as a Black feminist pop star concerned with fore fronting pleasure as a critical part of her identity. In doing so, Beyoncé joins other Black feminist pop stars, including Janet Jackson and TLC, in using music to elevate the consciousness of their audience while also being bold in their exploration of sexual themes. Pleasure is an integral part of Black feminist thought and central themes within Beyoncé's work exposes its importance. Overall, a hip-hop black feminist reading of Beyoncé pushes Black feminist scholars in a multitude of disciplines to incorporate pleasure in their analyses.

REFERENCES

Balaji, Murali. 2010. "Vixen Resistin': Redefining Black Womanhood in Hip-Hop Music Videos." *Journal of Black Studies* 41: 5–20.
Ball, Charing. 2013. "The Thing About Beyoncé's Feminism…." *Madame Noire*, December 16. Accessed November 3, 2015. http://madamenoire.com/333140/beyonce-feminism/
Beaudoin, Kate. 2015. "17 Times Nicki Minaj Perfectly Shut Down Sexism." *MIC*, April 3. Accessed October 20, 2015. http://goo.gl/unW7Iu.
Bennett, Jessica. 2014. "How to Reclaim the F-Word? Just Call Beyoncé." *Time*, August 26. Accessed October 25, 2015. http://time.com/3181644/beyonce-reclaim-feminism-pop-star/.
Blay, Zeba. 2015. "Rihanna's '#BBHMM' Video is Brilliant, Terrifying, Complicated." *The Huffington Post*, July 2. Accessed October 26, 2015. http://goo.gl/mFOjUQ.
Brooks, Daphne A. 2008. "All That You Can't Leave Behind: Black Female Soul Singing and the Politics of Surrogation in the Age of Catastrophe." *Meridians: Feminism, Race, Transnationalism* 8: 180–204.
Carroll, Rebecca. 2015. "Rihanna's Video Puts a Black Woman in Control—No Wonder There's a Backlash." *The Guardian*, July 6. Accessed October 25, 2015. http://goo.gl/zra7wI.
Carter-Knowles, Beyoncé. 2014. "Gender Equality Is a Myth!" *The Shriver Report*, January 12. Accessed November 10, 2015. http://shriverreport.org/gender-equality-is-a-myth-beyonce/.
Cliff, Aimee. 2015. "7 Reasons Why Janet Jackson Is an OG Pop Feminist Icon." *The Fader*, June 3. Accessed October 25, 2015. http://www.thefader.com/2015/06/03/janet-jackson-is-an-og-pop-feminist-icon.

Collins Hill, Patricia. 1986. "Learning from the Outsider Within: The Sociological Significance of Black Feminist Thought." *Social Problems* 33: 14–32.

Collins Hill, Patricia. 1990. *Black Feminist Thought: Knowledge, Consciousness and the Politics of Empowerment.* New York: Routledge.

Crunk Feminist Collective. 2011. "Man Down: On Rihanna, Rape, and Violence." *Crunk Feminist Collective*, June 2. Accessed October 20, 2015. https://goo.gl/XBfNAE.

Durham, Aisha. 2010. "Hip Hop Feminist Media Studies." *International Journal of Africana Studies* 16: 117–139.

Durham, Aisha. 2012. "Check On It: Beyoncé, Southern Booty, and Black Femininities in Music Video." *Feminist Media Studies* 12: 35–49.

Durham, Aisha, Brittney C. Cooper, and Susana M. Morris, 2013. "The Stage Hip-Hop Feminism Built: A New Directions Essay." *Signs* 38: 721–737.

Ellison, Jo. 2013. "Mrs. Carter Uncut." *Vogue*, April 4. Accessed October 28, 2015. http://goo.gl/tXegHs.

Gallo, Phil. 2013. "Beyoncé's Superbowl Halftime Show Draws Estimated 104 Million Viewers." *Billboard*, February 4. Accessed November 1, 2015. http://goo.gl/nr6ssw.

Freeman, Hadley. 2013. "Beyoncé: Being Photographed in Your Underwear Doesn't Help Feminism." *The Guardian*, January 15. Accessed October 20, 2015. http://goo.gl/NAVUoK.

Gordon, Jane. 2010. "Beyoncé: The multi-talented star reveals what she is planning next." *The Daily Mail*, August 15. Accessed October 28, 2015. http://goo.gl/Hss7rn.

Harris-Winfrey, Tami. 2013. "All Hail the Queen." *Bitch* Magazine, May 20. Accessed October 10, 2015. https://goo.gl/xiy7fQ.

Harris, Laura A.1996. "Queer Black Feminism: The Pleasure Principle." *Feminist Review* 54: 3–30.

Hobson, Janell. 2003. "The 'Batty' Politic: Toward an Aesthetic of the Black Female Body." *Hypatia* 18: 87–105.

_____. 2014. "Beyoncé's Fierce Feminism." *Ms. Magazine*, March 7. Accessed October 25, 2015. http://msmagazine.com/blog/2015/03/07/beyonces-fierce-feminism/.

hooks, bell. 1992. "Selling Hot Pussy: Representations of Black Female Sexuality in the Cultural Marketplace." In *Black Looks: Race and Representation*, edited by bell hooks, 61–79. Brooklyn: South End Press.

hooks, bell, Shola Lynch, Janet Mock and Marci Blackman. 2014. "Are You Still a Slave: Liberating the Black Female Body." Panel discussion, the New School, New York, NY, May 6.

Lewis, Helen. 2015. "Let's Talk About Rihanna's Video." *New Statesman*, July 3. Accessed November 9, 2015. http://goo.gl/KXkjJE.

Lindsey, Treva B. 2013. "Complicated Crossroads: Black Feminisms, Sex Positivism, and Popular Culture." *African and Black Diaspora: An International Journal* 6: 55–65.

Lorde, Audre. 1984. *Sister Outsider: Essays and Speeches.* Freedom: The Crossing Press.

Lordi, Emily. 2013. "Beyoncé's Boundaries." *New Black Man (in Exile)*, December 18. Accessed December 7, 2015. http://www.newblackmaninexile.net/2013/12/beyonces-boundaries-by-emily-j-lordi.html.

Mastrangelo, Francesca. 2013. "TLC's 'No Scrubs' Helped Make Me a Feminist." *Bitch* Magazine, October 9. Accessed November 1, 2015. https://bitchmedia.org/post/tlcs-no-scrubs-helped-make-me-a-feminist.

McVeigh, Tracy, and Edward Helmore. 2015. "Feminists Fall Out Over 'Violent, Misogynistic' Rihanna Video." *The Guardian*, July 4. Accessed November 2, 2015. http://goo.gl/EG7USs.

Menza, Kaitlin. 2014. "One year later: How Beyoncé's surprise album ended up changing the music industry forever." *Marie Claire*, December 12. Accessed November 1, 2015. http://www.marieclaire.com/culture/news/a12729/how-beyonces-surprise-album-changed-music-industry-forever/.

Morgan, Joan. 1999. *When Chickenheads Come Home to Roost: A Hip-Hop Feminist Breaks It Down.* New York: Simon & Schuster, 1999.

_____. 2015. "Why We Get Off: Moving Towards a Black Feminist Politics of Pleasure." *The Black Scholar* 45: 36–46.

Qureshi, Bilal. 2013. "Feminists Everywhere React to Beyoncé's Latest." *NPR*, December 19. Accessed November 2, 2015. http://goo.gl/eta4jE.

Rio, Carmen. 2014. "Nicki Minaj's Feminism Isn't About Your Comfort Zone: On 'Anaconda' and Respectability Politics." *Autostraddle*, August 25. Accessed November 1, 2015. http://goo.gl/Ue1xYa.

Sandell, Laurie. 2015. "Nicki Minaj Wants All Women to Demand More Orgasms." *Cosmopolitan*, May 29. Accessed November 3, 2015. http://goo.gl/HFrkDp.

Smith, Brannon. 2014. "Funky Fresh and Feminist: A Look Back at Janet Jackson's 'Control.'" *Ebony*, March 19. Accessed October 25, 2015. http://goo.gl/iVOyxZ.

Smith, Mychal D. 2014. "Nicki Minaj's Butt and the Politics of Black Women's Sexuality." *Feministing*, July 29. Accessed October 25, 2015. http://goo.gl/BgxEhy.

Sosa, Chris. 2013. "Beyoncé Continues to Reign as Mrs. Carter." *The Huffington Post*, December 23. Accessed October 26, 2015. http://goo.gl/JHH3uT.

Traister, Rebecca. 2014. "Beyoncé's VMA Performance Was the Feminist Moment I've Been Waiting For." *The New Republic*, August 26, 2014. Accessed October 28, 2015. https://goo.gl/ncVJF3.

Vogel, Joseph. 2014. "The Nation that Janet Jackson Built." *The Atlantic*, September 15. Accessed October 25, 2015. http://goo.gl/EV3F9j.

Wallace, Amy. 2013. "Miss Millennium: Beyoncé." *GQ*, January 10. Accessed November 7, 2015. http://goo.gl/ObYCHc.

Winsor, Ben. 2014. "Why a Professor Is Teaching an Entire Class About Beyoncé." *Slate*, October 24. Accessed November 2, 2015. http://goo.gl/LQ0Imt.

Creole Queen

Beyoncé and Performing Plaçage in the New Millennium

KIMBERLY J. CHANDLER

> Honey, de white man is de ruler of everything as fur as Ah
> been able tuh find out. Maybe it's some place way off in de
> ocean where de black man is in power, but we don't know
> nothin' but what we see. So de white man throw down de
> load and tell de nigger man tuh pick it up. He pick it up
> because he have to, but he don't tote it. He hand it to his
> womenfolks. De nigger woman is de mule uh de world so
> fur as Ah can see.
>
> —Hurston 1937, 19

One could argue that Zora Neal Hurston's words concerning the positioning of African American women within a white supremacist patriarchy are never truer than what we see today. Black women's bodies are policed in ways that discount their humanity. Black women's choices are critiqued against a malleable standard of morality that is strategically tenuous at best. The lack of security black women endure concerning every aspect of their being is relentless. As a result, many chose performances of gender that create a sense of agency that is unidentifiable, in terms of its presumed respectability, to others outside of their lived experiences.

The constant barrage of monikers placed on black women's lives—Baby Mama, Gold Digger, THOT, Bitch, Ho, Ball Slut, Wifey, Jumpoff, Chicken Head, Dime, Hoochie, Skank, MILF, GILF, etc.—simultaneously disparage their personhood and often diminish their ability to create performances of the self that represent their authenticity. The personhood created by others often forces black women into places where they can be the convenient "mule uh de world" Hurston so aptly characterizes as the black woman's legitimized space of performance in a white world. So, what is a black woman to do in order to have agency? How does she negotiate the confining contexts she has been handed by those that only seek her services, not her self-ness? How does she create personal power that will not be commodified for public consumption and/or for exoticized spectacle? I suggest some black women use the marginalizing tools they have been given in service to themselves. One woman who has crafted an entire career doing just this is multi-platinum mogul and musical phenom Beyoncé.

Critics contend that Beyoncé Knowles reflects all that is wrong with the conceptualization of feminism as the power to own one's sexuality through public exhibition. Others suggest Beyoncé pushes the boundaries of dated perceptions of feminism that equate power with sex. However, the fact that Beyoncé comes from Creole heritage, is considered a "black" woman in American, and embodies her sexuality as a form of feminist gender performance suggests she is more than pure spectacle. While these seeming contradictions pervade the narrative about Beyoncé, I suggest they are not informed by her intersectional identity. This essay looks at the ways in which Beyoncé embodies a culturally informed performance of gender by functioning as what I term a "new millennium placèe" within a continuing American appropriation of the practice of plaçage; an institutionalized system of extralegal marriage primarily practiced in 19th century New Orleans.

Beyoncé and the Performance of Gender

To understand the performance of gender Beyoncé produces, we must first understand the nature of performativity. Hamera's states "performativity is a specific means of material and symbolic social production that centers on the repetition and apparent stability of a particular kind of embodied utterance" (2006, 6). To unpack that notion, performativity is the act of doing something over the course of time, consistently and repetitively, that creates for its actor a method of becoming. That becoming *is* the performance. For Beyoncé, the act of embodying her particular brand of gendered identity over the course of her career has rendered Beyoncé Giselle Knowles-Carter, the person, synonymous with Beyoncé the mediated image. Every incarnation of her gendered identity acts as a performative, i.e., the enduring quality of the behavior that produces Beyoncé. Therefore, what she does is what she *is*, i.e., the word Beyoncé is defined by all that she has and is continuing to perform as the *human* Beyoncé.

Beyoncé also embodies a performance of gender that is characterized by the concept of restored behaviors. Schechner suggests restored behaviors are "… physical or verbal actions that are not-for-the-first time, prepared, or rehearsed" (2002, 22). Just as a woman wearing a white dress is not a new performance of bride; restored behaviors suggest performances of gender are continually embodied in ways that create particularized identities for their actors. The person performing the behavior *becomes* the behavior. A woman in a white dress *is* a bride. Likewise, the image Beyoncé produces for public consumption is who we know as Beyoncé. However, restored behaviors suggest Beyoncé's performance is not new, but is historically informed by performances associated with the past or of the past.

Beyoncé and Creole Performances of Plaçage

Collectively, the notion of performativity and restored behaviors is connected to the historical context and heritage of Beyoncé's ancestors. Several writers note Beyoncé's Creole roots emanate from her mother's lineage (Daniels 2014; Dhillon 2012; Smolenvak 2012). Tina Knowles' side of the family was of French Creole heritage inclusive of Indian, Spanish, African, French and Native American cultures. Creoles in Louisiana, the place of birth for Tina Knowles' ancestors, often engaged in plaçage: a form of marital relationship practiced by Creole women and often slaveholding European and white men (Guillory 1998). Women engaged in these common-law type marriages were characterized as placèes (meaning "to place with") due to the arrangements that were made on their behalf. A placèe's mother or older aunt would negotiate her placement with a prospective wealthy suitor during social events known as quadroon balls. The name quadroon reflected the mulatto and white ethnicity of the young women intended for placement. Assets were given to these young women that were unheard of during this time in America when slavery was commonplace. Financial payments were made to the placèe and her mother; the placèe was given a home in her name; and for some, recognition of any children born throughout the union was promised in the will of the suitor (Guillory 1997).

What is most salient to the discussion concerning plaçage is the economic foundation of the extralegal arrangement. Economically, these young women were of high value because of their light skin, the same light skin that would make them of high value as a slave (Guillory 1997). These women used their physical image as bargaining chips within the economic exchange of slavery during their day. It was their only means to distinguish themselves in a society fraught with inequities. More importantly, it was their only way to build wealth within a society and culture that only deemed them valuable as property. In many ways, they were still property. However, they used the agency their ethnicity allowed them to maintain some power over their lives and the destinies of their children. In this regard, Guillory states,

The most a mulatto mother and a quadroon daughter could hope to attain in the rigid confines of the black/white world was some semblance of economic independence and social distinction from the slaves and other blacks [1997, 83].

These women became expert business persons and marketers of their own image, even their bodies. Since many were able to economically maintain themselves even after the plaçage system was no longer in place, it is clear they learned how to use the system they were bound to—or play the hand they were dealt—in order to create a life of wealth and privilege in keeping with their social status.

I contend Beyoncé's performative is that of what I term a "New Millennium Placèe." Just as a placèe is used in the slave economy as a means to ascertain wealth, status and a modicum of security, so has Beyoncé demonstrated this same performative through the use of her carefully crafted image. She exhibits a restored behavior—the placèe—that was commonplace in Creole culture. She is strategic in her use of her mixed heritage as a selling point in her music, interviews, and advertising endorsements. For example, in a L'Oreal commercial for True Match foundation, she states, "There's a story behind my skin. It's a mosaic of all the faces before it" (Stodghill 2012). Underneath her photo are the words "African American, Native American and French." While she is known as an African American woman to the masses, she intentionally plays up her ancestry to connect her image to a product that sells beauty. The use of what was once termed "mulatto" as her ethnic identity allows Beyoncé to connect herself to the same exotic image enjoyed by Creole women engaged in plaçage. While shrewdly disconnecting herself from being *just* black, she can claim and reap the benefit of an elevated social status based simply on skin privilege. In doing so, she brings the performance of plaçage into the new millennium and the public eagerly consumes it because she represents a standard of beauty that contains enormous social currency.

While Beyoncé is not at the mercy of the marginalizing context perpetuated during American slavery, she is still marginalized due to her intersectional identity as a black woman in a white supremacist patriarchy. However, Beyoncé uses the same tools a placèe uses to build a life of economic security through wealth and status quite effectively. Her Eurocentric standard of beauty (light skin, long blond hair, a sexualized body, etc.) and a hypersexualized performance of gender provide enormous opportunities for her to live beyond her blackness. As long as she performs as a "New Millennium Placèe," using her body in service to others first, she can continue to reap the benefits her Creole ancestry provide.

Clearly, there are many similarities between Beyoncé's career trajectory and the historical practice of plaçage. First, Beyoncé's parents were the impetus for her career just as the mother moves her daughter into the role of placèe in the plaçage system. With her father as her first manager and her mother as confidant and stylist, Beyoncé's trajectory as a placèe was probably crafted before she was born. What's interesting in her mother-daughter relationship is the power her mother held in creating and promulgating her image. Tina Knowles created Destiny Child's, and later Beyoncé's, costumes and stylized image. Being a hairdresser and stylist herself, surely she understood the ways in which the body can be manipulated in order to perform an alluring and seductive presence. As well, it is clear Tina Knowles is influenced by her Creole heritage in that she was not only a purveyor of Beyoncé's body; she was a business owner with a salon herself. She was not a novice to using the body as a tool within which to obtain social power. She created Beyoncé's style icon identity which has always been perceived as sexually provocative. One could even say in the beginning that she created Beyoncé's entire persona which was *founded* upon sex appeal. Add to this the carefully choreographed images fed to the media foregrounding Beyoncé's sexuality—not her singing—and you have the creation of a marketing machine reminiscent of the quadroon balls. The only difference is that Beyoncé's ball has not ended. She continues to use her sexually charged image as a tool to be commodified by the dominant power structure that controls the entertainment business.

Second, one could argue that Beyoncé obtains the spoils from the historical war over ownership of black women's bodies. She reaps the benefit of wealth, status and privilege within her global circle of influence. As the placèe bargains with her body in order to obtain a privileged place in society, so Beyoncé bargains with her body of talents to achieve superstardom. However, like the Creole placèe, Beyoncé does not hold the deed to her place of power. She is dependent on the small group of white male entertainment industry owners for the proliferation of her image and the reproduction of her wealth. Yes, she owns a great deal of herself when one considers song royalties, movies, tours, appearances, and other activities associated with her career. Forbes approximates her earnings at $54.5 million, listing her as #29 on the top 100 celebrities in 2015. Her net worth is approximated at $250 million (Forbes 2015). However, Sony Music Entertainment, the parent company of her record label, is the second largest music company in the world worth *billions* of dollars. When weighing her power in sheer dollars, it is clear who holds the upper hand.

Beyoncé's Performance of Feminism: Plaçage Redux

Finally, the "… semblance of economic independence and social distinction…" (Guillroy 1997, 83) refers to in her writing on Creoles of color may be the most pervasive characteristic of plaçage that is reflected in the ways in which Beyoncé performs gender. Many of Beyoncé's songs reflect a presumed independence and fierce determination to be a woman on her own terms. Even her alter ego's name is Sasha Fierce. She speaks of feminism in interviews and even uses the word as a backdrop on one video. In her retrospective short film, "Yours and Mine" (Beyoncé 2012) she states:

> I always considered myself a feminist, although I was always afraid of that word because people put so much on it, when honestly it's very simple. It's just a person that believes in equality for men and women. Men and women balance each other out, and we have to get to a point where we are comfortable with appreciating each other.

Wait! Beyoncé is a feminist? This woman who has repeatedly used sex and sensuality to purvey an image reminiscent of Eurocentric standards of beauty is claiming feminism? This woman, who has continuously put her body before her intelligence in order to sell the product that is her image, is a feminist? Contending with the answers to these questions is no easy exercise. If one equates feminism with equality, it is easy to discount Beyoncé's contention that she is a feminist. However, we must deal with the continuing macro structures of political and economic power that inherently reproduce the marginalized place of women in the world. Even with all of the gains women have made within the last century, they still do not claim equal earning power with men. As well, they are still objectified in the media and experience an uneven playing field across all domains, be they religion, education, politics, or economic security. Therefore, it is necessary to expand the limits of the definitional nature of feminism to understand Beyoncé's performance of gender. While she contends women and men should "balance each other out," it would seem her notion of balance has more to do with equilibrium than equality.

Noted feminist author and intellectual, bell hooks, routinely provides scathing critiques of Beyoncé and her brand of feminism. *Clutch* magazine (Danielle 2014), in its reporting of a dialog about images of women of color in media, highlighted the feminist tensions Beyoncé creates. In a conversation between filmmaker Shola Lynch, author Marci Blackman, activist and author Janet Mock and hooks, the magazine reports:

> hooks, argued Beyoncé's sexy, partially-clothed *Time* cover did little to bolster her pro-woman bona fides. "Let's take the image of this super rich, very powerful Black female and let's use it in the service of imperialist, white supremacist capitalist patriarchy because she probably had very little control over that cover—that image," the professor argued.

Herein is the chief issue with Beyoncé's brand of feminism. Who does it serve? Does Beyoncé promulgate an image as if it is her possession to commodify?

Or, does she fall prey to macro structures of marginalization through the (ab)use of the black body? Is she playing the game that is white heterosexist capitalist patriarchy or is she being brilliantly played? In everything she does in her career, Beyoncé performs at the pleasure of someone else. Her stage performances are crafted to provide pleasure for consumers. She projects a hypersexual, vixen-like image which is not her everyday reality. She makes her living being objectified, but will blast the word "FEMINIST" in bold letters on her stage backdrop. She performs in ways most feminists would simply balk at, but sees it as her way to combat oppression through economic security. With Beyoncé, these contradictions live side by side. From the dyed hair, lightened skin on magazine covers and technological tricks that make her seem bigger than life to the carefully crafted narrative that reconceptualizes the selling of black bodies as an exercise in independence, Beyoncé seems to represent a living, breathing contradiction.

The other overwhelming issue within the contradiction that is Beyoncé is the subject of ownership. Historically, the practice of plaçage gave Creole women a measure of ownership in that they had some economic freedom. Their names were often on deeds to their homes. Some even owned slaves. Within the context of image driven society, their skin held great privilege. They were the standard of beauty, but only Creole beauty. They could claim some control over their existence. Beyoncé's carefully crafted image seems to suggest she is in control. But, who really has the control here? Concerning hooks comment about her wardrobe on the previously mentioned *Time* cover, Janet Mock (Danielle 2014) states:

> I think she had control over what she wore.... I would argue that she has a power now that she has final-cut approval and she chose that image. I don't want to strip Beyoncé of her agency, of choosing that image, of being her own manager, of all of this stuff.

Mock certainly brings up several salient points. First, Beyoncé could be asserting a sense of agency by providing extensive input on the various elements of her performance (e.g., selecting and designing her wardrobe). In fact, it would be hard to believe that an artist at her level is passive in what the audience consumes or gets to digest. Even the release of her last CD supports this notion as she decided how, when, and in what way consumers could access her music. She has ascended to a level of power that allows her decision making power concerning her image. However, she is still at the mercy of those she serves. She gives the public what they want to consume. She provides the commodity that is mediated through the power structure that distributes her global presence. She knows and accepts that she willfully gives them what they want every time. She may be her own manager, but there are several layers of management above her that hold the power to produce her image for public consumption. Clearly, there are tensions between the macro power structures that empower Beyoncé to have more than average control of her image and those that create those structures. Beyoncé knows this and works within the slippery slopes of these competing structures to the tune of millions while the architects of those structures make billions.

What is most interesting to note is the relationship created through the social agreements between Beyoncé and dominant power structures. Sex still sells and it would seem that Beyoncé is a willing salesperson. hooks describes this as "colluding the construction of herself as a slave" (Danielle 2014). The operative word here is "slave." It would seem that even as Beyoncé has profited from those that enable her celebrity and wealth, she is simultaneously beholden to their favor in order to maintain her status. Beyoncé seems to use her image as a tool. However, dominant power structures also use her image as a tool. Here, again, lies what seems to be the contradiction and tension due to what some might say are competing goals: Beyoncé and dominant power structures' control of her image. Marci Blackman and bell hooks argue these marked contradictions by stating:

> Blackman: … She's using the same images that were used against her, and us, for so many years and she's taken control of it and saying, "If y'all are going to make money off it, so am I." There's collusion, perhaps, but there's also a bit of reclaiming if she's the one in control.
> hooks: Well, of course, I think that's fantasy. I think it's a fantasy that we can recoup the violating image and use it. I used to get so tired of people quoting Audre [Lorde], "The master's tools will never dismantle the master's house." But that was exactly what she meant that you are not going to destroy this imperialist white supremacist capitalist patriarchy by creating your own version of it. Even if it serves you to make lots and lots of money [Danielle 2014].

I would suggest that Beyoncé *is* using the master's tools, not to dismantle the master's house, but to claim agency within the confines of that house. Clearly, Beyoncé is playing what some might say is the hand that she's been dealt because of her status as a black woman. However, reading Beyoncé's performance of gender in this way without understanding the historical context that may inform her choices renders her just another pretty face to sell songs and sex. It is within this historical context, the practice of plaçage, that we find an explanation for the complexities and contradictions that inform Beyoncé's performance of gender.

Beyoncé the *Creole Queen*

It may be erroneous to assume Beyoncé does not understand the downside to capitalist gamesmanship. However, what is not clear is her understanding of her contribution to the reification of this form of slavery. She is a slave to the plaçage system that is the white capitalist patriarchy. She reflects a new millennium sort of plaçage where her ownership leaves her with much more power and wealth than could ever be imagined by her ancestors. No, she is not elegantly dressed in order to catch the eye of a wealthy slave-owner or European suitor at the quadroon ball. One might say that was the place she held in the earliest days of her career under the direction of her father and tutelage of her mother, both acting as her chief negotiators. Today, she seemingly has a seat at the tables of power, albeit a conditional seat as the talented placèe or producer of the product. She is a sheer reflection of the standard of beauty and social acceptability her ancestors enjoyed during the time of plaçage. Her image, her stage personae even, reproduces a contemporary form of plaçage within the entertainment industry that is purely driven by economics, yet historically informed by preferential treatment based on skin color and in this case Creole ancestry.

When considering her declaration of feminist leanings, one must also consider another statement Hare (2014) retells in a CNN article stating: "No one is immune to the price of fame, and that includes Beyoncé. With global stardom, 'you become the property of the public,' she laments. 'There's nothing real about it.'"

Might the unity of these aforementioned statements explain not only Beyoncé's brand of feminism, but also provide a particularly useful context for understanding how her heritage informs her choices. Simply, it would seem that Beyoncé knows exactly what she is doing. She believes she takes ownership over her body and her image. However, that ownership comes with a price because the public and is her business partner. She seems to clearly understand the limits of her ownership within the confines of a white patriarchy. Greater still, she willingly engages in the social agreement required for her measure of economic independence. When she states, "there's nothing real about it," one wonders where the deception lies? Is her presumed independence a lie or is the perception of her placèe-ness within the wealth producing economy that is her career fictitious?

I would suggest reading Beyoncé's performance of gender is not quite as easy as it may appear. It seems to be an agreed upon contradiction in which each side has willingly and willfully entered into an agreement based upon historically defined roles of power and status. To read Beyoncé's performance of gender as traditionally feminist simply does not work. One must consider the players in the predefined game of politicizing black women's bodies in order to understand the losers and winners. It appears that Beyoncé—the true Creole Queen—has decided the winners circle is where she belongs.

References

Danielle, Britni. 2014. "bell hooks on Beyoncé: She Is a Terrorist Because of Her Impact on Young Girls." *Clutch* Magazine, May. Accessed November 18, 2015, http://www.clutchmagonline.com/2014/05/bell-hooks-beyoance-terrorist-impact-young-girls/.

Daniels, Cora, and John L. Jackson. 2014. *Impolite Conversations: On Race, Politics, Sex, Money, and Religion.* New York: Atria Books.

Dhillon, Georgina. 2012. "Beyoncé Knowles: A Creole Queen." *Kreol* Magazine, October 3. Accessed November 18, 2015, http://www.kreolmagazine.com/arts-culture/spotlight/beyonce-knowles-a-creole-queen/.

Guillory, Monique. 1997. "Under One Roof: The Sins and Sanctity of the New Orleans Quadroon Balls." In *Race Consciousness: African American Studies for the New Century*, edited by Judith Jackson Fossett and Jeffrey A. Tucker, 67–92. New York University Press.

Hamera, Judith. 2006. *Opening Acts: Performance In/As Communication and Cultural Studies.* Thousand Oaks: Sage Publications.

Hare, Breeanna. 2012. "Beyonce Opens Up on Feminism, Fame and Marriage." *CNN* December 12. Accessed November 18, 2015, http://www.cnn.com/2014/12/12/showbiz/music/beyonce-feminism-yours-and-mine-video/.

Schechner, Richard. 2006. *Performance Studies: An Introduction.* New York: Routledge.

Smolenyak, Megan. 2014. "A Peek into Blue Ivy Carter's Past." *The Huffington Post* January 12. Accessed November 1, 2015, http://www.huffingtonpost.com/megan-smolenyak-smolenyak/a-peek-into-blue-ivy-cart_b_1200346.html.

Stodghill, Alexis. 2012. "Beyoncé L'Oreal Ad Controversy Inspires Black Community Backlash." *The Grio,* February 10. Accessed November 18, 2015, http://thegrio.com/2012/02/10/beyonce-describes-herself-as-african-american-native-american-french-in-new-loreal-ad/#beyonce-true-match-loreal-adjpg.

Sex(uality), Marriage, Motherhood and "Bey Feminism"

Elizabeth Whittington Cooper

Beyoncé has shown, as bell hooks expressed in her epochal 2000 text, that "feminism is for everybody." By lifting verses from Adichie's TED talk on gender equality and using it to inspire her own music, Beyoncé is bridging the gap between academic feminism and everyday feminism. If young women attendees at her On the Run tour can scream out the lyrics to "Flawless" and mean every word, who says they can't eventually read Audre Lorde?

—Little 2014

Beyoncé has released five albums starting with her first solo album in 2003. Since that time, she has won several Grammys, played in numerous movies, completed several world tours, got married, and had a baby. This is no small feat for any women, especially a Black woman. Over the years, Beyoncé has suffered her fair share of ridicule from feminists, conservatives, and pop culture. From the way she talks to the clothes she wears, she is constantly under the microscope. Yet, through family drama and media criticism, Beyoncé has risen to the top to rub elbows with President Obama and First Lady Michelle.

In December 2013, Beyoncé did what no other artist has done. She released an album without any promotion and no leaks to the public at the stroke of midnight. Within the album, she released 14 songs and 17 videos to go along with each of the songs including bonus video. The album quickly reached the top of the charts with songs like "Drunk in Love," "Pretty Hurts," "Mine," and "Flawless." Also with this album came even more criticism for the images she was releasing in her videos and how she was branding feminism.

Whittington and Jordan (2014) began to explore Bey feminism (coined for Beyoncé's brand of feminism) with Black feminism. They argue that Bey feminism is a type of feminism Beyoncé promotes which combines traditional feminism with the everyday woman. It allows a more grassroots platform for women to start discussing feminism and even embrace it in a world where feminism has remained rather elitist. As mentioned in the quote at the beginning of the essay, Beyoncé has created a feminism that allows women to accept it and just as she began to explore other feminist works, this is now a chance for other women to do the same.

This essay seeks to explore how Bey feminism examines topics such as sex(uality), marriage, and motherhood, concepts that were discussed by feminists in particular and women in general with the release of *Beyoncé: The Visual Album*. While analyzing what some of the feminist blogs said about Beyoncé's image as a wife and a mother, I seek to understand how Bey feminism allows Beyoncé to situate herself among feminists as a confident and secure woman who claims feminism as her own without being branded as a traditional feminist. By exploring feminist theory, Black sexual identity, and Black feminism, I unpack these identities that Beyoncé holds in order to understand how Bey feminism applies. First, I will examine feminist theory through the lens of sex(uality). Then I will juxtapose what some traditional feminists are saying about Beyoncé portrayal of sex(uality) in her most recent album.

Sex(uality) and Feminist Theory

Sexuality is a key variable within feminist research especially in terms of examining power dynamics. Beyoncé is a woman who some would consider to still be ruled by the male gaze and seen as an object by male fans. When Trier-Bieniek (2014) wrote about Beyoncé for the blog *Feminist Reflections* she said, "Beyoncé is challenging the passivity of the male gaze, setting a foundation for a new wave of feminists who simultaneously celebrate their bodies and provide cunning intellectual fodder." Additionally, as Alicia Little (2015) of *Ms.* magazine blog states, "When feminists hone in so closely on racy lyrics and music videos, they're only seeing one part of her message." Both of these authors are exploring the idea that how Beyoncé uses her body and how she portrays sexy is not an attack against feminism and not for the attention of male fans. Instead, it should be seen as a woman who is comfortable in her own skin and challenging this idea that her body is situated in the male gaze.

Some of the other criticisms Little addresses range from the "problematic representation of the feminist movement" (this representation meaning how Beyoncé represents feminism) to criticizing "her overly sexualized dance moves and skin baring-costumes." Sandole-Staroste states, "Feminist theory and practice value diversity and deeply respect differences that are necessarily reflected in the questions feminists formulate, the analyses they attempt, and the solutions they suggest" (2002, 227). However, when Beyoncé was featured on the cover of the Spring 2013 *Ms.* magazine there was tremendous uproar on her brand of feminism as a misrepresentation of true feminism (Hobson 2013). If feminist theory allows for the diversity of perspectives and a safe place for feminism to be explored, then it is a wonder that these feminist called Beyoncé a "stripper" and a "whore" (Hobson 2013). It seems when it comes to things such as sex or sexuality, Beyoncé's brand is not tolerated or accepted.

Feminist theory examines gender influences on how individuals view who they are within the society in which they live (Lorber 2005). In this society, historically, "our culture has enforced rigid sex roles, accepted interpersonal violence, and viewed women as property" (Humphreys 2011, 10), which has led to the various gender inequities. This society has tolerated and even glorified "masculine violence, encouraging men and boys to be aggressive and competitive," which has also led to a society that perpetuates rape culture and myths (Humphreys 2011). The society that operates like this sets up a system that "affords men a dominant position or role with respect to initiating sexual encounters, negotiating desired sexual activities and deciding the start and end of such encounters" (Humphreys 2011, 11).

However, when we examine how Beyoncé is policed by feminists for how she portrays her body, it is as if these feminists are becoming the patriarchal dominating force created to tell Beyoncé how much she should and should not show in her clothing choices, how her body should move, and how her sexuality should be displayed. In writing for the *Ms.* magazine blog, Hobson explores some of these relationships. It seems that in feminist theory or traditional feminism some

> want to regulate the bodies of women of color in order to eradicate difference. Since when did feminism reinforce dress codes instead of women's autonomy and solidarity with other women, in which we support all of our choices while also recognizing how those choices are sometimes limited by intersectional oppressions (and no one is immune from this)?" [Hobson 2013].

Karen and Sonja Foss argue, "The feminist perspective challenges communication research through its use of methodologies that allow women to speak their own voices, rather than through the traditional lenses of more traditional paradigms" (Waggenspark 2007, 466). Feminist perspective allows for the breakdown of gender construction in a way that challenges the traditional and allows for a new contemporary form that seems to still prefer one perspective over another. The Fosses state that "gender functions as a lens through which all other perceptions pass," but the argument should also include that race is in conjunction with gender especially when one operates through both lenses (Waggenspark 2007, 466). In this case, this policing done of one woman of color's body leaves a hole in this acceptance of feminism by everybody.

In another example of a female artist, Alicia Keys, told her story this summer in an essay written for Bet.com.

> For as long as I can remember, I've hidden myself. It might have started in school when I realized that I caught on to things a little quicker, and teachers started to show slight favor to me, or use me as an example I remember feeling like my friends would make fun of me or look at me as if I was different from them and so … I started hiding. Not intentionally, I didn't mean to, but I did. Little pieces at a time.
> I definitely started hiding when I got old enough to walk down my NY streets alone. I started to notice a drastic difference in how men would relate to me if I had on jeans, or if I had on a skirt, or if my hair was done pretty. I could tell the difference, I could feel the animal instinct in them and it scared me. I didn't want to be talked to in that way, looked at in that way, whistled after, followed.
> And so I started hiding. I chose the baggy jeans and Timbs, I chose the ponytail and hat, I chose no makeup, no bright color lipstick or pretty dresses. I chose to hide. Pieces at a time. Less trouble that way [Ramos 2015].

The way Keys saw herself in her music career was very much influenced by how she saw herself in her personal life. Although Keys is just one example, this isn't an uncommon view many women have for themselves. By Beyoncé not being ashamed, she allows Bey feminism or her brand of feminism to give girls and women a platform to feel comfortable with their bodies no matter how much or how little clothing they wear. Feeling as Keys did and having to wear male clothing to avoid the male gaze left her feeling even more confused because people then started to question her sexuality. This link to clothes, sex appeal, and sexuality is something feminists are supposed to help women realize that what matters is what makes them comfortable and that should be the ability to wear whatever they want.

Marriage, Motherhood, and Black Sexual Politics

Next, I want to examine how Black sexual politics plays a role in the concept of marriage specifically in the backlash Beyoncé has gotten for her roles in her videos for the *Visual Album*. Hill Collins argues that the way that Western culture defines African bodies in relation to Black women's agency illustrates how they seek to control how and when their bodies are displayed (Hill Collins 2005). A prime example is when feminists have sought to call Beyoncé a "stripper" and a "whore" for the lack of clothing she chooses to wear and how she performs in her videos. Further down in the comment section a reader says she does not understand how the author links the two because being a wife and a mother has nothing to do with being a "stripper" and a "whore." However, this illustrates that within Western culture Black women's bodies are not their own. When there is a deviation from the traditional scope of what a wife and a mother should be, in many cases, their sexuality then becomes examined. Yet, in what context has Madonna, Jennifer Lopez, or Brittany Spears been criticized for their overly sexualized performances in conjunction with their role as a mother and/or wife?

While writing for Madame Noire in December 2013 Ball examined Beyoncé's more sexualized songs, "Partition," "Blow," "Drunk in Love," and "Haunted." Ball argues Beyoncé "spits in the face of what we chiefly believe to be an appropriate display of a woman's sexuality (i.e., asexual) post-motherhood." Although, I believe she is sarcastically referring to how society as a whole believes women should act specifically after becoming a mother, what does hold true is that many feel this way when watching the videos. Also in the lyrics Beyoncé isn't shy about talking about sex, including oral sex. She makes no apologies for wanting to please her man and she does it in seductive clothing. She illustrates various dimensions of sexual prowess from aggressive to submissive. African Americans have historically been known for being deviant when it comes to gender ideology and sexual practices (Hill Collins 2005, 44). This is evident with the criticism of Beyoncé both from both White and Black audiences. She seems to be held to a platform that other White artists have not been held to all because she is a Black woman exploring her sexuality through her music.

In Christina Coleman's 2013 article for the website *Global Grind*, she discusses how *The Visual Album* ended all arguments that Beyoncé was not a feminist. Although this is not my argument, she does highlight two things that are important to my argument. One that some feminists feel like motherhood cannot be put first if one does call herself a feminist. In college, I told one of my friends that if I had children I would like to stay home and raise them for at least the first five years. I remember her cringing and saying that feminists everywhere were rolling over in their graves. This type of feminism (she proclaimed to be a traditional feminist) argues that if motherhood is put before feminism then one cannot call herself a feminist. As Coleman (2013) states, "How anti-feminist of a feminist to say that being a mom is anti-feminist." However, there are many feminists who echo this emotion. In a 2008 essay for the *Daily Mail* Rebecca Walker, Alice Walker's daughter, writes about her mother's feelings toward marriage and motherhood, expressing that both were a waste of Rebecca's time when there are women across the world who need help. Walker stated:

> The truth is that I very nearly missed out on becoming a mother—thanks to being brought up by a rabid feminist who thought motherhood was about the worst thing that could happen to a woman. You see, my mum taught me that children enslave women. I grew up believing that children are millstones around your neck, and the idea that motherhood can make you blissfully happy is a complete fairytale.

Walker goes on to say she has not spoken to her mother since she became pregnant. Her mother has disowned her for becoming what Alice Walker feels is a slave to motherhood.

Given these attitudes it is not surprising that Beyoncé received such push back for her embracing motherhood and her sexuality all in one album. For some feminists, this is an abomination to their very belief system thus they reject her brand of feminism because it allows more women to get the idea that motherhood and feminism can go together. While embracing motherhood, embracing her career, and showing that she can do both well, Beyoncé gives other working Black mothers the hope that they too can achieve something which, for so long, seemed unattainable. Many times working class Black mothers are sometimes seen as Bad Black mothers (Hill Collins 2005, 131). They are neglecting their children in some way and therefore not taking care of their responsibility and although Beyoncé is not considered a working class Black mother she does give space for these women to feel some connection to her. Bey feminism allows them to embrace motherhood and not feel guilty for also having to work to provide for their child(ren).

The other idea that Coleman highlights is that some feminists assume that feminists cannot be wives. When Beyoncé named her tour "Mrs. Carter," feminists were outraged that she was placing her identity in her husbands (Coleman 2013). The idea that being linked to a man further perpetuates the patriarchal system of male dominance over women is one argument. Historically, Black women have been stereotyped as Mammies, Jezebels, and Sapphires, but never as a loving wife who values her relationship and works to make it successful. As Schmidt (2014) writes for the blog *Chimes*,

> Her incredibly successful tour was even named "The Mrs. Carter" tour, a move emphasizing her married status that earned her opponents from the other end of the feminism spectrum. Critics claimed that Beyoncé was defining herself by Jay-Z and her marriage to him, rather than being an independent woman … and the fact that Beyoncé doesn't need to show she is independent: she reminds us in every song that she is. She also happens to be in love with her husband, and—as she claims herself—wouldn't be "Beyoncé" if it weren't for him. Barack Obama has said similar things about Michelle and he's never been called an anti-feminist.

Even though some critics do not like the fact that Beyoncé embraces both her marriage and her feminism, she once again gives a platform that many feminists have not given the everyday woman, a place to celebrate their womanhood, independence, and marriage. Bey feminism allows the everyday woman to be proud of her role as a wife, to still embrace her sexuality, and to strive for career achievements without being ashamed. These are things Black women have not had the opportunity to achieve. White feminists have been allowed to be wives, career women, and sexual beings, but when it comes to Black women any of these seem a subversion or a deviation that needs to be handled. However, as Christina Coleman (2013) states:

> But there's something else that's extremely feminist about the way Beyoncé celebrates her marriage. It's the idea that women have to play a certain role in a relationship … an idea that Beyoncé is neutralizing every single time she does something like drop an album in the middle of the night with no promotion or warning. She might make Jay Z a steak at night and rock Blue to sleep, but she's still making history, breaking barriers….

Black Feminism and Bey Feminism

Where does Black feminism fit in this argument? Black feminism seems to embrace and celebrate all these roles of Black women. Hill Collins states, "As a critical social theory, Black feminist thought aims to empower African-American women within the context of social injustice sustained by intersecting oppressions" (2002, 22). In this sense, examining how gender, race, and class operate within the context of Beyoncé and her latest album, Black feminism should be able to understand Bey feminism. However, Reynolds takes a critical perspective of Black feminist thought arguing for changes in the way that Black feminist thought is examined, requiring promotion of a more inclusive model of Black womanhood (2002, 604). Black feminist thought must take a "more contextual, more reflexive, fluid and locally based approach to understanding Black women's lives so that the scope of complexities and diversity of Black women's lives can be successfully captured" (Reynolds 2002, 604).

This is where Black feminism falls short of Bey feminism. For some Black feminists, they feel the same as traditional feminists (i.e., White feminists). That is Beyoncé's brand of feminism harms rather than helps young Black girls because of the over sexualized performances and lyrics. In particular, bell hooks defines Beyoncé as a "terrorist" (Jonas 2015). hooks argues that Beyoncé comes from a place of privilege and is able to embrace certain identities such as these that most Black girls do not come from. Although, hooks does have a point, Black feminism has not been able to reach young

Black girls. For many Black girls, they do not learn about feminism at all much less Black feminism until college, and that is if they go to college. As Mikki Kendall wrote for the online website *The Guardian*:

> This album makes it clear that her feminism isn't academic; isn't about waves, or labels. It simply is a part of her as much as anything else in her life. She's pro-woman without being anti-man, and she wants the world to know that you can be feminist on a personal level without sacrificing emotions, friendships or fun [2013].

The question remains, how is Black feminism reaching the masses when Bey feminism is able to reach young girls, especially young Black girls wanting to learn more about feminism when one of their favorite artists embraces the term?

bells hooks, Patricia Hill Collins, Audre Lourde, Alice Walker, all these women have been influential in the Black feminist movement, but most of their movement stays behind the walls of Academia. They are not in elementary schools, middle school, high schools, YMCAs, or Boys and Girls Clubs talking to Black girls about Black feminism, but Beyoncé's music is being heard across the country in these same institutions and on the radio, television shows, etc. Black feminism is failing the Black community with the lack of exposure to the everyday woman. Beyoncé is addressing topics like sex(uality), marriage, and motherhood in very public forums that Black feminism still struggles to reach. Victoria Jonas (2013) states, "Beyoncé's contribution to the re-imagination of mainstream feminism as an intersectional practice has meant an incredible expansion and furthered understanding of the movement." As a self-proclaimed Black feminist, I see the limitations in Black feminist not learning to embrace Bey feminism. Her feminism starts the conversations surrounding feminism that can continue to lead to change. As Qureshi writes for NPR music, "The majority of women that need feminism listen to Beyoncé.... They don't take women's studies classes."

Conclusion

Beyoncé has been claimed as iconic. At age 34, she has broken down barriers and made a name for herself in the music industry. The following essay examined how sex(uality), marriage, and motherhood are illustrated in Beyoncé's album *The Visual Album*. Through different theoretical frameworks, I analyzed some of the blogs and articles that discussed these topics in relation to Beyoncé's feminism coined Bey feminism and the current feminist conversations. These topics are areas that women, especially Black women deal with in their everyday life. The process of deciding to marry or not, becoming a mother or not, and constantly negotiating sex(uality) in a culture that denigrates Black women's sexuality in pop culture and society. Beyoncé has developed a platform, which she has built up through the years to finally proclaiming herself as a feminist at the 2014 VMAs. Though several critics have denied Beyoncé a place within feminism, Beyoncé has created her own platform. She has created a space for girls and women to explore feminism where feminism has stayed locked within the walls of academia. In Beyoncé's song "Flawless," she samples feminist Chimamanda Adichie's speech (and eventual book) *We Should All Be Feminists*, which illustrates all of the concepts discussed within this essay. The words of Adichie made their way into several reviews of the album, including one for *Time* magazine. Adichie states:

> We teach girls to shrink themselves, to make themselves smaller. We say to girls, you can have ambition, but not too much. You should aim to be successful, but not too successful. Otherwise, you would threaten the man. Because I am female, I am expected to aspire to marriage. I am expected to make my life choices always keeping in mind that marriage is the most important. Now marriage can be a source of joy and love and mutual support but why do we teach girls to aspire to marriage and we don't teach boys the same? We raise girls to see each other as competitors not for jobs or accomplishments, which I think can be a good thing, but for the attention of men. We teach girls that they cannot be sexual beings in the way that boys are. Feminist: a person who believes in the social, political, economic equality of the sexes [Dockertman 2013].

Adding Adichie to her song "Flawless," Beyoncé sets the stage for her feminism. Not only does she hit some of the major points of feminism, she introduces her audience to feminism from a feminist who is not well known in popular culture. Beyoncé sets the tone of Bey feminism, not by arguing for every woman to be a feminism, but to try and live it through her life and her music. She never says she is perfect and that is not what feminism is about. Feminism was created to reach all women, but unfortunately it does not. In this essay, I sought to analyze how Bey feminism is created for the everyday woman surrounding topics of sex(uality), marriage and motherhood. By also looking at the limitations of Black feminism in reaching a more diverse audience, the conversation has been started on how Bey feminism can also have a platform among feminism in its ability to reach more women across the country.

REFERENCES

Ball, Charing. 2013. "The Thing About Beyoncé's Feminism." *Madame Noire.* Last modified December 16. http://madamenoire.com/333140/Beyoncé-feminism/. Accessed October 12, 2015.

Coleman, Christina. 2013. "That Time Beyoncé's Album Invalidated Every Criticism of Feminism EVER." *Global Grind.* Last modified December 11. http://global grind.com/2013/12/13/that-time-beyoncés-album-invalidated-every-criticism-of-feminism-ever/. Accessed October 12, 2015.

Cavanagh, Shannon. 2007. "The Social Construction of Romantic Relationships in Adolescence: Examining the Role of Peer Networks, Gender, and Race." *Sociological Inquiry* 77:572–600.

Dockterman, Eliana. 2013. "Flawless: 5 Lessons in Modern Feminism from Beyoncé." *Time.* Last modified December 17. http://time.com/1851/flawless-5-lessons-in-modern-feminism-from-beyoncé/. Accessed October 12, 2015.

Hill Collins, Patricia. 2000. *Black Feminist Thought: Knowledge, Consciousness and the Politics of Empowerment* (2nd ed.). New York: Wadsworth.

_____. 2005. *Black Sexual Politics.* New York: Routledge.

Hobson, Janell. 2013. "Policing Feminism: Regulating the Bodies of Women of Color." *Ms. Magazine Blog.* Last modified June 10, 2013. http://msmagazine.com/blog/2013/06/10/policing-feminism-regulating-the-bodies-of-women-of-color/. Accessed October 13, 2015.

Humphreys, Terence Patrick. 2001. "Sexual Consent in Heterosexual Dating Relationships: Attitudes and Behaviours of University Students." Doctoral dissertation, University of Guelph.

Jonas, Victoria. 2015. "Beyoncé's Self Titled: A Black Feminist Text." *Medium.* Last modified April 28, 2015. https://medium.com/black-feminism/beyoncé-s-self-titled-a-black-feminist-text-7d2b1120527e#.jt65isfbt. Accessed October 14, 2015.

Kendall, Mikki.2013. "Beyoncé's New Album Should Silence Her Feminist Critics." *The Guardian.* Last modified December 13. http://www.theguardian.com/commentisfree/2013/dec/13/Beyoncé-album-flawless-feminism. Accessed October 12, 2015.

Little, Anita. 2014. "Beyoncé at the VMAs: Feminist and Flawless." *Ms. Magazine Blog.* Last modified August 25. http://msmagazine.com/blog/2014/08/25/Beyoncé-at-the-vmasfeminist-and-flawless/. Accessed October 14, 2015.

Lorber, Judith. 2005. *Breaking the Bowls: Degendering and Feminist Change.* New York: Norton.

Qureshi, Bilal. 2013. "Feminists Everywhere React to Beyoncé's Latest." *NPRMusic.* Last modified December 19. http://www.npr.org/sections/therecord/2013/12/19/255527290/ feminists-everywhere-react-to-beyonces-latest. Accessed October 15, 2015.

Ramos, Dorkys. 2015. "Alicia Keys Pens Essay on Confronting Her Insecurities." *Bet.Com.* Last modified August 12. http://www.bet.com/news/lifestyle/2015/08/12/alicia-keys-pens-essay-on-confronting-her-insecurities.html. Accessed October 15, 2015.

Reynolds, Tracey. 2002. "Re-thinking a Black Feminist Standpoint." *Ethnic & Racial Studies* 25: 591–606.

Sandole-Staroste, Ingrid. 2002. *Women in Transition: Between Socialism and Capitalism.* Westport, CT: Praeger.

Schmidt, Meg. 2014. "Opinion: Is Beyoncé a Feminist." *Chimes.* Last modified November 20. http://www.calvin.edu/chimes/2014/11/20/opinion-is-Beyoncé-a-feminist/. Accessed October 13, 2015.

Trier-Bieniek, Adrienne. 2014. "Should Beyoncé's Feminism Be Flawless." *Feminist Reflections: The Society Pages.* Last modified December 4. http://thesocietypages.org/feminist/2014/12/04/should-beyoncés-feminism-be-flawless/. Accessed October 15, 2015.

Waggenspack, Beth. 2007. "Into the Twenty-First Century: Contemporary Directions in Women's Rhetoric." In *The Rhetoric of Western Thought* edited by James L. Golden, Goodwin F. Berquist, William E. Coleman, and J. Michael Sproule, 491–501. Long Grove, IL: Kendall Hunt Publishing.

Walker, Rebecca. 2008. "How My Mother's Fanatical Views Tore Us Apart." *Daily Mail.com*. Last modified May 23. http://www.dailymail.co.uk/femail/article-1021293/How-mothers-fanatical-feminist-views-tore-apart-daughter-The-Color-Purple-author.html. Accessed October 13, 2015.

Whittington, Elizabeth, and Mackenzie Jordan. 2014. "'Bey Feminism' vs. Black Feminism: A Critical Conversation on Word-of-Mouth Advertisement of Beyoncé's Visual Album." In *Black Women and Popular Culture: The Conversation Continues*, edited by Adria Goldman, VaNatta Ford, Alexa Harris, and Natasha Howard, 155–174. New York: Lexington Books.

About the Contributors

Melissa **Avdeeff** is a scholar of all things popular. Her research examines the sociability of digital music technologies, including the role of music in social media platforms. She teaches popular music at the University of Victoria, including a course that examines Beyoncé's position in the music industry, popular music history, and society.

Evette Dionne **Brown** is a culture writer, editor and scholar. She uses black feminist thought, critical race theory and other critical methods to examine black female sexualities and pleasure within media texts. She is also a writer and editor whose work has been published in the *New York Times*, *The Toast*, *Clutch* magazine, *VIBE*, *Bitch* magazine, *The Root*, *Bustle* and a number of other digital and print publications.

Kimberly J. **Chandler** is an assistant professor of communication studies at Xavier University in New Orleans and a faculty contributor to the Women's Studies program. Her research interests and publications are focused on gender and communication, specifically African American masculinities as well as black women and identity negotiation. She is working on a book-length autocritography based on her experiences as a survivor of abuse.

Jamila Akilah **Cupid** is an assistant professor of strategic communication at Lincoln University. Her research is focused on international and intercultural public relations, communications and digital media.

Noel Siqi **Duan** is a writer and editor who has been published in *Bitch* magazine, *Yahoo*, *ELLE*, *Teen Vogue*, *Oyster*, *Oxford Times*, *xoJane*, and other publications. Her research involves the role of women and feminism in environmental movements, the transnational effects of capitalism on local beauty practices, and the gendering of East Asian migrant workers contracted by overseas corporations.

Nicole **Files-Thompson** is an assistant professor at Lincoln University who entered academia after having worked in television as a producer and writer. Her research focuses on the theoretical and practical concerns of empowerment for marginalized groups in mediated and human communication.

Janell **Hobson** is the author of *Venus in the Dark: Blackness and Beauty in Popular Culture* (Routledge, 2005) and *Body as Evidence: Mediating Race, Globalizing Gender* (SUNY Press, 2012). She regularly contributes to the *Ms. Magazine* blog and wrote the 2013 cover story on Beyoncé for *Ms.* Her research focuses on iconography and popular representations—both historic and contemporary—of women of color.

Natalie **Jolly** is an assistant professor of sociology and gender studies at the University of Washington, Tacoma. She is interested in pregnancy, childbirth, and motherhood and her research focuses on how women's experiences of these events are shaped by various social forces.

Marla H. **Kohlman** is a professor of sociology and the director of African diaspora studies at Kenyon College. Prior to teaching at Kenyon, she was an attorney practicing in Maryland and Washington, D.C. Her primary area of research has been intersectionality in the experience of family and in the reporting of sexual harassment and sexual assault in the civilian labor market and the military.

Kristin **Lieb** is an associate professor of marketing communication at Emerson College. She has held numerous marketing and business development positions in the music industry. She worked as a researcher for Harvard Business School and as a freelance writer for *Billboard* and *Rolling Stone*. She is the author of *Gender, Branding, and the Modern Music Industry: The Social Construction of Female Popular Music Stars* (Routledge, 2013).

Anne **Mitchell** teaches in the departments of Ethnic Studies and Women's, Gender, and Sexuality Studies at Bowling Green State University. Her academic interests include black women in the Civil Rights Movement, autobiography, queer theory, and popular culture.

Sonita R. **Moss** is a Ph.D. candidate in sociology at the University of Pennsylvania. Her research examines food, health, media, and inequality in post-racial America.

Adrienne **Trier-Bieniek** is the department chair and a professor of sociology at Valencia College. Her first book was *Sing Us a Song, Piano Woman: Female Fans and the Music of Tori Amos* (Scarecrow Press, 2013). She has also written for online magazines.

Tia C.M. **Tyree** is an associate professor at Howard University. Her research interests include African American and female representations in media and music. She has published articles in several journals, including *Women and Language, Howard Journal of Communications*, and *Journal of Black Studies*.

Elizabeth **Whittington Cooper** is a visiting assistant professor at Xavier University in New Orleans. She teaches public speaking with an emphasis on social justice issues, intercultural communication, and other classes dealing with race and gender within human communication.

Melvin L. **Williams** is a telecommunications professor at Alabama A&M University. His research examines the role of social media in the process of identity formation for historically marginalized social groups.

Index

219